Voices and Values in Joyce's *Ulysses*

The Florida James Joyce Series

Florida A&M University, Tallahassee
Florida Atlantic University, Boca Raton
Florida Gulf Coast University, Ft. Myers
Florida International University, Miami
Florida State University, Tallahassee
University of Central Florida, Orlando
University of Florida, Gainesville
University of North Florida, Jacksonville
University of South Florida, Tampa
University of West Florida, Pensacola

The Florida James Joyce Series
Edited by Zack Bowen

Voices and Values in Joyce's *Ulysses*

Weldon Thornton

University Press of Florida
Gainesville · Tallahassee · Tampa · Boca Raton
Pensacola · Orlando · Miami · Jacksonville · Ft. Myers

05 04 03 02 01 00 6 5 4 3 2 1

Library of Congress Cataloging-in-Publication Data

Voices and values in Joyce's Ulysses / Weldon Thornton.
p. cm. — (Florida James Joyce series)
Includes bibliographical references and index.
ISBN 0-8130-1820-X (alk. paper)
1. Joyce, James, 1882–1941. Ulysses. 2. Joyce, James,
1882–1941 — Literary style. 3. Joyce, James, 1882–1941 —
Technique. 4. Narration (Rhetoric). I. Thornton, Weldon. II. Series.
PR6019.O9 U765 2000
823'.912 — dc21   00-061520

The University Press of Florida is the scholarly publishing agency
for the State University System of Florida, comprising Florida
A&M University, Florida Atlantic University, Florida Gulf Coast
University, Florida International University, Florida State University, University of Central Florida, University of Florida, University
of North Florida, University of South Florida, and University of
West Florida.

University Press of Florida
15 Northwest 15th Street
Gainesville, FL 32611–2079
http://www.upf.com

To my students at Chapel Hill
these forty years

Contents

Foreword

Weldon Thornton, one of the most respected critics in Joyce studies, offers a view of the narration of *Ulysses* that is the product of a lifetime of classroom interaction and hard and thoughtful scholarship. His thesis is that in the proliferation of narrative patterns in the novel, which are far from being collectively simply ingenious experimental examples, each narrative style constitutes its own discrete set of meanings in the episode in which it is employed. His thesis depends on the intuitive meaning or subtext to be derived from the way Joyce chose to present his material, from the truths that arise from the form in which it is presented as much as the wealth of realistic and personal detail that is its subject. Taking the discussion of narrative form back to basics and building on those assumptions, Thornton has presented what will be the most complete assessment of the subject to date.

Thornton begins with the historical criticism surrounding the rise of the novel in the seventeenth and eighteenth centuries, a criticism that stresses the dichotomy between a realism born of the resurgence of scientific observation and the increasing reliance upon empirical fact that permeated the new scientific way of thinking. He traces the evolution of "realism" into the broader and more intuitive aspects of meaning in creative fiction, and sees Joyce's narrative voices—rather than being the production of a disinterested artist standing aside paring his fingernails—as being expressions of his "deepest artistic intentions." Thus, the way his narrators relate the details of *Ulysses* becomes for Thornton a major aspect of the meaning of the book.

Thornton outlines in the first two chapters the historical context, the issues, and the definitions of what comprise formal narrative form—point of view, narrative voice, and authorial omniscience—and in the third chapter he explains how these definitions apply to *Ulysses*. Much of this material is already known to Joyce scholars, but its application to individual episodes of *Ulysses* is often unique to Thornton. While he accepts the concept of an "initial style" to describe the narration of the first six episodes of the novel, his readings of the text and applications of the thesis to Joyce's words produce new explications that are sometimes startling, if always reasoned and absolutely believable, insights that for me are alone worth more than the price of the book. Thornton builds on a thorough knowledge of existing critical exegesis to discover nuggets of insight that I have not read anywhere else.

The last two chapters, discussing the discrete narrative styles of the remaining episodes of the book, constitute an authoritative, balanced defense of his thesis. Although in the individual discussions his formulations of philosophical and moral constructs sometimes differ from my own (comic) view of the world, they provide an exceptionally coherent framework for this splendid, thoughtful masterwork on the narration(s) of *Ulysses*.

Zack Bowen
Series Editor

Acknowledgments

My thinking about the ideas in this book has spanned several decades and draws upon many classroom sessions, *Ulysses* seminars, conversations, and arguments with students, colleagues, and critics. To these I owe a debt I cannot acknowledge, much less repay.

My thanks to Zack Bowen for his encouragement and support of this manuscript and to Patrick McCarthy and Stanley Sultan for their careful and thoughtful scrutiny of an earlier stage of this work. And my thanks to my copy editor, Sharon Damoff, whose sharp eye and understanding mind saved me from many errors and inconsistencies.

I thank the Institute for the Arts and Humanities of the University of North Carolina for providing me a semester free from teaching duties.

Once again, I express my appreciation to Frances Coombs for her indispensable help in formatting and preparing this manuscript.

I gratefully acknowledge permission from the following persons and firms to use the following copyrighted material:

Associated University Presses, for permission to reprint material from Weldon Thornton, "Voices and Values in *Ulysses*," which appeared in *Joyce's "Ulysses": The Larger Perspective*, edited by Robert D. Newman and Weldon Thornton (copyright 1987 by Associated University Presses); and from Weldon Thornton, "Authorial Omniscience and the Cultural Psyche: The Antimodernism of Joyce's *Ulysses*," which appeared in *Irishness and (Post)Modernism*, edited by John S. Rickard (copyright 1994 by Associated University Presses).

Princeton University Press, for permission to reprint material from Karen Lawrence, *The Odyssey of Style in "Ulysses"* (copyright 1981 by Princeton University Press).

The University of Pittsburgh Press, for permission to print excerpts from Erwin R. Steinberg, *The Stream of Consciousness and Beyond in "Ulysses"* (copyright 1958, 1973).

My appreciation to Stephen James Joyce and the Estate of James Joyce for permission to use material from Joyce's letters and his literary works.

Abbreviations

The following abbreviations are used for frequently cited sources. Other clear, short-title citations are used in the notes. Full publication information is given in the bibliography.

JJII	*James Joyce*, rev. ed. (1982), by Richard Ellmann
JJMU	*James Joyce and the Making of "Ulysses,"* by Frank Budgen
Lts	*Letters of James Joyce*, ed. by Stuart Gilbert and Richard Ellmann
MM	*"Ulysses": The Mechanics of Meaning,* by David Hayman
PoA	*A Portrait of the Artist as a Young Man*
SoC&B	*The Stream of Consciousness and Beyond in "Ulysses,"* by Erwin R. Steinberg
Sel Lts	*Selected Letters of James Joyce*, ed. by Richard Ellmann
TM	*Transparent Minds: Narrative Modes of Presenting Consciousness in Fiction,* by Dorrit Cohn
U	*Ulysses* (Gabler edition, 1986), cited by episode and first line number of the quoted material

Introduction

This book has evolved out of several decades of trying to understand for myself and to clarify for my students the narrative techniques and authorial voices in James Joyce's *Ulysses*. I must confess that for a long time I tried assiduously to separate "authorial" and "figural" elements in the initial style—as the annotations and markings in my first copy of *Ulysses* attest. I was puzzled and offended by Joyce's using such a chameleonic narrative voice and his indiscriminately mixing authorial and figural materials. But after trying for many years to grasp Joyce's techniques in terms of modernist ideas about point of view and authorial effacement—some presumably derived from Joyce himself—I found a different approach to the text. Taking seriously Joseph Warren Beach's insistence in *The Twentieth Century Novel* that technique arises out of intention, I began to ask not what the techniques of *Ulysses* should do according to modernist critical dicta, but what those techniques in fact do, what effects they achieve, and what intentions on Joyce's part they fulfill.

As a result I have come to see that the distinctiveness of *Ulysses* lies not simply in the absence of conventional exposition, nor in the use of the "mythical method," nor even in the bewildering variety of styles of the later episodes, but rather in the complex, unified array of techniques by which the novel presents its characters' psyches and the collective psychic milieu of their fictive world. Though many novels use some mode of stream of consciousness or free indirect discourse or authorial exposition, I know of no other, including *A Portrait of the Artist*, that adapts and unifies these techniques so as to achieve certain distinctive effects in *Ulysses* that I believe express Joyce's deepest artistic intentions. Most important among these intentions and effects are the subversion of various dichotomies that are endemic to the modernist worldview—"inner" and "outer," personal and cultural, conscious and unconscious—and the simulation of a cultural milieu that serves as the psychic medium of the characters and events of the novel.

In the following chapters I shall develop three related claims involving techniques of narrative presentation in *Ulysses*. The first concerns the unobtrusive, carefully effaced primary narrator who is present in the first six episodes, in episode eight, and in parts of several other episodes. Even though the primary narrator lacks certain traditional signs of omniscience, such as the overt persona that we find in Fielding or Thackeray or George Eliot, this narrator is best described as "omniscient," and is best understood as a simulation of the collective cultural psyche of the novel. My second claim concerns the distinctive techniques by which the characters' psyches are presented to us in the opening episodes. The techniques of Joyce's "initial style" cannot be adequately described by any single label, such as "interior monologue" or "free indirect discourse" or "omniscient presentation"; rather, this style is a carefully crafted blend of such devices.

My third thesis involves those later episodes of *Ulysses* that are presented through various distinctive narrative voices—secondary narrators, or "presenters." Contrary to the common critical view that these styles or voices reflect Joyce's linguistic relativism, or that they represent self-indulgent tours de force on his part, I argue that each of these voices represents a contemporary literary mode or theory or style that Joyce reveals as deficient or distorting. Each of these voices, that is, represents a perspective that is confused or mistaken, and that in some way inhibits or distorts our engagement with reality. The deficiencies of these styles are revealed both by their inherent limitations and by our realizing how inept each of these styles is in comparison with the initial style.

One theme that I find runs through this book is the insufficiency of our critical categories and terminology to do justice to our experience as readers. I know this both from having read innumerable critical discussions of *Ulysses,* and from having wrestled with articulating my own experience of the novel. And I am convinced that the constraints imposed by our critical vocabulary ultimately affect not just our formulation of our reading experience, but the very experience itself. It is ironic and disturbing that we critics and academics, we "professional thinkers," remain hamstrung by our own categories; it provides an example from within our own sphere of how difficult it is (to adapt Stephen's phrase) to "free our minds from our minds' bondage." One critical statement that has become for me a pillar of cloud and of fire is Derek Attridge's observation that "our activities as readers are usually more complex than the terms in which we represent those activities to ourselves" ("Reading Joyce," 5). Messer Attridge, I thank thee for the word.

Part I

Contexts, Issues, Clarifications

Literary Mimesis and the Realism of the Novel

In order to set the context for the ideas about voices and values in *Ulysses* that I develop in subsequent chapters, I must first explain my understanding of two issues: what is involved in literary mimesis, and the nature of Joyce's literary realism. This discussion builds upon claims about Joyce's life attitudes and literary aims that I present in *The Antimodernism of Joyce's "Portrait of the Artist"* (1994). Because that book deals with Joyce's simulation of Stephen Dedalus's individual psyche, my emphasis there is upon the relationships among language, thought, and reality (see the index of *Antimodernism,* s.v. "Language and thought"). My present interest in how the omniscient authorial voice of *Ulysses* simulates the cultural milieu requires that I explore the relationships among language, cultural entities, and values, especially as these relate to literary mimesis and realism.

Literary Mimesis

The way that literature, and the novel genre especially, imitates life involves inherent paradoxes, for there are significant senses in which literature is, and is not, mimetic. It is mimetic in that literature more than any other art, and the novel more than any other genre, necessarily re-presents and simulates a wide range of experience, individual and cultural. Such representation is possible because the medium of literature is language, which is itself inherently social and historical, and because the distinctive modality of literary art, as over against painting or music or sculpture, is verbal meaning, which necessarily evokes complex human experience, and undergirds all cultural entities.

The inherently social nature of language means that every child acquires language within a society, enabled and prompted by other human beings who comprise a language-based community, and thus children's learning of a language initiates them into a social and cultural nexus. Even simple words such as *bird* or *bottle* or *Mama* necessarily involve concepts and familial and social roles, so that the whole cultural milieu is embedded in the language a child comes to speak. Cultural immersion occurs all the more fully when the words the speaker encounters represent concepts (e.g., private property, equal opportunity) or involve narrative schemata that are integral to the culture (e.g., the establishment of the Magna Carta, the Hebrews' struggles in Egypt, Ulysses' adventures on the way home from the Trojan War). As a result, in acquiring language, speakers necessarily internalize their distinctive culture, whether that be Ethiopian or Japanese or American. To learn a language is to be acculturated. And conversely, without language as the base and the enabling medium, none of the other metalinguistic dimensions of culture—institutions, ideals, physical structures—could evolve; creatures without language are creatures without culture.

Many novelists and critics have claimed that the novel is distinctively capable of representing human experience. In "The Art of Fiction" Henry James proclaims point-blank: "The only reason for the existence of a novel is that it does attempt to represent life" (*Theory of Fiction,* 30). Taylor Stoehr specifically links this mimetic capacity with its linguistic medium. He points out that the ease with which we readers imagine and inhabit the world of a novel "comes of its being a verbal medium, continuous with everything else that fills the consciousness"; literature thus is unique among the arts in the facility with which it "can represent events in a wider context of history and culture, motive and consequence" (*Words and Deeds,* 169, 170). The crucial role of language in enabling the imagination to make such a world has been shown by Paul Ricoeur in "The Function of Fiction in Shaping Reality"; as Ricoeur says, "Imagination at work—in a [fictional/literary] work—produces itself as a world" (128). Since language is the medium of literature as well as the substrate of culture, and every literary work is grounded in words, concepts, images, and schemata that already exist in the culture, literary creation is never ex nihilo—it is imitative, in that it necessarily evokes in the mind of the reader a wide array of preexisting sociocultural entities.

Because language also inherently involves an immaterial aspect—the aspect of meaning—the mimesis within a realistic novel simulates intangible, meaningful aspects of the world. A language, that is, can never be equated with the physical sounds uttered by its users or with the print or markings on paper, for what makes it a language, rather than gibberish or an arbitrary display of ink, is that it involves meaning, which necessarily exists within the cultural milieu. This dimension of language is of course inexplicable—even imperceptible—in positivistic terms. But every language utterance is both an array of sounds traceable on a spectrograph, and an expression of meaning, and in this way each utterance (as Walker Percy puts it) solves the Cartesian dilemma, since it is simultaneously matter and mind. This immaterial dimension of language, this dimension of meaning, is an inherent part of the "world" that the novel imitates and re-presents. I emphasize this because, as we shall see, evoking this immaterial, meaningful element is an essential part of Joyce's literary realism.

Moreover, the novel's mimesis of experience invokes elements beyond those explicitly referred to by the words on the page, so that we readers respond to the language of the literary work by imagining a "whole world"—that is, a world sufficient to provide context and continuity for whatever is specifically described by the text. Precisely how the reader projects an imaginative plenum from the printed pages of a literary work is a mystery akin to the acquisition of language itself or to the ways in which "mere language" can be constitutive of psychic and cultural entities such as the self or culture. But though we cannot explain the process of evocation and projection, recognizing this imaginative re-creation of a world is crucial to our understanding both the novel's distinctive "realism," and the importance for Joyce of simulating a cultural milieu within the fictive world of *Ulysses*.

The novel genre is capable of this simulation, seems naturally fitted to it, by virtue of its length, the ordinariness of its language, and its characteristic evocation of a full-scale setting in which to place its characters and its narrative. A lyric poem is not expected to provide the detail necessary to simulate a whole cultural milieu, and, appropriately, charges of unrealism are virtually never brought against works from other genres, even narrative poetry, whereas they are commonly leveled against novels.

Roy Harvey Pearce, in the foreword to *Experience in the Novel,* notes: "Thus we now freely say of all literary forms that they create 'worlds.' But I think it most significant that we did not get into the habit of so saying until we perforce tried to comprehend the novel. For par excellence it is the novel that creates a 'world,' even as it is created directly out of a 'world'" (vi). Ruth Ronen, approaching this issue philosophically, concurs, speaking of "the generally held belief that among literary genres, narrative fiction most clearly constructs those systematic sets and states of affairs to which the concept of *world* pertains" (*Possible Worlds,* 13).

A number of writers and critics have testified to this world-evoking capacity of the genre. George Eliot, whose novels—especially *Middlemarch*—show such concern to simulate a locale and a cultural milieu, explained: "It is the habit of my imagination to strive after as full a vision of the medium in which a character moves as of the character itself."[1]

Percy Lubbock argues that the presentation of Yonville and of the world of provincial life is a large part of Flaubert's purpose in *Madame Bovary* (*Craft of Fiction*, 80, 84–85). And in his "London Notes" of July 1897, Henry James observes: "The great thing to say for them [novelists] is surely that at any given moment they offer us [readers] another world, another consciousness" (*Theory of Fiction*, 23–24).

The ease with which we readers construct an imaginative world from a verbal text is reflected in how much a skillful writer does *not* have to tell us in order to evoke a fictive world.[2] If the work-as-apprehended-by-the-reader consisted only of what is explicitly spelled out by the text, the result would be an aggregation of atomic points or details, without coherence. But in the mind of an acculturated reader, the printed book—what Hugh Kenner calls "100 cubic inches of wood pulp"—becomes a plenum, evoking continuity and wholeness out of a narrative that is necessarily only partially given. By the time we have read the first page of any novel, we have already imagined (*inferred* seems an imprecise, thinly logical, term) a great deal that is not stated in the text, thus bringing into being the fictive world or plenum. In the opening lines of the "Calypso" episode of *Ulysses*, for example, we read: "Kidneys were in his mind as he moved about the kitchen softly, righting her breakfast things on the humpy tray" (*U*, 4.6). Responding to the words of that sentence (in context), we are immediately involved in a world of mental/psychic phenomena, of objects, activities, relationships, all of them understood by virtue of an acculturation presumed by the author and evoked by the text. To try to spell out for someone from another realm everything that is implicit in the first fifty lines of this episode—that is, to provide what artificial intelligence researchers call an "effective procedure" sufficient for a totally unacculturated reader (or a computer) for whom everything had to be specified—would require many pages of detailed explanation.[3]

The fictive world of a novel cannot, then, be identified with what is given on the page. (Franz Stanzel expresses admiration for the reader's capacity to maintain in his imagination "an even and continuous flow of action" in spite of a discontinuous narrative presentation; see his *Narrative Situations*, 114–15.) The fact that we do not accompany Stephen and Bloom throughout the day, or that they are presented through a variety of styles, does not render them discontinuous as characters. And this plenum in all realistic novels involves not only the characters' unexpressed or quasi-conscious experiences and motives, but the implicit values and schemata of the cultural milieu. As we shall see, Joyce took pains in *Ulysses* to develop an array of techniques and devices to evoke not only the subconscious dimensions of the characters, but the collective psychic milieu in which they exist, thus immeasurably enriching our sense of the fictive world of the novel. Moreover, the integrity and resilience of the fictive plenum, the virtual world, of *Ulysses* enables us in the later episodes to discern what the characters say and do, even through the obfuscating stylistic veils of "Sirens" or "Oxen of the Sun."[4]

Sportive, audacious Joyce even flaunts the reality and fullness of his fictive world by relegating some crucial events and dialogue to offstage status. And while some of these events are adumbrated, others are left very largely to our inference. Moreover, while we cannot determine such elided events with certainty, we do not regard questions about those events as meaningless. We are not, for example, explicitly told the Irish phrase that Haines speaks to the old milkwoman, though Stephen understands its gist as "bid[ding] her be silent" (*U*, 1.422); trying to infer it involves interesting questions about how much Irish Haines really knows—probably little more than the citizen, who presumably uses this same elementary tag later (*U*, 12.265)— and thus about the relationship that exists between him and Stephen at this point. A more important elided event is the early morning conversation between Bloom and Molly regarding the time of Boylan's visit, subsequently reflected on furtively by Bloom. And since we have no scene describing it, we cannot be certain how or why the furniture in 7 Eccles Street got moved about during the day—whether by Molly or Boylan or both—but we cannot say that it was not moved (Bloom does encounter a solid object in an unexpected place), or that it moved itself, or that it was moved by Stephen Dedalus or by Gypo Nolan (from another Dublin novel, not yet written in 1922).

Other important elided events are acknowledged by Jennifer Levine, who notes: "Something has happened at Westland Row Station, but neither 'Oxen of the Sun' nor 'Circe' chooses to reveal what it is"; and she points out that the crucial assignation of Boylan and Molly is not explicitly given, and we are told so little about the repercussions of this event in the minds of Bloom and Molly that we continue to argue over what it all means, uncertain whether Molly's thinking of bringing Bloom breakfast in bed signals repentance or a simple misunderstanding of Bloom's somnolent murmuring (*"Ulysses,"* 155). The importance to the novel of such events, and the continuity among depicted and undepicted events, shows the insufficiency of the idea of narrative "completeness" proposed by Robert Champigny.[5]

To say that literature is mimetic, then, means that it is impossible for us to read a work without projecting a world that mirrors our own, that the imaginative world we project involves meanings, and that it is a "whole world."

This leads to the other side of the paradox—the several ways in which literary works are not mimetic. First, we do not expect a literary text to reproduce or replicate the psychological processes or cultural milieu it depicts; second, a literary work brings something unique into being— something that has not existed before and that originates from a specific creative endeavor; and third, the literary work critiques the cultural milieu it depicts.

In regard to the first point, I have argued in *The Antimodernism of Joyce's "Portrait"* that techniques such as stream of consciousness and interior monologue always simulate rather than replicate the character's psychic processes. Here I would extend that claim to any novel's evocation of a cultural milieu; even in the most detailed and "realistic" text, we expect only simulation of the social scene, not replication. This point should be obvious, both because any cultural milieu is too extensive to be replicated within the few hundred pages of a novel, and because every culture involves elements that a verbal medium cannot possibly replicate. That is, while language is the necessary substrate without which no culture can evolve, cultures involve institutions, rituals, familial and social relationships, distinctive modes of aspiration, success, and failure—even physical structures—none of which can be replicated by the most detailed and extensive literary text.

A second way in which literary works are not mimetic is that they bring something new and unique into being. This aspect becomes clear if we consider the essential difference between the kind of entity that a writer creates and the kind discovered or developed by a scientist—the difference between a literary work, such as *Hamlet* or *Ulysses,* and the calculus or an invention such as the airplane. Sir Isaac Newton was a towering genius, but if he had not developed the infinitesimal calculus, it would have been developed by someone else—was in fact being developed simultaneously by Leibniz—and had Newton not discovered the laws of motion, someone else would have articulated them, in a form mathematically identical to Newton's formulation. Even in the case of a complex invention such as the airplane, it is clear that the machine would have been invented and would have evolved into its present-day form had the Wright brothers never lived. But a literary work such as *Hamlet* or *Ulysses,* no matter how "derivative" from earlier material, is a unique creation, and had its author not lived, it would not exist. We value these works not because they skillfully retell a known story, but because of the quality of the literary experience they offer to us. A literary work is not the kind of entity that is discovered or invented, nor is it simply the result of a convergence of cultural forces—in spite of recent attempts to argue the redundancy of the author or to dissolve him or her into the milieu.[6]

This point suggests a third sense in which the literary work does not simply imitate the reality it depicts—and leads us to the question of the novel's realism. The reality that the novel imitates is (as we have seen) imaginative and cultural, involving not just objects and events and persons, but an array of values and meanings and schemata. In its necessarily selective and evaluative imitation of a complex cultural reality, the novel participates in, critiques, and thus modifies the very cultural reality that it simulates, and in this sense the novel is never merely mimetic. For this reason, the question of whether the novel is "natural" *or* "conventional"—whether it imitates life *or* has reference to earlier literary works or to itself—involves a specious dichotomy and fails to acknowledge that the novel always participates in and alters the very cultural reality it imitates. Erich Kahler makes precisely this point when he says of the arts:

> They are also more than forms of expression, and they do more than merely register. By giving expression to latent reality, and thus bringing it to consciousness, they make wholly real what has been only potential. They create the cultural atmosphere of each given age. And by virtue of this function they play as active a part in man's development as other, seemingly more practical human activities such as science, technology, and politics. The evolution of artistic forms of expression is one of the most important evidences we have for the changes in man's consciousness and the changes in the structure of his world. (*Inward Turn*, 3; see also Paul Ricoeur's substantial and carefully argued essay "The Function of Fiction in Shaping Reality")

What Does a Realistic Novel Simulate?

Many critics of the novel have said that its distinctiveness as a genre, its very raison d'être, is its "realism." Ian Watt, for example, in a famous statement in *The Rise of the Novel*, says that "historians of the novel . . . have seen 'realism' as the defining characteristic which differentiates the work of the early eighteenth-century novelists from previous fiction" (10); he goes on to claim, "There are important differences in the degree to which different literary forms imitate reality; and the formal realism of the novel allows a more immediate imitation of individual experience set in its temporal and spatial environment than do other literary forms" (32). And many other critics and writers have in various ways concurred.[7] But the term *realism* is chameleonic, and has in fact involved diametrically opposed ideas about the reality that the novel is presumed to imitate.[8] Pursuing this issue carefully will help us to appreciate the distinctive "realistic" achievement of Joyce's *Ulysses,* especially in its simulation of the collective cultural milieu.

While the term *realistic* in literary discussions often refers to a mode of presentation or a style, or to "the writer's attitude towards and treatment of his subject matter" (Stang, *Theory of the Novel,* 145), the underlying issue in regard to fictional realism is not stylistic or even epistemological (*pace* Watt, *Rise of the Novel,* 11) but ontological—that is, it involves the kind of *reality* the novel aims to re-present. More specifically, because this issue has emerged within the recent Western intellectual tradition, it predictably involves modernist (Cartesian) dichotomies. That is, the debate turns on whether the reality that the novel depicts is essentially the "objective" physical reality described by the new science and philosophy of the seventeenth and eighteenth centuries, or whether the reality that the novel aspires to capture involves such immaterial, "subjective" entities as values and cultural phenomena, attitudes and judgments, including the "meaning" of its subject matter. Out of this fundamental ontological divergence arise other questions, such as the kinds of subjects that are appropriate for novelistic representation and the style in which the material should be presented.

To survey conflicting opinions about realism over the past 150 years is to realize how much the term reflects the underlying metaphysical issues that Western thought has wrestled with since the Renaissance. The novel emerged in the seventeenth and eighteenth centuries partly in response to the philosophical ferment and claims generated by the new ways of thinking fostered by Galileo and Descartes and scientific empiricism. But the debate over what is involved in the novel's "realism" did not emerge until the mid-nineteenth century, perhaps because it took that long for the implications of the new philosophy to filter down into our thinking about the ontological status of human consciousness and of cultural entities. While the eighteenth-century novelists were sometimes concerned to present their works as "histories" (e.g., *The History of Tom Jones, A Foundling,* or *The Life and Adventures of Robinson Crusoe*), such titles referred more to the purported truthfulness of their stories than to any ontological question about the kind of reality their work presented—in

Michael McKeon's terms, more to "historicity" than to "verisimilitude" (*Origins of the English Novel,* 53).

The nineteenth-century debate about realism, then, is best understood as part of a larger philosophical debate stemming from the increasing metaphysical authority of the materialism inherent in the thinking of Galileo and Hobbes and in Newtonian mechanics, and in the so-called empirical method. Under the influence of this growing authority, novelists who aspired to be "realistic" found themselves called on to emulate the presumed clarity and objectivity of the sciences and of critical, rational thought generally. As the positivist worldview that was succeeding so well in physics and chemistry grew in authority, the question arose of what possible claim to reality could be made by a literary work, since it is the product of one individual's imagination and consists of mere language and cultural phenomena—entities whose "reality" was suspect in the eyes of the materialistic metaphysic. Predictably, some literary critics emulated the new science, claiming that literature to be best, most realistic, that came closest to an unbiased, documentary presentation of its material. Others were dissatisfied with this, believing that literature is inherently interpretive and that the aim of "realistic" writing is to convey some underlying gist or meaning within what it depicts. The objectivist view, however, grew in prestige and manifested itself later in the century in the naturalism of the brothers Goncourt and of Zola, who aspired to write an "experimental novel"—by which he meant a novel grounded in the methods of the social and medical sciences (see Zola's 1880 essay "The Experimental Novel").

If we keep this issue in focus, we can see how writers of the past 150 years have wrestled with these alternatives, some of them pushed toward documentary realism by the growing authority of the physical sciences and by the narrow understanding of *rationalism* and *experience* that developed in the Enlightenment, but others drawn toward a selective, interpretive realism involving intangible psychological and cultural entities and a concern for the *meaning* of the events they were depicting.

These antithetical senses of *realism,* and the evolution that certain writers' opinions underwent in regard to this issue, are clearly shown in Richard Stang's *The Theory of the Novel in England, 1850–1870* (1959; Stang's coverage is broader than the dates in his title suggest). The letters, essays, and reviews that he draws upon clearly show the developing schism between realism understood as a transcript of actual life (eschewing imagination and even selectivity), and realism understood as fidelity to human experience (thus necessarily involving judgment and interpretation). In a section entitled "The Reductio ad Absurdum" Stang quotes a number of critics who called for the novel to replicate society, without any admixture of imagination or interpretation or even of selectivity. For example, the *Quarterly Review* of 1855 praised Thackeray's *The Newcomes* as "the most minute and faithful transcript of actual life which is anywhere to be found" (qtd. in Stang, 149). An 1855 essay by Fitzjames Stephen, "The Relation of Novels to Life," called for the novel to be a biography, and to have no more plot than a bona fide biography (Stang, 150). And Stang cites an 1860 essay on George Eliot "that complained that the number of deaths in her first three books was out of proportion to the number in real life" (151).

Particularly revealing of the assumptions of documentary or positivist realism is an anonymous review article in *Westminster Review* in 1853, entitled "The Progress of Fiction as an Art":

> It has been the tendency of modern writers to restrict themselves more and more to the actual and the possible; and our taste would be offended were they greatly to overstep these limitations, for a scientific, and somewhat sceptical age, has no longer the power of believing in the marvels which delighted our ruder ancestors. The carefully wrought story, which details events in orderly chronological sequence; which unfolds character according to those laws which experience teaches us to look for as well in the moral as the material world; and which describes outward circumstances in their inexorable certainty, yielding to no magician's wand, or enchanter's spell, is essentially the production of a complex and advanced stage of society; nor do we meet with it until science and letters have reached a high place and are established firmly enough to influence the popular mind. . . .
>
> There is an instinct in every unwarped mind which prefers truth to extravagance, and a photographic picture, if it be only of a kitten or a hay-stack, is a pleasanter subject in the eyes of most persons (were they brave enough to admit it), than many a glaring piece of mythology, which those who profess to worship High Art find themselves called upon to pronounce divine. (Stang, 146–47, quoting from *Westminster Rev.* 60 [1853]: 343–44, 358; I have corrected and extended Stang's quotation)

While some of the terms are metaphysically ambiguous— "laws" of the moral world (by analogy with the physical) and "truth"—the clear thrust of this passage is to set science, skepticism, photography, inexorable certainty, and the laws of the material world over against the marvels and enchantments and mythology that deluded our uncritical and self-indulgent "ruder ancestors."[9] These positivistic and reductionistic views did not go unchallenged—see Stang's sections headed "Art Is Not Life" and "Bulwer and Dickens—The Attack on Realism" (151–59)—but the point is that the sense of "reality" that informed these critics' conception of realism was grounded in a metaphysic of objective reality that stemmed from Galileo and Hobbes and Newton and that has grown in authority and continues today to pervade our thinking.

Equally interesting is Stang's documentation of the views of three writers—George Eliot, George Meredith, and G. H. Lewes—as they evolved from an austere realism espousing objective documentation to one that acknowledged the necessity of selection and interpretation (Stang, 159–76). Each of the three began under the influence of positivistic philosophy and rhetoric, claiming to see art as documentation, but each came to understand that art is inherently selective and imaginative and that it neither can nor should forgo interpretation of the material it presents. Of George Eliot, Stang points out, "At the beginning of her career as a novelist, she thought one of the most important requirements of a novel was that it image the world outside the artist's mind, the world of external reality, as faithfully as possible" (160). But he traces—through various comments in her essays, novels, and letters—her evolving realization that the novel must be "ideational" and interpretive (see esp. Stang, 166, citing Eliot's *Letters*, 4:300–301).[10] Stang then traces this same evolution from documentary to interpretative realism in the thinking of George Meredith and G. H. Lewes (166–76). The later ideas of Eliot, Meredith, and Lewes reflect their understanding that realism in fiction involves the writer's going beyond the "unessential details" in order to evoke some qualitative dimension or meaning that lies beneath the surface of experience—that is, the understanding of the writer's task (and of realism) that Joyce embraced.

This debate about realism was not resolved with the passing of the nineteenth century. A concern over the reality status of the imagination and its creations, including literature and culture, underlies many of the literary manifestos of the early twentieth century, most of which involve attempts by the writers to clarify the kind of reality that literature involves. And not surprisingly some of these proclamations reflect confusion in regard to the paradigms of science and objectivity and the necessarily interpretive nature of literature.[11]

Though the ideas in it are not clearly presented, the gist of Conrad's famous author's note to *The Nigger of the "Narcissus"* is that literature aims to bring to light the "truth"—he uses the term several times—that underlies every aspect of the visible universe. When, in the most famous line of this note, he says that his aim is "to make you hear, to make you feel—it is, before all, to make you *see,*" it is clear that he is referring not to enhancing our sensations, but to conveying understanding. Similarly, Virginia Woolf, in her important essay "Modern Fiction," refers to Bennett, Galwsorthy, and Wells as "materialists," because they "spend immense skill and immense industry making the trivial and the transitory appear the *true* and the *enduring*" (153; my emphasis). In adjuring the younger writers to be faithful to the inner realities, she suggests "that the proper stuff of fiction is a little other than custom [i.e., documentary realism] would have us believe it" (154), and she goes on to cite Joyce's *Ulysses* (then appearing in the *Little Review*) as embodying such an intention.

So pervasive is the authority of the scientific metaphysic and of the paradigm of objectivity, that some critics still talk as if the reality that fiction should represent is that of Galileo and Newton and as if that reality should be presented without any "distortion" by interpretation. George Levine, who has written extensively on realism, reflects this ontological confusion when he says that realism assumes that "the firmest realities are objects rather than ideas or imaginings" ("Realism Reconsidered," 340). If this is so, then the novel can never be more than a shoddy substitute for the account of the world given by the sciences, and all literary imitation, literary realism, is consigned to a second-rate presentation of a dubious aspect of reality. A similar capitulation to an utterly literal criterion of realism is reflected in Robert Scholes's claim that "Realism exalts Life and diminishes Art, exalts things and diminishes words. But when it comes to representing *things,* one picture *is* worth a thousand words, and one motion picture is worth a million. In the face of competition from cinema, fiction must abandon its attempt to 'represent reality' and rely more on the power of words to stimulate the imagination" (*The Fabulators,* 11–12).

In such a positivist climate of opinion, describing literature as "realistic" implies that it can and should be veridical as regards objects and facts, but denigrates its selective simulation of a culture or its evocation of a characteristic milieu (which is always imaginative and qualitative) or its attempt to convey meaning. Admittedly, to say that literature presents the meaning of an event or the spirit of a milieu, or even that it interprets reality, involves ontological assumptions that are difficult to defend in our present climate of opinion. What does it mean to say that a work "gets beneath the surface" or "goes to the heart of the matter" or "captures the essence of its subject"? When we praise *Dubliners,* or Hemingway's short stories, for how deftly they capture the gist of a character or a situation or a milieu, what exactly are we claiming—that is, what (ontologically) distinguishes the "gist" from the "surface"? Or when we say that a social historian such as Tom Wolfe has captured what is crucial about a given social milieu, what do we imply about the reality of other less-than-crucial aspects? Such phrasing (and it is quite common) suggests that the critic who speaks this way believes in some "essential" quality that may be obscured by the "unessential details"—and yet there are very few Platonists among us nowadays. (A random example recently encountered: the jacket blurb of Tom Howard's *Hardy Country* claims, "Hardy unerringly captures the character of this part of England"; few of us balk when we read such a phrase, but what do we think it means, and how do we reconcile our understanding of it with the reigning positivism of our day?) All such claims about *interpretive* realism involve metaphysical dilemmas that the modernist climate of opinion has great difficulty dealing with.

Joyce, however, rejected this materialistic view of reality and regarded the acts of the imagination, and the cultural milieu that sustains them, as the true and appropriate objects of the imitation that "realism" involves. That is, for Joyce the novel's mimesis, its realism, refers not to its capacity to represent any physical reality (which leads to the fallacy of imitative form, pilloried by Joyce in "Oxen of the Sun"), but its capacity to evoke, to simulate, and to *interpret* a whole imaginative-cultural world. What we value in "realistic" writing such as that of Joyce—or of George Eliot or Trollope—is not exhaustive mechanical detail or verisimilitude. Quite the contrary, it is their capturing the spirit or the essence of the scene or the meaning of the events that their works so skillfully re-present.

Joyce's literary realism in *Ulysses* depicts something other than Newtonian objects—that is, it evokes ideas and imaginings and other cultural entities, all of which are sustained by the same psychic-linguistic medium that sustains literary works and is ontologically continuous with those works (again, the point made by Taylor Stoehr, above). When a (realistic) writer does depict an "object," what he is evoking is not some discrete Newtonian entity, but the object as it exists within a psychic/cultural continuum, in its distinctive *quidditas* (or "radiance," as Stephen calls it in *Portrait*).

In my book on Joyce's *Portrait,* I argue that one of Joyce's basic aesthetic aims was to capture the gist or meaning of the things he wrote about (see esp. 47–50 of *The Antimodernism of Joyce's "Portrait"*). That Joyce construed "realism" in such interpretive and imaginative terms is revealed in his lecture on that great realist Daniel Defoe. Discussing Defoe's *The Storm*, Joyce points out how much tedious detail is involved, but then notes: "The modern reader does a good deal of groaning before he reaches the conclusion, but in the end *the object of the chronicler has been achieved*. By dint of repetitions, contradictions, details, figures, noises, *the storm has come alive, the ruin is visible*" (*Daniel Defoe*, 16; my emphasis). As the italicized phrases show, for Joyce the hallmark of Defoe's realism is not accuracy of meteorological detail, but a transubstantiation of details into something experiential, something meaningful.

Similarly, drawing on Joyce's lecture on Blake, Robert Kellogg argues that for Joyce, "the artistic representation of external reality amounts to much more than the products of the photographer and the court stenographer, which reproduce *only* visual and verbal surfaces," and he points to a passage in this same lecture in which Joyce ridicules an overly naive realism by citing "those very useful figures" [i.e., photographer and stenographer] ("Translating Dublin," 1; Kellogg cites *CW*, 220). Immediately before this passage, Joyce asserts: "If we must accuse of madness every great genius who does not believe in the hurried materialism now in vogue with the happy fatuousness of a recent college graduate in the exact sciences, little remains for art and universal philosophy." Tim Cribb makes essentially this same point when he notes: "In Joyce's early work, then, these moments [i.e., epiphanies] only appear to owe allegiance to realism, if realism means only fidelity to fact; their true allegiance is to reality, and that is located beyond common understanding in some realm of cognition at first accessible only to the artist" ("James Joyce," 66). And S. L. Goldberg argues that "if Joyce *is* a Realist, the world he pictures is not the simplistic mechanical nightmare it is commonly assumed to be, a world in which people merely register passively 'objective' impressions and 'subjective' associations, but one in which action, the moral action of the individual spirit, is not only possible but fundamental" (*Classical Temper*, 247).

Such an understanding of Joyce's realism is implicit in Frank Budgen's perspicacious reflections on the kind of reality that literature presents, and on how Joyce captures and conveys "Dublin" in *Ulysses*. Noting that in *Ulysses* Joyce "neither paints nor photographs it for our guidance" (important to Budgen, who was himself a painter), he says, "It must grow upon us not through our eye and memory, but through the minds of the Dubliners we overhear talking to each other. . . . Here and there we get a clue to the shape and colour of this place or that, but in the main Dublin exists for us as *the essential element in which Dubliners live*. It is not a décor to be modified at will, but something as native to them as water to a fish. Joyce's realism verges on the mystical even in *Ulysses*" (*JJMU*, 71; my emphasis). Budgen's reference to the "essential element in which Dubliners live" and his saying that it is to them as "water to a fish" concur well with claims I shall subsequently develop about Joyce's intention to evoke the cultural milieu or collective psyche of the world he writes about. Nor does Budgen's use of *mystical* here imply anything occult; rather, it shows that he felt the need to acknowledge some spiritual quality in what Joyce has achieved, in order to distinguish it from "objective" or documentary realism. Budgen's point—and my own—is that the realism of *Ulysses* captures the very spirit of the place.

As we shall see more fully in chapter 4, the simulation of cultural milieu in a novel is done through an array of devices—description, exposition, evocation of distinctive objects or schemata that embody the culture, use of narrative voice, and so forth. Perhaps we have hidden from ourselves this cultural or "psychic" dimension of the novel by using such terms as *atmosphere* (thus implying that the novelistic world consists largely of evocative physical setting), or *tone* or *mood* (thus implying that it consists of an attitude on the part of the authorial voice). But while setting (e.g., in *The Return of the Native* or *Heart of Darkness*) and authorial tone (e.g., in *Pride and Prejudice* or *Madame Bovary*) are essential aspects of the fictive world, there is something more pervasive, if less tangible, which I am calling the psychic milieu of the work. Not that this is separate, or even separable, from atmosphere, tone, and so on, but neither is this psychic milieu identical with these other aspects of the work.

Finally, to prepare a broader base for my subsequent claims, I want briefly to explore the relationship between the emergence of the novel and the intellectual climate of the seventeenth and eighteenth centuries. Specifically, I want to explore whether the relationship between the new genre and the various philosophical currents that we have mentioned—especially the impact of the ideas of Galileo, Bacon, Descartes, Locke, and Hume—was one of congruence and complicity, or of resistance and counterstatement.

While I accept the idea that the novel arose in response to cultural and intellectual currents, I am skeptical of Ian Watt's claim in chapter 1 of *The Rise of the Novel* (1957) that the relationship between the philosophical/ scientific ideas of the day and the genre of the novel is one of continuity and of mutual reinforcement. For example, summarizing Locke's and Hume's views on personal identity and continuity of selfhood, Watt claims, "Such a point of view is characteristic of the novel" (21). While the relationship between philosophical milieu and literary works varies from one literary period or tradition to another and cannot easily be generalized, I believe that the great literature of the English tradition (in contrast to that of the Gallic?) has more often challenged contemporary abstract thought than it has been complicit with it. And in his *Conrad in the Nineteenth Century* (1979), Watt himself says that "the greatest authors are rarely representative of the ideology of their period; they tend rather to expose its internal contradictions or the very partial nature of its capacity for dealing with the facts of experience" (147).

I would argue that the novel emerged not to illustrate the ideas of Descartes and Locke and Hume, but in reaction against those ideas and the underlying intellectual currents that they expressed. Those skeptical, analytical philosophies involve a view of reality and of the self that is not compatible with the complex characters and the richness of milieu that novels can effect. That is, had Fielding and Richardson—and especially Swift and Sterne—accepted the implications of Descartes's belief in clear and distinct ideas, and Locke's "punctual" or "neutral" self, they would have had nothing to write about.[12]

There may be another dimension of this counterstatement, one more directly related to the genre's capacity for evoking a whole world, a cultural milieu, that I have been insisting on. Perhaps one impetus for the emergence of the novel at the same time that science and philosophy were articulating the subject/object division and the claim that the outer world (i.e., everything beyond the individual brain/mind) is utterly objective and Hobbes was articulating his materialistic view of the state, was a need to affirm, to demonstrate, that such an intangible, intersubjective reality does in fact exist. That is, it may be because the reality of culture was being called into question by the reductionistic modernist metaphysic, and some confirmatory experience of this whole world was wanted, that the novel arose and has become the genre of choice in recent centuries. Whether conscious of it or not, those who read Cervantes' *Don Quixote* or Fielding's *Tom Jones* enter thereby into a public, qualitative world that is far more than the sum of its parts and far more than motions of particles impinging upon the sensorium of the "individual" person. The readers of these novels experienced, that is, a living refutation of the partitioning of the world into inner and outer, mind and matter, carried out by Galileo and Descartes, and of the discrete totally self-aware self of Locke, and of Hume's demonstration that we have no experience of causation. And as these reductionistic ideas became the reigning ideas of the modern worldview, the novel's confutation of these ideas has remained one of the mainstays of the genre and one of the reasons that we have valued it.

Hillis Miller notes that the novel arose at a particular time and place "and therefore expresses the personal, social, and metaphysical experiences of man during that time. The rise of the novel is associated with a new discovery of the isolation and autonomy of the private mind, with a sense of the absence of any preestablished harmony between the mind and what is outside the mind, with a diminishing faith in the existence of any supernatural power giving order and meaning to this world . . ." ("Three Problems of Fictional Form," 22). Yet Miller goes on to describe the nature of the novel in ways that seem inherently to counter or balance this isolation and autonomy. He asserts, "The novel is the form of literature developed to explore the various forms intersubjective relations may take. If reading a novel is consciousness of the consciousness of another, the novel itself is a structure of related minds. To read a novel is not to encounter a single mind but to take part in an interaction among several minds. . . . Intersubjectivity is an important dimension of fictional form, and a sensitive discrimination of the ways minds are related to one another in a given novel is a primary requirement in the interpretation of fiction" (22).

Similarly, Georg Lukács argues, "The novel is the epic of an age in which the extensive totality of life is no longer directly given, in which the immanence of meaning in life has become a problem, yet which still thinks in terms of totality" (*Theory of the Novel,* 56). Ian Watt says in passing that "Spengler's perspective for the rise of the novel is the need of 'ultrahistorical' modern man for a literary form capable of dealing with 'the whole of life'" (*Rise of the Novel,* 22, citing *Decline of the West* [London 1928], 1:130–31.) And John Warner, in *Joyce's Grandfathers,* says of Defoe, Smollett, and Sterne: "Writing in an era of epistemological dislocation, they 'divined' that in the synchronisms of myth they could find ways to resist the pressures of an encroaching positivism and empiricism" (2). My point is that the novel genre—and especially Joyce's *Ulysses*—refutes such abstract, dichotomous, modernist claims as the isolation and autonomy of the private mind and the absence of harmony between mind and what is "outside."

2

Point of View, Narrative Voice,
Authorial Omniscience

Because my analysis of *Ulysses* will deal at length with the novel's narrative point of view and with the omniscience of the primary narrator, and because the critical literature involves confusion and even contradiction in characterizing various modes of point of view, I must address those concepts and terms. But I have no wish to trace here the rise of the critical concern with point of view, nor to develop a coherent schema of points of view.[1] I regard point of view as a technical concept that justifies itself through the light it can cast on individual novels, and it seems clear that consistency of point of view and attempts to schematize or rationalize it have been of concern to critics far more than to novelists.[2] Moreover, I agree with R. H. Fogle that the concept has been overextended and misapplied.[3]

James Joyce/Implied Author/Primary Narrator/Secondary Narrator

The complex narrative situation in *Ulysses* calls for certain distinctions in regard to modes of authorial presence. I follow Wayne C. Booth and Seymour Chatman in distinguishing between the flesh-and-blood author James Joyce and the "implied author" of *Ulysses*, and between the implied author of the text and the narrator(s).[4] James Joyce (1882–1941) is the person whose genius and whose struggles from 1914 to 1922 brought *Ulysses* into being—but he did other things as well during that time: he played the roles of son, brother, husband, father, friend, cajoler, antagonist, and he displayed an array of strengths, foibles, virtues, and superstitions. James Joyce is also the man who wrote several works that are quite different in theme and technique from *Ulysses*. In short, he was what W. B. Yeats, in making a similar distinction between poet and person, referred to as "the bundle of accident and incoherence that sits down to breakfast" ("General Introduction," 509).

The implied author of *Ulysses,* while undeniably an aspect of the person James Joyce, is an entity whose traits can be inferred only from the text of *Ulysses,* and who may be quite different in his artistic aims, techniques, and demands upon the reader from the implied author of other texts by this same James Joyce. (Both Booth and Chatman illustrate "implied author" by contrasting several works by the same writer—e.g., Fielding's quite different novels.) The implied author of *Ulysses* manifests those aspects of the mind of James Joyce that conceived and carried out the novel and give it whatever degree of artistic and thematic integrity and whatever values it has. Moreover, the values of this implied author (i.e., the values of the novel) may be different from those of the flesh-and-blood James Joyce (established by biographical study), and this in itself is reason enough to distinguish between these two entities.

How such a difference can exist is not easy to understand, but it is undeniable that writers can project saner values into their works than they manifest in their lives. To cite one clear example: the works of F. Scott Fitzgerald persistently warn us of the baneful effects of worshipping money and social status, and yet Fitzgerald himself continued throughout his life to pursue these hollow ideals. Conversely, evidence that Joyce himself was misogynistic becomes beside the point—perhaps even an impediment—when we are reading *A Portrait* or *Ulysses,* for the implied authors of those books present misogyny as one of Stephen's besetting stumbling blocks (discussed below in chapter 4). This distinction between author and implied author, then, helps us to understand that in order to determine the values of a literary work, we must go to the work, not to the biography of the writer. And Joyce himself seems to have recognized such a distinction; during the time he was writing *Ulysses* he responded to Stanislaus's objections to his intemperance by calling himself "the foolish author of a wise book" (*JJII,* 471).

It is this implied author of *Ulysses* whose choices and judgments and values inform the whole of the work. He does not—indeed, cannot—appear in the text overtly—that is, as a character or even as a discrete, characterizable narrative voice—for each character or voice is necessarily one facet of this larger and more complex authorial entity. Rather, the implied author manifests himself in every one of the events and characters and situations and structures of the novel, in the allusive frames of reference, even in the crucial fictional choices about setting, emphasis, perspective, and so forth. As Seymour Chatman explains, "He [the implied author] is not the narrator, but rather the principle that invented the narrator, along with everything else in the narrative, that stacked the cards in this particular way, had these things happen to these characters, in these words or images. Unlike the narrator, the implied author can *tell* us nothing. He, or better, *it* has no voice, no direct means of communicating" (*Story and Discourse,* 148).

Since this implied author exists pervasively in the novel, we must (with Chatman) be prepared to distinguish between the implied author and the narrator. Such a distinction is easy when the narrator assumes figural status—for example, Nick Carraway in *The Great Gatsby,* or Charley Marlow in "Youth"—or even when the narrator speaks in a tangible, consistent nonfigural voice, as in James's *The Ambassadors.* But the distinction must be acknowledged even when the distance between the implied author and the narrative voice is not so obvious—for example, in the opening chapters of *Ulysses.* Since the narrative voice in these opening chapters is so effaced and implicit, this distinction may seem unnecessary or specious, but there is nonetheless a discernible narrative voice in these episodes, and this voice cannot be identified with the far more comprehensive implied author. (For reasons I shall discuss later, I do presume continuity of values between the implied author and this highly effaced primary narrator of the opening episodes.) Moreover, one reason that we must distinguish the narrator of the opening episodes of *Ulysses* from the implied author is that in the later episodes this primary narrator is displaced or occluded by various secondary narrators, whereas the implied author necessarily persists throughout the novel. These secondary narrators, manifested by their distinctive stylistic traits, project quite different values from those of implied author and primary narrator. Such a secondary narrator has been recognized by a number of critics, including David Hayman, who has called it "the arranger."[5]

Having drawn these lines between Joyce, the implied author, and the primary narrator, I must acknowledge that, since I see so great a continuity of values among these three entities, I will not insist on maintaining a terminological distinction where there is often no substantial difference. I will, that is, refer to Joyce, or the implied author, or the primary narrator, as the source of various attitudes or techniques.[6]

Critical Rejection of Omniscient Point of View

In order to appreciate the distinctiveness of Joyce's literary aims and techniques in *Ulysses,* we must examine two reiterated modernist critical claims in regard to omniscient point of view. The first is that modern authors disdain the omniscient point of view that was a staple of fiction-writing for virtually all earlier novelists; the second is that this purported disdain of omniscience reflects the death of God, on the assumption that traditional omniscient point of view simulates an omniscient God, whose late-nineteenth-century demise is generally acknowledged. Morton P. Levitt reflects both claims when he speaks of "the Modernists' endeavor to develop narrative techniques which place modern man in his true set-ting—principally their development of a point of view that removes the omniscient-omnipotent Victorian God at the center of the narrative and replaces him with limited, representative man."[7] But omniscient point of view is quite common in twentieth-century literature—indeed, in *Ulysses* itself—and identifying the omniscient perspective with God obscures some interesting uses of that narrative perspective by many twentieth-century writers.

So strong is the wish to expunge "omniscience" from modern fiction—to believe that modernist narratives restrict themselves to "a plausible observer placed at the realistic level of the action" (Morrisette, see n. 7 above)—that it draws otherwise perspicacious critics into error. For ex-ample, Caroline Gordon and Allen Tate discuss "The Dead" as an ex-ample of the Jamesean method of "Central Intelligence," in which a "single Central Intelligence is used throughout the action; the hero (Nar-rator) registers and evaluates everything that happens, including what happens *to* and *in* himself" (*The House of Fiction*, 443). They go on to claim, "The hero is never off the stage and everything that happens is, in the end, referred to him and evaluated by him" (444), showing their great concern to confine all evaluations to some plausible, realistic observer, rather than to some disembodied (deific?) entity.

But in fact "The Dead" is not restricted to Gabriel's physical or mental perspective. The story begins before Gabriel arrives at the party, and some of the language of the opening paragraphs clearly reflects the perspective of Lily, the maid. Even after Gabriel's arrival we do not remain in his presence—for example, the scene between Mr. Browne and the ladies while Gabriel is downstairs with Freddy Malins (*Dubliners*, 182–84). Moreover, we are given exposition about the history of these parties that does not come from or through any character (175–76), and the extensive description of the dinner table involves an array of martial metaphors that seem authorial rather than figural (196–97). In short, the third-person voice that presents the story cannot be identified with the presence, much less the perspective, of any single character. It provides exposition; its description of events and of characters (including Gabriel himself—e.g., the description of his "delicate and restless eyes" [178]) involves qualitative, evaluative, and metaphoric terms; and certainly this voice tells us more of Gabriel than he would himself be capable of telling. Most important, this nonfigural, yet evaluative, perspective evokes the milieu of the event—the Dublin hospitality that Joyce himself acknowledged he had left out of the earlier stories (letter to Stanislaus, 25 September 1906; *Lts*, 2:166), which Gabriel, in his limited and defensive posture, is incapable of appreciating, much less of evoking.

Similarly, Bernard Benstock refuses to attribute omniscience to the text or author of *Ulysses* (*Narrative Con/Texts*, 31–32), and resorts to various circumlocutions to avoid using the term *omniscient* to account for aspects of the text that are not attributable to some character. He speaks, for example, of "the narrational presentation in *Ulysses*" (99), "the textual presentation" (105), or "the narrational style" (106). At one point Benstock acknowledges that "a repository of information exists outside the perspectives of any of the characters, an encyclopaedic knowledge of reference and resource materials unretainable in the average—even highly knowledgeable—mind, but readily recuperable from other sources: reference books, guides, maps, directories, programmes, brochures, newspapers, journals, circulars and advertisements" (108), but he declines to acknowledge any authorial omniscience since he presumes such a tactic should be available only to a "nineteenth-century novelist" (111). But the idea that modern fiction disdains authorial omniscience is a misapprehension, stemming presumably from the critics' identification of omniscient point of view with explicit, suprafigural statements of information and values and tangible authorial personas such as we find in the novels of Fielding or Thackeray. Perhaps modern novels do not often *appear* so traditionally omniscient as *Tom Jones* or *Vanity Fair*, but most are nonetheless omniscient in very meaningful ways.[8]

It is not clear why critics are so reluctant to acknowledge the omniscient perspective within much modern fiction, and especially in Joyce's work. Perhaps the reluctance reflects contemporary biases against authority generally—perhaps, that is, the critics presume an omniscient perspective is outmoded in fiction as well as in religion and metaphysics. Probably it stems as well from our positivistic unease about a collective mind or milieu, or about disembodied qualities and values. In part, though, this reluctance involves confusion as to what comprises "omniscient" point of view. That is, surveying traditional fiction, one might presume the hallmarks of omniscient point of view to be a tangible authorial persona and explicit valuational statements, and this might suggest that any narrative lacking such a persona or apothegms is not "omniscient." But as Wayne Booth says, "There is a curious ambiguity in the term 'omniscience'. Many modern works that we usually classify as narrated dramatically, with everything relayed to us through the limited views of the characters, postulate fully as much omniscience in the silent author as Fielding claims for himself" (*Rhetoric of Fiction,* 161). Similarly, David Goldknopf notes that "seldom does the author overtly assert the authority of his omniscience. Usually he stands *beside* the reader, as he discloses his story, and side by side they remain, in a mutuality of viewpoint and interest" (*Life of the Novel,* 32).

The fact that the author withholds *some* information does not, however, rule out omniscience, since even the most overtly omniscient authors do not tell us everything. In *Tom Jones,* Fielding, for all his volubility about persons and events, withholds crucial information about Tom's identity, allowing it to emerge in its own time. As Booth observes, "very few 'omniscient' narrators are allowed to know or show as much as their authors know" (*Rhetoric of Fiction,* 160). The term, that is, has always referred to a conventional literary device and never to thoroughgoing (or theological) omniscience.

Another label that critics prefer to (or confuse with) *omniscient* is *third-person,* some suggesting that the two terms are mutually exclusive, while others conflate them. For example, Mitchell A. Leaska proclaims that in both *Mrs. Dalloway* and *To the Lighthouse,* Woolf "maintains the third-person angle throughout," and he asks "how precisely this differs from an omniscient-author-point-of-view novel." His answer is less than satisfactory: "The difference, though often not susceptible to detection, is chiefly this: While in the omniscient-author-point-of-view novel, the author looks into the minds of his characters and relates to the reader what is going on there, the information is presented as *he* sees and interprets it, rather than as his people see it. Moreover, in the traditional omniscient novel, the information is narrated as though it had already occurred" ("Concept of Point of View," 265).[9] Richard Brown's *James Joyce* contains a chart describing the point of view of the various episodes in *Ulysses,* in which most episodes are characterized as "3rd person" and/or "inner monologue" (66). Brown explains that "Joyce's 'third-person' narrative is never merely conventional" (67), but he takes no notice of its omniscience or of the extensive degree to which this "third-person" mode presents the inner life of the characters.

While certain carefully restricted modes of third-person presentation may avoid omniscience, rarely are the two categories mutually exclusive. Traditional omniscient novels are usually narrated in the third person, and the third-person narration of Joyce's *Portrait,* for example, should not cloud the fact that its authorial voice is, in meaningful ways, omniscient. Wayne Booth, for example, speaks of the "omniscient, infallible author" in *Portrait* (*Rhetoric of Fiction,* 163). James Moffett and Kenneth R. McElheny, in the afterword to *Points of View,* criticize the mixed principles behind classification schemata and argue, "Some 'omniscience' is more omniscient than other, and no third-person narration can really be limited to the point of view of a character" (566). Keith Booker, in clarifying Conrad's point of view in *Heart of Darkness,* says that he declined to tell the story "in the authoritative voice of the nineteenth-century omniscient third-person narrator" ("Horror of Mortality," 4).

Descriptions of traditional omniscient point of view usually presume a narrator who can be ubiquitous in space and time, can reveal the thoughts and feelings of any of the characters (as well as their "true qualities"), typically "tells" rather than "shows," provides broad thematic statements or apothegms, and—perhaps most important—appears as a tangible narrative persona not identifiable with any character in the work. When such an authorial persona is present, critics regard the point of view as omniscient, even if there are restrictions on the perspective of the persona or on the information that is provided.

But while the overt presence of an authorial persona or explicit thematic statements are the most salient signs of omniscience—and in the absence of these signs, critics often use some other label—they are by no means essential to it. Any authorial perspective has a good claim to omniscience if it can move freely among locales or characters (even if these shifts come between episodes); if it provides information or exposition that does not come through the characters; if it presents the characters' thoughts and feelings in more depth than they themselves could; and if it involves value judgments and qualitative descriptions that do not stem from any "plausible observer." A novel involving these traits is omniscient, even if it lacks the homilies or the overt persona often associated with traditional omniscient fiction. I dwell on this because I shall argue that the primary narrative voice of *Ulysses* possesses every one of these traits, and thus is omniscient, but that for specific reasons Joyce is careful not to let this omniscient perspective manifest itself in a tangible persona.

Joyce's Primary Narrator as Cultural Psyche

Several of the critics I quoted earlier characterize the omniscient narrative persona in deific terms and link the purported modernist disdain of omniscience with the death of God. But rather than seeing the omniscient narrator as an all-knowing deity, I propose a perspective that better expresses Joyce's distinctive purposes and modes of presentation in *Ulysses*—that is, that the omniscient primary narrative voice simulates the cultural psyche, or collective mind, of the world of the novel. This is not a new idea, either about the traditional novel or about *Ulysses,* but it is one that has not been pursued as it deserves and that seems especially appropriate in light of the carefully effaced primary narrator of *Ulysses.*

One insightful example of this claim in regard to earlier novelists is that of J. Hillis Miller in *The Form of Victorian Fiction* (1969). In a chapter entitled "The Narrator as General Consciousness," Miller discusses the role of the omniscient narrator in Thackeray, Eliot, Dickens, Meredith, Hardy, and Trollope. Arguing that in these writers, all of whom use some form of omniscient narrator, the narrative voice reflects a "collective mind" (63), Miller asserts:

> The Victorian novelists tend to assume that each man finds himself from his birth surrounded by a transindividual mind, identical with the words he learns. This mind surrounds him, embraces him, permeates him, from the first day of his life to the end. To write a novel is to identify oneself with this general consciousness, or rather to actualize a participation in it which already exists latently by virtue of a man's birth into the community. . . . The reader of a Victorian novel in his turn is invited by the words of the narrator to enter into complicity with a collective mind which pre-exists the first words of the novel and will continue when they end, though without the novel it might remain invisible. (67)[10]

Miller supports this claim by quoting passages from these authors that implicitly or explicitly involve such a collective mentality. For example, Thackeray at one point says of the "I" narrator of *Vanity Fair,* "'I' is here introduced to personify the world in general—the Mrs. Grundy of each respected reader's private circle" (73), or consider Meredith's explicit statement in the prelude to *The Egoist* that the "comic spirit" is "the spirit born of our united social intelligence" (79), or Trollope's repeated invocation of "'the world'" (87). Similarly, Miller argues that one manifestation of Feuerbach's influence on George Eliot is that "the narrator of *Middle-*

march is precisely that all-inclusive 'consciousness of the species' which was Feuerbach's definition of Christ" (84).

Miller recognizes that some of these authors achieve the effect of a general mentality better than others. He sees Thackeray as less effective in this regard than Trollope, in part because of the "highly individualized voice" in which Thackeray often speaks—for example, referring to himself as the puppet master (69–70). Trollope's more effaced narrator, by contrast, "is perhaps the most perfect example in Victorian fiction of the omniscient narrator as a collective mind" (85), and Miller's explanation of this is relevant to my subsequent claims about *Ulysses:* "Trollope's narrator watches his people with an equable sympathy, a sympathy so perfect and so neutral in temperature that it insinuates itself into the reader's mind until the reader identifies himself with the narrator's consciousness and is no longer aware of it as something other than himself. The narrator becomes invisible in a union of reader and narrator" (85).[11]

Many novelists evoke a collective mentality or cultural milieu in their works, thus manifesting one of the most distinctive and appealing features of the genre (discussed above in chapter 1). One of Eliot's purposes in *Middlemarch*, for example, is the evocation of just such a collective mind (see the quote from her, above, in chapter 1, about her aim to present "the medium in which a character moves"). But while the traditional novel does evoke a milieu and even a collective mentality, it usually does so by virtue of setting, of mood and atmosphere, of incorporating cultural rituals or schemata, of direct invocation of "society" or "tradition" or "common attitudes," rather than by scrupulous use of the narrative voice or persona. While Eliot, for example, evokes a milieu in *Middlemarch* in a variety of ways, she does not deploy her authorial voice specifically toward this end. The result—which incurs the disdain of Michael Levenson, noted above—is that her omniscient narrative voice emerges as a persona rather than an ambience, and we incline to see it as representing an omniscient deity. By contrast, one of the most important, pervasive techniques by which Joyce evokes a collective mind or cultural psyche in *Ulysses* is through careful effacement of the omniscient narrative voice.

The Purported Disappearance of the Author

The refinement of the narrator out of (apparent) existence in some modern fiction has generated one recurrent critical confusion that I must address. It has caused some critics to talk as if not only the narrator but the author has absconded, leaving behind a text that has written itself, or been written by one of its characters, or been generated by the circumstances of the day. This confusion has been fostered by critics' talking loosely about the "disappearance of the author" when they mean the *effacement of the narrative persona*. One early, influential example of such imprecise language is the chapter "Exit Author" in Joseph Warren Beach's *The Twentieth Century Novel* (1932), which begins: "In a bird's-eye view of the English novel from Fielding to Ford, the one thing that will impress you more than any other is the disappearance of the author" (14). Another is to be found in Scholes and Kellogg's statement: "The great trick of modern literary magicians of the Jamesean school is said to be the disappearance of the author" (*Nature of Narrative*, 268). But Roy Pascal, more perspicaciously, quotes a critic who claims that the author has withdrawn from a novel, and then notes: "It is the slogan 'exit author' that we have so often heard . . . ; *by 'author' is meant narrator* (*Dual Voice*, 16; my emphasis).

In a climate of ideas where critics can talk seriously about novels as "self-generating," we may have to restate the obvious.[12] In the most fundamental way, the author's presence manifests itself in the very characters and events comprising the novel, in the ordering of those events, in authorial choices as to the relative prominence given to various characters and events and the perspective from which they are presented. This pervasive authorial presence is of course quite different from the (more or less) palpable presence of a narrator within the work. While such a caveat should not be needed, it nonetheless is appropriate, even necessary, since some critics have collapsed these categories. But even in such experiments with narrational authority as Flann O'Brien's *At Swim-Two-Birds,* where the narrator tells us that a good book may have three openings and a hundred times as many endings (and proceeds to illustrate), or John Fowles's *The French Lieutenant's Woman,* where we have a choice of endings, the underlying fiction is nonetheless generated entirely by O'Brien and Fowles, and the "options" exist only within parameters those authors have created.

Given human ingenuity, it is inevitable that there should be works of fiction—not all of them modernist—that assiduously, if playfully, explore the limits of authorial/narrational control. These include characters who seem to become autonomous or self-generating (O'Brien's *At Swim-Two-Birds*), or hiatuses to be filled in by the reader (as in *Tristram Shandy,* volume VI, chapter 38), or variant endings (Fowles's *The French Lieutenant's Woman*). But such playfulness should not confuse us about who is responsible for the existence of the work that contains these ca-prices. To put such experiments in perspective, we need simply ask our-selves where all of these apparent options would be if O'Brien or Sterne or Fowles had not lived to write the novels that contain them. Critics may talk about "self-generating texts," or about the reader's role in "creating" the novel, but had Joyce died as young as Keats, all the world's readers and all the world's critics could not have brought *Ulysses* into being out of the quotidian events of Edwardian Dublin.

Part II

The Styles, Voices, and Values of *Ulysses*

3

Authorial Voice and Point of View in *Ulysses*

No aspect of *Ulysses* has been more extensively debated than the styles or voices of the various episodes.[1] That the debate has not, however, resulted in consensus about the purpose or meaning of these styles is acknowledged by some of the best critics of the novel. Hugh Kenner observes in the preface to *Joyce's Voices* that *Ulysses* "commences in tacit adherence to the canons of naturalism, of Objectivity, and then disorients readers by deserting them, for reasons that have never been satisfactorily explained. Its profusion of styles—what are we to make of *that?*" (xii–xiii). David Hayman says that "discontinuities like the abrupt style changes that punctuate each chapter" are among "the most intriguing and disturbing features of *Ulysses,*" and that "they have been noted but never fully studied or explained" (*MM*, 1982, 132). In fact, critical debate about the styles of *Ulysses* has widened the rift between those who see the book as a novel reflecting the experiential world through character and event, and those who see it as a self-referential text whose technique is its real subject. And in recent decades the current of that debate has undoubtedly run in favor of those critics who see the technique, the style, as the "subject" of *Ulysses.*[2]

In this book I propose three claims about the various narrative styles and voices of *Ulysses.* My first two points involve the distinctive, carefully wrought "initial style" of *Ulysses,* which I take to include not just the narrative voice of the opening episodes, but the novel's basic authorial choices, strategies, and techniques.[3] About this initial style I will argue, first, that Joyce's careful effacement of the omniscient primary narrator is crucial to his simulation of the cultural psyche, or collective mind, of the novel and, second, that his complex, distinctive techniques of presentation in the initial style of *Ulysses* achieve an inextricable blending of various modernist dichotomies—individual/cultural, conscious/unconscious, inner/outer.

My third point deals with the voices of the obtrusive secondary narrators in later episodes, which I see as far more limited in scope or agency than the primary narrator or the initial style. These voices, I believe, represent styles or literary modes or agendas that Joyce exposes as deficient or mistaken. This evaluation of these secondary voices is grounded in the context provided by the initial style (including the primary narrator), and in the norms and values of the novel as a whole. I will develop these claims by an analysis of the initial style and the primary narrative voice in the opening episodes (chapter 4), by brief discussions of the secondary narrative voices in the later episodes (chapter 5), and by fuller readings of "Wandering Rocks," "Oxen of the Sun," and "Circe" (chapter 6).

To understand the distinctive nature of the initial style in *Ulysses,* we must recognize that it consists of much more than the diction, syntax, and voice of the first six episodes. We must see that it includes character, event, structural patterns, and narrative focus and emphasis, as well as Joyce's carefully crafted techniques of psychological presentation. The critics' emphasis on such salient entities as "voice" and point of view, and on word- and sentence-level linguistic/stylistic traits, has resulted in neglect of more implicit and important modes of authorial presence. As Christine Brooke-Rose puts it in her critique of linguistics as an approach to narrative: "linguistics seemed unable to go much beyond the structure of the sentence and remain significant, despite attempts at discourse analysis. For in fact all, all is text, and textuality is a far richer concept than is syntax or lexic" (*Stories, Theories, and Things,* 25). Similarly, David Trotter says of grammatical descriptions of the language of *Ulysses,* such as those of John Porter Houston or Roy K. Gottfried, that all of them "suffer from a similar vagueness. They admit that grammar won't explain everything, but have no terms for what it won't explain" (*The English Novel in History,* 101).

In *Ulysses,* as in all novels, the most basic expressions of authorial presence and of the novel's values are the characters, the plot events, and the distinctive techniques of the book. Even in modernist or postmodernist fictions, where voice and language are so carefully crafted, these underlying choices and strategies are the most fundamental manifestation of the author within his novel. In *Ulysses* the very personalities of Stephen and Bloom are profound expressions of Joyce's authorial purposes and values—as is his decision to make these characters central to the novel, rather than, perhaps, Deasy and his wife. Moreover, the fact that the paths of Stephen and Bloom cross several times during the day, and that the two ultimately come together, is entirely Joyce's doing, and while we may argue about its meaning, we cannot deny that for some reason Joyce created *this* set of events, rather than another. By contrast, in Woolf's *Mrs. Dalloway* (1925)—whose one-day, urban setting and psychological techniques show its affinity with *Ulysses*—the central characters, Clarissa and Septimus, never meet, thus making the "rapport" between those two utterly different. As a result, Clarissa must (almost mystically) intuit the purposes behind Septimus's suicide, thus enabling him to serve as her "double," as Woolf says in her preface to the Modern Library edition of the novel. Such plot decisions about whether their central characters do or do not meet are fundamental expressions of Joyce's and Woolf's authorial presences and fictional purposes.

We must also recognize that, whatever authority the secondary narrator or "arranger" has in the later episodes, that authority does not extend to fundamental levels of character and plot—for example, to altering Bloom's character from what it is in "Calypso" and "Lotus-Eaters." We may have difficulty in "Oxen of the Sun" making out exactly what Bloom is saying or doing, but we are nonetheless puzzling over *Bloom*, attempting to see how his statements and actions in this episode cohere with his personality as we know it from all other parts of the novel. (For fuller discussion of the characters' continuity and integrity, and their independence of the secondary narrative voices, see chapter 5.)

The point, then, is that the most stable and pervasive modes of authorial presence in *Ulysses* are not the "speaking voice" or the diction or syntax of any episode, but the very characters and events and structures and techniques of the novel. These aspects of the book, attributable to Joyce, substantiate and give coherence to the fictive world of *Ulysses,* saving the novel from arbitrariness or caprice. They are the real "rock of Ithaca" underlying the other strata of the novel, both in the early episodes, where the primary narrator's voice is "reliable," and in the later episodes, where the voices of the secondary narrators are not. In this sense, then, the stability of character and event and of the cultural milieu evoked by the novel's fictive world—that is, by Joyce's continuous agency in the book— is an integral part of the initial style that remains firm beneath our feet even after the voice of the early episodes has been obscured by that of other narrators.[4]

Furthermore, these events and structural correspondences and especially these characters provide the most pervasive manifestation of the values of the novel, since, as Franz Stanzel points out, an author's work never simply presents reality—it always interprets it (*Narrative Situations,* 7–10). I agree, then, with Wayne Booth that "the author's judgment is always present, always evident to anyone who knows how to look for it" (*Rhetoric of Fiction,* 20) and with Marilyn French that "it is impossible to write a sentence, much less a novel, without making value choices" (*Book as World,* 36), and I concur in her inference of the values of *Ulysses* from the characters. (See her discussion of Stephen's intellectual acumen [82] and of Bloom's *caritas* [85].) Nor does Joyce abjure the role of interpreter and evaluator that authorship requires of him; *Ulysses* does endorse certain values, not only in the way it disposes the characters and events that it selects for dramatization, but even in the narrative voice of the opening episodes, which (as we shall see) is persistently evaluative. This is not to say that Joyce presents the values of the novel simply or unambiguously; it is to say that the fictive world of *Ulysses,* of which James Joyce is the creator, involves a cultural milieu that is suffused with values. And while the styles of some of the later episodes may obscure the characters and events and the implied values, these values nonetheless remain fundamental to the novel and provide the basis of our recognizing the limitations and distortions of the later styles.

Another crucial aspect of the initial style involves the techniques and strategies of psychological presentation that Joyce so carefully developed, modifying those he had used in *Dubliners* and *Portrait,* to achieve in the opening episodes of *Ulysses* a mode of presentation that is uniquely suited to his artistic purposes. Critics who see nothing normative or paradigmatic about the initial style have not reflected enough about the implications of these carefully crafted techniques of psychic presentation and do not realize how profoundly and effectively these techniques express the novel's worldview and values—far better than any of the secondary styles of later episodes. Similarly, those who argue about whether the "styles" of the various early episodes are the same or different—that is, whether the diction or sentence structure of "Telemachus" is consistent with that of "Nestor" or "Calypso" or "Lestrygonians"—concern themselves with details while overlooking more fundamental continuities, and thus they fail to recognize how the techniques of all of the opening episodes are so appropriate to Joyce's intentions and so finely attuned to the subject matter. Moreover, the distinctive capacity of the initial style to fulfill Joyce's purposes becomes one standard by which each of the subsequent styles of the novel is shown to be deficient.

For many critics the claim that there is any normative style in *Ulysses,* or that Joyce stands behind any of the book's voices, is suspect, because it runs counter both to his presumed linguistic relativism and to his pride in his own protean stylistic capacities. Surely, this argument runs, Joyce knew that there is no objective or translucent style, and moreover, this master of all styles would never permit himself to be identified with any single style, which could subject the parodist himself to parody. Undoubtedly Joyce did reflect on these issues, and perhaps the role of a stylistic Proteus held some appeal for him. But I believe that Joyce weighed carefully the various alternatives available (in theory) to him as a novelist: first, to present his material "objectively"—without any coloring whatsoever of value; second, to assume a persistently relativistic and parodic stance, from which he could expose the insufficiency of others' values and styles without committing himself to any; or third, to ground his novel in narrative devices and techniques and in values that are admittedly neither objective nor absolute, but that manifest his own artistic purposes and values. Joyce recognized the first alternative as impossible, saw the second as superficially appealing but finally undesirable and irresponsible, and embraced the third—in the initial style of *Ulysses*.

We have already examined the first of these alternatives. The impossibility of an objective, value-free work of literature is self-evident; values are inherently expressed in the characters the author creates and attends to, in the events and situations he creates and emphasizes, in the structures linking the parts of the work together, and in the techniques by which he presents his material.

Joyce's rejection of valuational and stylistic relativism—the second alternative—is a broader and more complex issue, and in a sense this entire book is devoted to it, since I am arguing that Joyce persistently makes value judgments about the various styles of *Ulysses*. But there is evidence of several kinds that Joyce is not a relativist. One is that Joyce's earlier works—*Dubliners* and *A Portrait*—clearly do involve values, such as the wish to expose various sources of paralysis, including the ways that certain modes of language can paralyze us, and it seems plausible to see *Ulysses* as consistent with those human and aesthetic values, rather than having abandoned them. (I develop this point in chapter 5.)

Furthermore, *Ulysses* does espouse certain values over others. Among the values that the novel sanctions are the sincerity and commitment and intellectual courage behind Stephen's struggles to find a viable worldview, and the openness to experience and concern for others that are such deep features of Bloom's personality (in Marilyn French's terms, his *caritas*). Among the qualities that the novel criticizes are the materialism, mockery, and cynicism exemplified in Mulligan, the presumptuous and insular "wisdom" of Deasy, and the purblind chauvinism of the citizen. Recognition that the novel espouses certain values and abjures others does little to resolve specific textual cruxes, or to determine what tone Joyce evokes toward certain characters (seeing Deasy as sententious and narrow-minded, for example, does not erode all of our sympathy for the old man), but amidst claims that *Ulysses* is relativistic or value neutral, such recognition provides helpful guideposts.[5]

In addition, the parodic stance is itself measured and found wanting, both in the character of Buck Mulligan and in the "Cyclops" episode as a whole. Mulligan employs his considerable verbal powers to mock and undercut a variety of values, literary and religious, showing how little use he has for "Stephen's views on the eternal affirmation of the spirit of man in literature" (*U,* 17.29). But in the course of the novel, Mulligan's measure is taken, and his callow self-interest, reductionistic materialism, and cynical mockery are rejected. Through the secondary narrative voice of the "Cyclops" episode, Joyce exposes the hollowness of an undiscriminating addiction to parody, for if we ask what the underlying basis or purpose of this parody is—what substantial values the parody is grounded in, and what specious values it exposes—we find that there are none. Rather, we discover a narrative voice that parodies all qualities indiscriminately, whether pacifism or patriotism or love, and that uses mockery as a defense against commitment. (I develop these ideas in chapter 5 also.)

To say that Joyce sanctions the initial style is not, however, to see it as either objective or absolute. The style is interpretive and value laden in a variety of ways, from the choice of situations and perspectives it emphasizes, and the techniques and devices used to present the characters and events, to the tone and mood that it evokes, to the specific evaluative words (many of them undeniably authorial) it employs. Nor is the authorial judgment confined to such implicit devices as selection of perspective or juxtaposition; it emerges as an active quality, enabling, even requiring, us to evaluate Stephen and Bloom and Mulligan—that is, to respond to them with feeling and with discrimination. Through this narrative perspective we come to regard Stephen and Bloom with profound sympathy, but we also recognize their foibles and failings; we realize that they are in their different ways insecure and escapist, and as a result we hope that they will confront their fears and become what they are capable of becoming.[6] Through this same narrative perspective we see Mulligan as a superficially engaging but shallow and selfish materialist, and later in the novel, we see the pernicious effects of chauvinism in "Cyclops" and of sentimentality in "Nausicaa." Thus the full-fledged initial style provides a normative base that underlies even the later episodes, where the narrative voice becomes aberrant.

My point about the obtrusive narrative voices of the later episodes can be stated briefly but will require the whole of chapters 5 and 6 to illustrate—

that is, these voices represent styles and values that Joyce exposes as insufficient or distorting. In principle, this is by no means an unprecedented view; a number of critics have proposed that some chapters involve a narrative persona whose aims and values run counter to those of the novel. But my claim is at once broader and more specific: the style of each of the later episodes is the work of a secondary narrator who is permitted to serve as the *presenter* of the material of each episode.[7] This narrator's authority extends to the stylistic presentation of the characters and events of the episode—even to their obfuscation—but it does not extend to liberties with the personalities of the characters or with the content of their thought or with what events occur in the novel, all of which are the continuing domain and responsibility of the implied author/primary narrator.

My claim, then, is that each of the various narrative voices of the later episodes of *Ulysses* illustrates some literary mode or theory about language that Joyce does not sanction. I make this claim for the "headlines" in "Aeolus," for "Scylla and Charybdis," for "Wandering Rocks," for "Sirens," for the parodic voice in "Cyclops," for the first half of "Nausicaa," and for "Oxen of the Sun," "Circe," "Eumaeus," "Ithaca," and "Penelope." The normative narrative style or some derivative of it exists in the first six episodes, in "Aeolus" apart from the headlines, in "Lestrygonians," in the second half of "Nausicaa," and behind the first-person narration of "Cyclops." Joyce's disdain of the styles of certain episodes is generally acknowledged. But if most critics recognize that Joyce abjures the sentimentalism of "Nausicaa" and the circumlocution of "Eumaeus," they do not accept a similar claim for "Oxen of the Sun" and "Circe," or for other later episodes. The consensus about these episodes is that, whatever is going on there, Joyce stands behind it. I will challenge that idea in subsequent chapters.

4

The Initial Style of *Ulysses*

The initial style of *Ulysses* consists not simply of voice (i.e., narrator's presence/point of view) and language (i.e., diction/grammar/syntax), but involves as well Joyce's authorial choices and strategies for the whole book. These include the characters and events of the novel, the hundreds of parallels and links that exist among characters and episodes, the distinctive psychological techniques, the pervasive allusive and cultural schemata, and so forth. These choices and strategies generate the fictive world of *Ulysses,* which is the "rock of Ithaca" underlying the novel and providing for the reader a stable base that persists even in the presence of the unreliable secondary narrative voices of the later episodes. Acknowledging that the initial style includes these fundamental aspects of the novel enables us to recognize the inherent values implicit in these strategies and to see that, even in its later stylistic divagations, *Ulysses* does not involve linguistic or moral relativism, nor does it become merely self-referential. While I shall continue to draw upon the continuity provided by these undergirding elements of character and event, my focus in this chapter is on the narrative and psychological techniques of the novel, in order to show how these carefully crafted aspects of the initial style fulfill Joyce's aims in *Ulysses.*

Joyce's distinctive techniques in *Ulysses* remain insufficiently recognized because critical opinion has foisted upon Joyce orthodox modernist aims such as authorial effacement and "objectivity," or has presumed that his works subscribe to post-Cartesian dualisms.[1] Joyce, though, was guided throughout the writing of *Ulysses* not by modernist shibboleths or clichés, but by his own artistic purposes, and he strove constantly to adapt existing techniques and to develop new ones that would effect those purposes. Critical misunderstanding of Joyce's underlying intentions has fostered discussions of the style of *Ulysses* that focus piecemeal upon some single aspect—for example, the narrative voice or the interior monologue or the allusive parallels. But understanding the distinctive style of *Ulysses* depends upon recognizing the unity of its intentions and effects, especially in regard to the various techniques of authorial voice and of psychological presentation in the initial style.

My discussion of the technical aspects of the initial style will emphasize two congruent aims, both of them crucial to Joyce's intention to remedy certain deficiencies or distortions of the dualistic, positivistic worldview that we have inherited from Galileo, Descartes, Locke, and Hume. One of Joyce's aims is to simulate the collective cultural milieu that is the psychic medium bridging and sustaining self and world; the other is to show the inextricable unity of aspects of experience that the modernist climate of opinion regards as dualistically opposed— that is, to resolve the Cartesian split. In *A Portrait of the Artist* Joyce subverted the Cartesian dualisms through exploring the psyche of a "single individual" (a major thesis of my *Antimodernism of Joyce's "Portrait"*); in *Ulysses* he does this on a broader canvas that involves many individuals, a city, and a cultural milieu. For all the differences in scope and technique between these two novels, Joyce's fundamental purpose in both is the subversion of modernist dichotomies. The more clearly we grasp this purpose in *Ulysses,* the better we understand how skillfully and distinctively Joyce's stylistic and technical devices fulfill that aim.

The distinctiveness—or uniqueness—of the psychological techniques of *Ulysses* has been recognized by many perceptive critics. Leon Edel in *The Modern Psychological Novel* argues, "There has been a singular failure to recognize that the Joycean novel belongs to a separate category of fiction within the art of the novel" (vii). Later he says more specifically, "It was Joyce who, possessing an incomparable mastery of words, succeeded above all writers in capturing the atmosphere of the mind" (75). He adds, "His experiment transcended by far the first stages of the novel of subjectivity. Proust and Dorothy Richardson had confined themselves to a single consciousness. Joyce, at one leap, went beyond them to capture the atmosphere of the mind" (77). Franz Stanzel asserts that in the opening episodes of *Ulysses,* "Joyce opens new paths in the presentation of consciousness" (*Narrative Situations,* 155).

This distinctiveness is a persistent theme of Erwin R. Steinberg's *The Stream of Consciousness and Beyond in "Ulysses"* (1973). For example, Steinberg notes, "By developing the stream-of-consciousness technique so completely and so imaginatively, he made available to the novelists who followed him a very sensitive and very useful method of delineating character and simulating consciousness" (257). He adds that "the measure of Joyce as an artist is . . . in his responding to a challenge which his predecessors had barely begun to meet, recognizing the promise of what Dujardin and others had started, and developing techniques to simulate multidimensional reality" (269). Zack Bowen has described Joyce's "blend of the narrative line with interior monologue" as "unique among Joyce's books" and "one of the most prolonged and sophisticated innovative uses in literature of the blend of narrational description and stream-of-consciousness thought" (*"Ulysses,"* 434). Melvin Friedman, quoting a passage from "Telemachus," says of Joyce's technique of presentation, "This is at first quite disconcerting. There is really nothing in the novel before Joyce to prepare one for it" (*Stream of Consciousness,* 222–23). And much earlier W. B. Yeats perceptively said of the early episodes of *Ulysses* (appearing in the *Little Review*), "It is an entirely new thing—neither what the eye sees nor the ear hears, but what the rambling mind thinks and imagines from moment to moment. He has certainly surpassed in intensity any novelist of our time" (letter to John Quinn, 23 July 1918; *Letters of W. B. Yeats,* 651).

These claims are not mere hyperbole, and yet *Ulysses* criticism has never done justice to what this distinctiveness of technique involves. The more clearly I understand Joyce's fictional aims, the more I am convinced that he did specific things with narrative voice and with various techniques of psychological presentation that no other author has done and that we have not yet fully recognized and appreciated.

Before illustrating the distinctive techniques through which the initial style of *Ulysses* simulates the cultural psyche and resolves modernist dualisms, I wish to set some historical context, to clarify why Joyce felt these aims to be important, as well as why modernist critical opinion has been unresponsive to such goals. (The following paragraphs recapitulate an argument developed more fully in my *Antimodernism of Joyce's "Portrait,"* 22–38.)

Modernist Skepticism about a Collective Mind

Reviewing the distinction between primary and secondary qualities that was made by Galileo and built upon by Descartes, Locke, and Hume will help us appreciate the intellectual context that Joyce inherited and the nature and scale of the challenges that he took on in *Ulysses.* As new instruments made it possible to observe and quantify physical phenomena, Galileo felt the need to distinguish between those qualities "in the objects themselves" (such as mass and extension) and those engendered by the observer's response (such as taste, color, odor). The former Galileo called primary qualities, the latter secondary qualities, and of these secondary qualities he said, "I think that tastes, odors, colors, and so forth are no more than mere names so far as pertains to the subject wherein they reside, and that they have their habitation only in the sensorium. Thus, if the living creature were removed, all these qualities would be removed and annihilated" (from "The Assayer," in *The Controversy on the Comets of 1618*, 309). Galileo goes on to claim: "I do not believe that for exciting in us tastes, odors, and sounds there are required in external bodies anything but sizes, shapes, numbers, and slow or fast movements; and I think that if ears, tongues, and noses were taken away, shapes and numbers and motions would remain but not odors or tastes or sounds. These are, I believe, nothing but names, apart from the living animal" (311). In other words, the world consists solely of matter in motion, and all of the qualities that we attribute to it are "merely subjective."

From this momentous distinction, it was an easy step to Descartes's proclamation of two distinct modes of reality, mind and matter—*res cogitans* and *res extensa*—thus paving the way for the anti-experiential "empiricism" of Locke and Hume, and for the still-intransigent "mind/ brain problem." Under the influence of this Cartesian dualism, we have come to believe that psyche—mind, consciousness, self-awareness—exists (if at all) only in individual persons—that is, that a mind must be grounded in a brain, though how even that can be, we do not understand. The modernist perspective engendered by these ideas of Galileo and Descartes, then, not only involves an array of entrenched dualisms and denies any psychic dimension to physical nature (understood simply as matter in motion), it is profoundly skeptical as well of any collective mind or cultural psyche, since such a psyche can presumably have no physical locus or substrate other than the brains of *individual* persons. As a result of this reductionistic thinking, the cultural psyche that had always been taken as much for granted as the air we breathe became an object of skeptical scrutiny and was found by avant-garde thinkers to be an unsustainable, unnecessary hypothesis, as Hume had shown the ideas of substance, causation, and personal identity to be.[2]

As modern Western thought became permeated by this schizoid division between mind and matter, subject and object, personal and cultural, writers positioned themselves as symbolists or naturalists, and wrestled with the claims of interpretive versus documentary realism (as we saw in chapter 1). But Joyce, perhaps because of his grounding in Aristotelian/ Thomistic philosophy and his profound intuitions about human experience, rejected Cartesian dualism.[3] His response was to develop techniques to dramatize the speciousness of these presumed dichotomies and to illustrate the various confusions and contradictions that modernist thinking had fallen into, especially in regard to the subtle symbiosis of "self" and "world." The result was the distinctive style and strategies of *Ulysses*. Tim Cribb acknowledges this response when he speaks of Joyce's revolution against the imperialism of the Cartesian mind and the reactive regime of Romantic subjectivism, which prepared him for the writing of *Ulysses* ("James Joyce," 73). John McGowan similarly recognizes that *Ulysses* demonstrates the utter permeability of boundaries of self and world, conscious and unconscious, past and present ("From Pater to Wilde to Joyce," 441).

Three Aspects of the Initial Style of *Ulysses*

I shall focus on three aspects of the initial style of *Ulysses:* authorial presence or voice, techniques of psychological presentation, and the allusive method. I turn first to the narrative voice, because Joyce's disposition of this voice is crucial to other aspects of the initial style, such as his subtle blending of authorial and figural material, and his continuous evocation of allusive and cultural schemata. First I shall show that this voice is "omniscient"—that is, that it is distinguishable (though not separable) from the voices of the characters, that it moves among the minds of a number of characters, and that it involves qualitative terms and evaluative judgments. Next I shall show how this carefully (but not totally) effaced narrative voice is essential to Joyce's simulating the cultural psyche or collective mind of the novel's fictive world.

The Omniscience of the Authorial Voice

To many readers it is obvious that the opening episodes of *Ulysses* involve an omniscient narrative voice. But in light of critical comments that ambiguously describe this voice as "objective" or that flatly deny the existence of a narrational voice, this fundamental point cannot be taken for granted.[4]

Instead of the radical authorial effacement that first-person point of view or sheer interior monologue would permit (as in Dujardin's *Les Lauriers sont coupés* or the "Penelope" episode), Joyce chooses in the opening episodes of *Ulysses* to present his material through a narrator who speaks in third person and past tense: "Stately, plump Buck Mulligan came from the stairhead, bearing a bowl of lather on which a mirror and a razor lay crossed" (*U*, 1.1); or "Sitting at his [Sargent's] side Stephen solved out the problem" (*U*, 2.151); or "Mr Bloom went round the corner and passed the drooping nags of the hazard" (*U*, 5.210). These passages are spoken by a voice that is not that of Mulligan or Stephen or Bloom, an undeniable, persistent voice whose presence is not a flaw in Joyce's method, but an integral part of it.

For entire paragraphs in "Proteus" and "Lestrygonians," this voice is effaced and we have what appears to be a first-person interior monologue presentation. But the monologue nonetheless comes *through* the third-person, past-tense perspective of the primary narrator, which undergirds the entire presentation and reappears frequently—sometimes in the very midst of the monologue—thus making it inaccurate to describe the technique (as some critics have) simply as interior monologue. (For instances of recurrent, pervasive third-person, past-tense presentation in a variety of contexts, see *U*, 3.10, 3.61, 3.147, 3.437, 8.10, 8.295, 8.371, 8.414, etc.) Often this third-person authorial voice takes on the idiom or the attitude of the character (of which more shortly), but the voice remains for the most part distinguishable (mainly by grammatical form) even when it is not separable from the character. (Later in this chapter we shall examine sentences in which it is not even distinguishable.)

One traditional omniscient function of this voice is to provide exposition about characters or events. For example: "Buck Mulligan attacked the hollow beneath his underlip" (*U*, 1.115); "Talbot slid his closed book into his satchel" (*U*, 2.90); "Stephen closed his eyes to hear his boots crush crackling wrack and shells" (*U*, 3.10); "The cat walked stiffly round a leg of the table with tail on high" (*U*, 4.15); "Having read it all [the letter from Martha Clifford] he took it from the newspaper and put it back in his sidepocket" (*U*, 5.266); "An incoming train clanked heavily above his head, coach after coach" (*U*, 5.313); "Ned Lambert glanced back" (*U*, 6.692). Nor can this voice be explained as a third-person expression of the perspective of Stephen or Bloom, for they are not always present. For a brief portion of "Telemachus," we are with Mulligan, not Stephen (*U*, 1.1–10), and in "Hades" and "Lestrygonians" we are for a time in the presence of characters who talk about Bloom (*U*, 6.526–34, 6.690–738, and 8.937–1027). Such passages prevent our seeing Stephen or Bloom as the "Central Intelligence" even of the episodes they dominate.[5] The persistent third-person, past-tense statements in these early episodes demonstrate the existence of a distinct narrative voice.

Moreover, the omniscience of this voice is shown by its not being restricted to "objective" description and factual exposition; it presents the characters' thoughts and feelings. The opening paragraph of "Calypso," for example—entirely in third person—apprises us of Mr. Leopold Bloom's liking for the inner organs of beasts and fowls. The second paragraph, continuing in third person and past tense, omnisciently reveals what is going on in his mind: "Kidneys were in his mind as he moved about the kitchen" (*U,* 4.6). Similarly, when Stephen is talking with Mulligan, we are told: "He had spoken himself into boldness. Stephen, shielding the gaping wounds which the words had left in his heart . . ." (*U,* 1.216). Nor is such information provided only about the main characters; in "Hades" we are told: "Mr Power gazed at the passing houses with rueful apprehension" (*U,* 6.310). Such constructions clearly involve a voice other than that of the characters, and the kind and range of information this voice provides is "omniscient." And as we shall see later in this chapter, this authorial presentation of mental/psychic processes is profound and extensive.

Not only does this authorial voice tell us the characters' thoughts and feelings, it involves qualitative and evaluative terms that cannot be attributed to the characters. This practice of course contravenes the modernist imperative that if a novel uses a perspective that cannot be identified with any individual character, the authorial voice should confine itself to descriptive rather than evaluative statements. For the voice not to channel its evaluations through a character would presumably suggest the antimodernist idea of a discarnate (collective) psyche that is capable of sustaining evaluations or judgments. This is essentially the point that Michael Levenson makes about Conrad's *Nigger of the "Narcissus"*—that is, that Conrad "clings fastidiously to externals" until he brings in a first-person narrator to serve as an evaluator of the scene (*Genealogy of Modernism,* 5; see chapter 2, above, for other strictures against nonfigural judgments).

Before demonstrating the presence of "subjective" elements in the authorial voice of *Ulysses,* I must address a relevant point. For the modernist stance on this issue to be consistent, it should prohibit the disembodied authorial voice from indulging in not only evaluative terms, but all qualitative terms as well. That is, if we accept the idea that the world apart from any observer consists only of "objective" entities, then we should acknowledge, as Galileo insisted, that even qualities such as warm or cold or smooth or rough exist only in the sensorium of some observer, and thus that they have no more "objective" existence than do moral judgments or evaluations. To be metaphysically consistent with the modernists' dictum, then, any nonfigural authorial perspective—that is, any perspective other than that of an individual character—should avoid not only evaluative terms such as *Stately* (*U,* 1.1) or *vacant* (*U,* 6.721) or *civilly* (*U,* 8.1026), but qualitative terms such as *plump* (*U,* 1.1) or *swift* (*U,* 8.958) or *large* (*U,* 6.707). (All of the preceding are drawn either from descriptions of

Stephen and Bloom, or from passages where those characters are absent, and thus they are clearly "authorial.") To my knowledge, such disdain of all qualitative terms is a standard of objective rigor that no modernist critic has proposed, and that no novelist aspires to.[6]

In fact, the authorial voice in *Ulysses* does *not* disdain either qualitative or evaluative terms, for the novel contains many instances of both that are not attributable to any character and that are clearly "omniscient." A number of such terms occur in description of Buck Mulligan in "Telemachus." In the second sentence of the novel, we are told: "A yellow dressinggown, ungirdled, was sustained gently behind him on the mild morning air" (*U*, 1.2); and soon after: "Solemnly he came forward and mounted the round gunrest" (*U*, 1.9); "He added in a preacher's tone" (*U*, 1.20); "He skipped off the gunrest and looked gravely at his watcher" (*U*, 1.30); "A pleasant smile broke quickly over his lips" (*U*, 1.33); "he said gaily" (*U*, 1.34); "A tolerant smile curled his lips" (*U*, 1.95); "A flush which made him seem younger and more engaging rose to Buck Mulligan's cheek" (*U*, 1.200). These authorial sentences involve a wide array of qualitative and evaluative terms. Moreover, it seems unlikely any of these terms reflect Stephen's perspective, and those in the earliest sentences cannot, because they occur before Stephen appears on the scene. Moreover, Stephen himself is subject to authorial evaluation: "Stephen said with energy and growing fear" (*U*, 1.60); "Stephen said gloomily" (*U*, 1.90); "Stephen, depressed by his own voice" (*U*, 1.188); "Stephen listened in scornful silence" (*U*, 1.418).

Similarly, in "Calypso" the author tells us: "Gelid light and air were in the kitchen but out of doors gentle summer morning everywhere" (*U*, 4.7); in "Lotus-Eaters" we are told of Bloom: "While his eyes still read blandly he took off his hat quietly inhaling his hairoil and sent his right hand with slow grace over his brow and hair" (*U*, 5.20). Several words in this last sentence clearly are qualitative or evaluative, but do not stem from the mind of Bloom: *blandly, quietly, with slow grace.* We may be tempted by the unobtrusive appropriateness of these terms, or by their arising so directly from Bloom's acts, to see them as Bloom's own, or perhaps to call them an "objective" account, but neither judgment would be accurate. While Bloom is of course carrying out these acts, he is not using, even implicitly, these words to describe his own acts; the words come from the authorial voice. (Joyce's omniscient presentation often involves authorial description of what the character is immediately experiencing but does not articulate; cf. the discussion of Stephen's moving toward the Pigeon House, later in this chapter.) And in "Hades," as the cortege proceeds down Brunswick Street, we are told: "They went past the bleak pulpit of saint Mark's" (*U,* 6.183). Here *bleak* certainly involves a qualitative, even evaluative, response, but it is not appropriate to attribute the term to any individual in the carriage, especially in light of the plural "They."

These early episodes, then, involve a voice distinguishable from that of the characters; that voice provides not only exposition, but an account of the characters' thoughts and feelings; and it involves qualitative and evaluative terms that cannot be ascribed to the characters. It has, that is, the hallmarks of authorial omniscience.

Authorial effacement and simulation of cultural psyche

In chapter 1 I documented modernist critical insistence that the novelist should show, not tell, and should refine himself out of existence. Often invoked in support of this idea is Stephen's dictum in *A Portrait of the Artist* that "the artist, like the God of the creation, remains within or behind or beyond or above his handiwork, invisible, refined out of existence, indifferent, paring his fingernails" (*PoA,* 215; Stephen's phrase adapts ideas from Flaubert's letters; see Scholes and Kain, *Workshop of Daedalus,* 247–48). But though it has been presumed to describe Joyce's own intention, this brief phrase does not convey Stephen's full statement on this issue, much less Joyce's practice. Sheldon Brivic astutely points out that Stephen's statement doesn't preclude the author's going *into* his work: "the doctrine of authorial absence has led us to see Stephen in *A Portrait* as saying that an author disappears *from* his work rather than *into* it."[7] Brivic's point is confirmed by the context of Stephen's remark, for he has just said, "The personality of the artist passes into the narration itself, flowing round and round the persons and the action like a vital sea," and he goes on to claim that in the dramatic form, "the vitality which has flowed and eddied round each person fills every person with such vital force that he or she assumes a proper and intangible esthetic life" (*PoA,* 215). Stephen here is describing the *dramatic* form, where the author is most effaced, yet even within that form the authorial "personality" is said to subsist around and within every character. Thus by no means is the author absent; rather, he exists in his work in a form that sounds very much like a collective mind or cultural psyche.

That *Ulysses* involves some supraindividual entity has been recognized by a number of critics.[8] Such claims are usually grounded in the "meta-realistic" sharing of ideas among the characters (especially Stephen and Bloom), which strongly suggests a communal mind such as W. B. Yeats describes in his well-known 1901 essay "Magic."[9] I concur in this reading of such psychological evidence, but my present argument for a cultural psyche in *Ulysses* is based as well on considerations of narrative technique—on the carefully effaced authorial voice and the merging of figural and authorial perspectives—and on how the pervasive allusive schemata function in the novel.

The omniscient authorial voice in the early chapters of *Ulysses*, while undeniably present, does not attract attention to itself or project a characterizable persona. On the contrary, it remains carefully, but not totally, effaced. In contrast to traditional omniscient fiction where the narrative voice emerges as a tangible persona—*Tom Jones, Vanity Fair, Middlemarch*—in *Ulysses* the narrative presence remains unpersonified and implicit. I believe Joyce took pains to achieve this quality, and that it plays a crucial role in the novel's evocation of a collective cultural milieu, as well as in the presentation of the characters' psychic processes and in the many allusive schemata within the novel.[10]

There is critical testimony both positive and negative to how successfully Joyce keeps his narrative voice implicit and beneath our notice. For example, Erwin R. Steinberg asserts that Joyce "was probably concerned about not making the opening chapters seem too obviously written from the point of view of the omniscient author" (*SoC&B,* 34, reiterated on 35). He later states, "In the first eleven chapters, there is no sign of a narrator other than the rhetorical gestures" (120). W. J. Lillyman says of the technique of interior monologue (as exemplified in *Ulysses*) that it "represents the culmination of the trend to remove the narrator's voice from the novel or, more precisely, to remove those features of narration which make the reader *aware* of the narrator's mediating voice. I make this distinction since all parts of all novels are obviously 'narrated'. The important question is, however, to what extent the narrator makes his presence felt" ("Interior Monologue," 47–48). Similarly, Robert Humphrey says of a passage from "Telemachus," "It is notable that the manner in which the author appears in this monologue is such that it would be scarcely perceptible to a casual reader that he is there at all" (*Stream of Consciousness,* 28).

Joyce's success in effacing his narrator is shown as well by other critics' denying that any narrator exists in the novel. Shari Benstock, for example, claims that, apart from the "Cyclops" episode, "*Ulysses* proceeds without the mediation of narrators" ("Who Killed Cock Robin?" 261). In her and Bernard Benstock's essay "The Benstock Principle," they would eliminate by fiat any "narrator" that does not refer to himself as "I." They claim, "In order for a 'narrator' to exist in the text, he must be present in his person. In reality, this leaves only the choice of first-person narration ('I'), since second-person narration is almost unknown and third-person narration suggests in both its person and syntactical structure the absence of a present, personalized someone who tells us the story" (14–15). But any authorial presence that refers to itself as "I" necessarily emerges for the reader as a characterizable persona or a full-fledged character (as in "Cyclops"), forgoing its status as simply the text's narrator.

The Benstocks' fiat would prevent Joyce's doing exactly what I am claiming he takes pains to do in *Ulysses*—use a third-person voice that is clearly not that of any character (or any "present, personalized someone"), and that, in order to achieve specific effects, does *not* personify itself. Interesting in this regard is Bernard Benstock's statement: "Direct narration in *Ulysses* rarely displays any consciousness of its own, hardly comparable to the omniscience for which narrative sources are often credited in fictional texts. Essentially, Joycean narrative directions depend upon the limited consciousness of the 'centered' character . . ." (*Narrative Con/Texts*, 31–32). The first sentence here acknowledges how little "persona" Joyce's narrator takes on, but the second shows Benstock's wish to restrict all evaluative (and qualitative?) terms to the consciousness of some character. For example, Benstock quotes, "Gelid light and air were in the kitchen but out of doors gentle summer morning everywhere" (*U*, 4.7), and observes that "'summer' here is a subjective adjective"—presumably meaning that whatever qualities this term has originate in Bloom, not in a narrator.

As we saw in chapter 2, Benstock goes to great lengths to deny the existence of any omniscient voice; he concludes by claiming, "What masquerades as open and objective narration is often unmasked as the interplay between observable phenomena and the limited consciousness of the subjective character . . ." (38). But this statement overlooks the fact that the only "observable phenomena" that enter into any novel are those selected by the author. In any event, the Benstocks' claim that there is no narrator in these episodes testifies to how little attention this narrator draws to itself, as does the striking difference of critical opinion about whether the novel has a narrator, and whether that narrator is omniscient or "objective."

That the primary narrative voice of *Ulysses* remains beneath notice may seem a negative claim or a nonachievement, but this is by no means the case. It requires special care for an author to remain present but effaced, and especially to do so in a way that maintains an overall tone of sympathy toward his fictive creation—as Joyce does. Most authors' attempts at effacement result in distinct irony toward their characters, as in Flaubert's *Madame Bovary,* while Joyce's effacement in *Ulysses* achieves a very different tone—balanced and even sympathetic. The author must maintain a delicate balance if he is to remain unobtrusive while the text persistently uses an omniscient mode of presentation that involves qualitative and evaluative terms—as we have seen is the case. This effaced narrator must deny himself appearances "in his own proper person"—that is, referring to himself as I, speaking to the reader, or presenting overt truths about a character's nature—and must forgo as well pointed philosophical observations or distinctive words or metaphors that we might be tempted to attribute to a persona.[11]

In addition to denying himself overt appearances, Joyce (or the implied author) uses other devices to remain unobtrusive. Perhaps the most important such device, because it so effectively simulates the collective psyche, is effacement into a character's perspective—or more precisely, merging the authorial and figural perspectives. This technique is pinpointed by Erwin R. Steinberg, who says that "in effacing himself, in attempting to become 'invisible,' Joyce tried to make his omniscient author's sentences less obtrusive by flavoring them with the characteristics of the stream of consciousness of the character with which he was dealing at the time" (*SoC&B*, 121). We are all familiar with what Hugh Kenner has dubbed the "Uncle Charles principle" in Joyce's fiction, according to which the narrative voice approximates the perspective of a character so that the "exposition" itself takes on the coloring of that individual's personality.[12] Though this device is more common in *Dubliners* and *Portrait,* where free indirect discourse is the main mode of presentation, something similar does occur in *Ulysses.* In *Ulysses,* however, the aim is not simply to refine the author out of existence, but to evoke the cultural psyche, and so Joyce's third-person authorial presence remains distinguishable (if not always separable) from any character.

This technique enables various degrees of affinity between the individual character and the narrative voice, and thus involves something like a gravitational (or psychic) field that becomes stronger as we approach its origin. While this narrator may asymptotically approach effacement into a character's idiom and personality, the third-person authorial voice nonetheless remains detectable, and can subsequently withdraw from one character's psychic sphere and gravitate toward that of another, altering its quality in the process—as it does in moving between Mulligan and Stephen in the opening pages of "Telemachus." Thus the quasi-effaced authorial voice becomes the medium that bridges the psychic fields of the individual characters. It is important, though, to the simulation of the *collective* psyche that this voice is never totally subsumed into any one character, and that (as we have seen) many of the qualitative/evaluative elements in the text cannot be attributed to any character. (The next section of chapter 4 will show how this merging of authorial and figural perspectives is essential to Joyce's techniques of psychological presentation.)

Joyce's simulation of a collective mind or cultural milieu is best achieved if the narrator's voice is distinguishable from that of individual characters, but attracts no attention to itself. We should recall J. Hillis Miller's claim that, among the Victorian novelists who used their omniscient voice to represent a collective mind, Thackeray did this least well because of the salient personification of his narrator, while Trollope did it best: "He speaks far less as a single person than does the moralizing narrator of *Vanity Fair* or the sermonizing narrator of *Adam Bede*" (*Form of Victorian Fiction,* 86), so that Trollope's "narrator becomes invisible in a union of reader and narrator" (85). Not that this subtle effacement of the authorial presence is the only device by which Joyce simulates the cultural context. He uses a variety of means to evoke the circumambient milieu, including his detailed depiction of the city of Dublin, his implicit invocation of scores of contemporary customs and institutions and of cultural and allusive schemata, and his development of an intricate array of interconnections among his characters—including but not limited to their shared thoughts.

Joyce's distinctive achievement in *Ulysses* becomes clearer when we compare his techniques with those of George Eliot, who, as we saw in chapter 1, was also interested in "the medium in which a character moves." An important part of Eliot's fictional aim in *Middlemarch*—as the title itself suggests—is the evocation of the cultural milieu of the community, or as Hillis Miller describes it, a collective mind. Eliot goes to great lengths to make the social and cultural milieu a tangible presence in the novel, which she does by a variety of devices, some of them subtle, some quite overt. For example, *Middlemarch* includes authorial passages that refer explicitly to the "civic mind" or the "world's habits" or the "public mind"; passages that refer to social schemata or institutions such as courtship or love-making; explicit authorial mention or discussion of received opinions on many topics, such as the best (and second best) poets and novels; attention called to apothegms, maxims, proverbs, and so forth (i.e., common knowledge or communal wisdom).

But the salience of Eliot's narrator deprives her (and most traditional novelists) of one important means of evoking this milieu, since it causes the reader to attribute all suprafigural qualitative or evaluative elements to the authorial persona, rather than to the climate of opinion or collective mind. For example, when Eliot tells us of Dorothea's idealistic premarital estimate of Casaubon that "Dorothea's inferences may seem large; but really life could never have gone on at any period but for this liberal allowance of conclusion, which has facilitated marriage under the difficulties of civilization. Has anyone ever pinched into its pilulous smallness the cobweb of pre-matrimonial acquaintanceship?" (*Middlemarch*, 45), we feel we are dealing with a persona expressing judgments, rather than with a suffused cultural milieu. And such tangible emergence of the authorial persona occurs not only in traditional omniscient novels such as *Middlemarch* and *Vanity Fair,* but in modern ones as well. When, for example, the narrative voice of Woolf's *Mrs. Dalloway* speaks overtly against Proportion and Conversion (87–89), we envision some persona who is expressing this judgment, which undermines our sense of an implicit milieu. By contrast, the highly effaced primary narrative voice in *Ulysses* does not invite us to personalize the many qualitative and evaluative terms it involves, and thus is more conducive to evoking a collective cultural milieu.

The felt presence of the persona/narrator in a novel can vary greatly, from the tangible first-person narrator/character of Nick Carraway in *The Great Gatsby;* to the "I" who speaks in the first paragraph of James's *The Ambassadors* (and who is of course not Strether); to the distinctive voice that occasionally (and inconsistently) speaks as a villager in Trollope's *The Warden;* to the voice that certainly has a distinct tenor but never emerges as a character in Austen's *Pride and Prejudice* (and, rather strangely, uses the first-person pronoun only in the last paragraph of the novel); to the intermittent, sometimes impalpable but sometimes personified authorial voice in Woolf's *Mrs. Dalloway*. In contrast to all of these, Joyce's authorial presence in the early episodes of *Ulysses* never assumes sufficient tangibility to suggest a character or even a persona; we are not inclined to speculate about its personal traits, much less to hypostatize it as a Victorian deity.

It is important, however, that while he wishes his authorial voice to be unobtrusive, Joyce does not attempt to eliminate the narrator or to render him "objective." On the contrary, Joyce illustrates the perils and abuses of presumed authorial objectivity through the secondary narrators of three later episodes — "Scylla and Charybdis," "Wandering Rocks," and "Ithaca" (see the discussions of those episodes in chapters 5 and 6). The initial style of *Ulysses* does involve a narrator who can be discovered and, to some degree, characterized, in stylistic if not personal terms. *Ulysses* is, after all, a novel, and Joyce does not deny himself one of the genre's most useful prerogatives. All that Joyce's purposes require, in terms of effacement, is that his narrative voice be unobtrusive, but not that it should be utterly undetectable, or "objective."

However, in a work that so persistently blends narrator and character, or even narrator and situation, it is very difficult to attribute words or images unequivocally to the narrator. As we shall see later in this chapter, many words and images that appear to be authorial can be shown to be figural, or to hover indeterminately between author and character. Nonetheless, we can detect certain characteristic traits and tonalities and values of the primary narrator of *Ulysses,* even in passages that are colored by figural or situational elements. These traits include great precision and economy of presentation, which deflect our attention from the voice and toward the events or persons of the novel (when we do take note of the voice, it is often to admire its deftness); an unconventional syntax that revivifies our perceptions; and (perhaps most important) a tone that disposes us sympathetically toward virtually all of the characters.[13] It is, for example, a characteristic of this voice that the main characters are habitually referred to as "Stephen" and "Mr. Bloom," establishing a different degree of familiarity or respect for each. (It is interesting how this mode of reference carries over into the critical literature.)

We should not, then, feel compelled to exorcize from this narrative voice every vestige of distinctiveness or color or tone, or to regard the presence of such qualities as a sign of the usurping arranger/presenter already rearing his mischievous head. Moreover, we must remember that narrative voice is only one part of the initial style, and that even with the obvious variation in voice among the early episodes (reflecting different personages and situations), the underlying techniques that comprise the initial style remain essentially the same for all of those early episodes.

Some critics have detected eruptions of an alien secondary voice (e.g., the "arranger") even in the early episodes. Kenner, for example, finds such a voice in "Telemachus," saying that the style "gives off here and there an unmistakable ring of Edwardian novelese" (*Joyce's Voices,* 69). Insofar as such qualities exist, they do not reflect a secondary voice, nor are they inconsistencies on Joyce's part; rather, they arise from the coloration of the voice by the characters or situation that are being depicted. Undoubtedly the "voice" of "Lotus-Eaters" does feel very different from that of "Proteus" or "Telemachus," but that arises from differences between the character and situation of Stephen and Bloom, not from inconsistency or idiosyncrasy in the primary narrator, much less in the underlying techniques of presentation. What Kenner detects in "Telemachus" is, I believe, the reflection of Stephen's defensive posturing and of his situation as he conceives it, for Stephen is still enamored (especially in the presence of Mulligan and Haines) of the fin de siècle conception of the artist in which he was so deeply enmeshed in *A Portrait*.[14]

Karen Lawrence is skeptical of Kenner's specific claims about the disparate styles in "Telemachus" (which she shows have varied over time), but she makes a similar claim of her own. While acknowledging a "normative" style of great subtlety and flexibility in "Telemachus" (later discovered not to be normative at all), she detects as well a counter mode, manifested mainly in what she regards as naive and formulaic inquit phrases ("he said sternly," "he cried briskly")—a voice that parodies the process of creation (*Odyssey of Style*, 44–45). But she acknowledges that "after Chapter One, this naive parodic style vanishes" (48), not to resurface (apparently) until "Cyclops." In view of the anomalous quality of this voice in this single episode (which Lawrence does not explain), it would be simpler to explain the stylistic variation in terms of some local phenomenon within "Telemachus." That is, the tenor of this "parodic" narrative voice reflects the stylized and stereotyped fin de siècle scenario that Stephen and Mulligan are playing out—the misunderstood, unappreciated artist versus the glib, cynical materialist. It is well within the primary narrator's empathetic, mimetic capacities thus to reflect these characters and their situation.

The Distinctive Techniques of the Initial Style

Joyce's techniques of psychological and cultural presentation in the initial style of *Ulysses* are as distinctive as his handling of authorial presence, and they grow as directly out of his artistic and thematic intentions. When compared with the techniques of earlier novelists such as Dickens or Hardy, and even with those of contemporaries such as Woolf or Forster, Joyce's presentation of his characters and of their milieu emerges as an unparalleled achievement. Moreover, this technical achievement has been insufficiently appreciated, because of critics' failure to recognize Joyce's antimodernist aims, because of the unprecedented subtlety and complexity of his modes of presentation, and because our critical vocabulary atomizes and misrepresents a highly unified technique for which there is no appropriate name. Monika Fludernik accurately assesses the source of the problem: "The origins of the traditional views on Ulyssean prose are instructive. They rely on a narrative model that contrasts a 'simple' narrative of events with 'pure' interior monologue and a grey area of overlap in indirect discourse and free indirect discourse" (*Fictions of Language*, 332). Such a vocabulary, and such a conception, cannot do justice to Joyce's achievement in *Ulysses*.

My concern with the cultural aspect of Joyce's techniques reflects an essential part of my thesis—namely, that Joyce intends in *Ulysses* not simply to present individuals, but the collective mentality or cultural psyche as well—a milieu that is ideational, valuational, affective, conative, and thus generically "psychic." Because of Joyce's intention to simulate the collective psyche and to subvert the Cartesian division between the individual and the milieu, "psychic work" is being done by virtually all of the sentences of the initial style—not just the first-person, "subjective" sentences.

Erroneous characterizations of the initial style

Failure to recognize that the opening episodes of *Ulysses* involve a distinctive, unified technique has led to inaccurate characterizations of the technique and mistaken charges against it. For example, critics often describe the technique in *Ulysses* as a mixture of first-person interior monologue that does all the work of psychological characterization and third-person, "objective" exposition, thus reflecting modernist categories of inner/outer and subject/object. Moreover, the initial style of *Ulysses* is sometimes said to rely so fully on first-person sentences for psychological presentation that it is not as subtle as the free indirect discourse of *Portrait*; or it is even said that this "mixed" technique itself perpetuates an inner/outer, subject/ object, dichotomy—which is especially ironic (and imperceptive), since this dualism is exactly what Joyce intends to subvert.

Such inaccurate or erroneous accounts of the initial style are pervasive in the critical literature, coming even from knowledgeable critics who are attending specifically to Joyce's techniques of psychological presentation. (Ironically, detailed scrutiny of Joyce's psychological presentation often exacerbates the problem, because it atomizes a technique that must be understood holistically.) For example, Erwin R. Steinberg tries to separate sentences that simulate the character's stream of consciousness from omniscient authorial sentences—a separation that (as we shall see) the style will not sustain. Discussing a passage from "Telemachus," he notes sentences that are "not . . . meant to simulate the stream of consciousness," some of them "omniscient author's sentences" (*SoC&B*, 31). He then says of these omniscient author's sentences that they "*are often summary*, with no hint of the author's point of view," or "*often function as stage direc-*

tions . . . maintaining the author's objectivity" (32, my emphases). He concludes, "Thus even where Joyce uses omniscient author's sentences in a stream-of-consciousness passage, *they do not obtrude*" (32, my emphasis). Steinberg does not, that is, recognize any third-person (i.e., authorial) sentences that do meaningful psychological work. His view is epitomized by the following: "Joyce regularly locates or moves his characters in both Proteus and Lestrygonians by means of omniscient author's sentences, which, as summaries, take less time to inform the reader than do the simulated raw data of the stream of consciousness. Frequently, however, because he presents these sentences in the idiom and style of the character's stream of consciousness, they are not as obtrusive as they otherwise would be" (254; 279 is essentially the same).

Dorrit Cohn similarly describes Joyce's technique as a mixture of atomic components: "Whenever the monologue technique appears in *Ulysses*, it *alternates with narration,* and these narratorial *incursions,* no matter how brief, permeate the self-locution with *a discontinuous element,* even as they relieve it of certain notorious difficulties of the autonomous form (e.g., the description of the monologist's own gestures and surroundings)" (*TM,* 16; my emphases). Cohn claims that Joyce achieves "symbiosis" between narration and quotation through certain constraints upon the narrator: "The *Ulysses* narrator omits not only quotational signals before an interior monologue, but also all other forms of psycho-narration, so that we find hardly any verbs of consciousness in his vocabulary" (71). Cohn quotes a passage from "Proteus" and asserts: "Though the narrator in this passage describes Stephen's physical gestures and surroundings, the stream of Stephen's consciousness remains purely subjective, *unpolluted by authorial interference*" (72, my emphasis). In spite of her lauding of *Ulysses* as "the novel that brought the most radical change in the integration of quoted monologue with *the surrounding narrative text*" (62, my emphasis), and her speaking of the "symbiosis" of these elements, most of Cohn's comments show that she regards the two elements as distinct and separate (see esp. 62, 66).[15]

Each of the descriptions that I have quoted or cited involves an imprecise and inaccurate analysis of what is a carefully crafted and highly unified technique. More specifically, the common thread running through these critics' descriptions of the initial style is the claim that virtually all of the psychic work is done by the first-person, present-tense sentences ("interior monologue"), and that the authorial (i.e., third-person) sentences simply provide exposition of the external scene. If the initial style did consist of such separate modes, Joyce might properly be accused of succumbing to and stylistically sanctioning the various dualisms we have spoken of. But as we shall see, quite the opposite is the case.

I have cited so many of these characterizations of the psychological technique of *Ulysses* in order to establish my crucial (and perhaps suspect) assertion that we have not yet recognized Joyce's distinctive achievement. I do find it remarkable that so many critics have inaccurately described this technique. Perhaps the errors stem in part from the pervasive influence of the Cartesian dichotomy, or from our having ready labels that mandate the separateness of techniques such as interior monologue or free indirect discourse or authorial exposition, but lacking a term for Joyce's uniquely unified mode of presentation. Perhaps some critical confusion is caused by the reliance in *Ulysses* on first-person, present-tense presentation (e.g., "interior monologue") rather than the third-person, past-tense mode (free indirect discourse) that Joyce so skillfully used in *Dubliners* and *A Portrait*.[16]

The frequent claim that Joyce relies *solely* on first-person sentences for the presentation of figural psyche in *Ulysses* is especially puzzling, since this is demonstrably not the case. While the first-person mode is used extensively (and subtly) in these episodes, the presentation of psychic material is significantly extended via third-person authorial modes of presentation of various kinds, such as authorial exposition of figural psyche, or free indirect discourse, or a coloring of authorial diction, syntax, or imagery by figural psyche (the Uncle Charles principle). Even in "Proteus," where there are paragraphs entirely in first person and present tense, the third-person, past-tense authorial voice contributes significantly not just to the "exposition," but to the characterization of Stephen's psyche and of the cultural milieu. Several of the critics I have quoted even acknowledge figural material—or at least figural idiom—in the third-person sentences, or comment on the inextricability of authorial and figural perspective, but nonetheless regard everything except the first-person sentences as exposition or "objective narration."

Joyce's technique cannot, then, be understood as a mixture of interior monologue and objective exposition, for many of the sentences hover indistinguishably between first and third person, or blend the two modes in various ways, and many of the third-person "expository" sentences convey important information about the characters' psychic content as well as the cultural milieu. Moreover, even the third-person sentences that do not provide figural psychic characterization are not solely expository and descriptive; they involve authorial qualitative and evaluative elements that merge inextricably with those of the characters and that thus help to form the psychic milieu that contains and sustains those characters. Through its melding of these elements, Joyce's technique achieves the virtual inextricability of the authorial and figural perspectives—and thus (by implication) of inner and outer, individual and cultural, conscious and unconscious. Thus, rather than sanctioning modernist dualisms, this unified style carefully and systematically subverts them.

The first-person component of the initial style

Since critical misunderstanding of the initial style frequently involves the first-person component of that style, I must specifically discuss it, in order to show how subtle and flexible that component is, as well as how inextricably integrated it is with free indirect discourse and omniscient presentation in *Ulysses*.

In *Dubliners* and *Portrait* Joyce relied almost entirely on a third-person presentation of his characters' psyches, developing it into a technique of great depth and subtlety. That mode enables the author to tell us more than the character can about his own psychic processes and thus to explore the penumbra between the character's conscious and subconscious psyche to a degree that seems denied to sheer interior monologue. It also enables a fuller exploration of nonverbal aspects of the individual's psychic processes—for example, affective and somatic states and mental images.

Why, then, some critics ask, did Joyce abandon the subtle, well-developed technique of the earlier works for the presumably more limited first-person mode he employs in *Ulysses*? Joyce's presumed reliance on "interior monologue" has given rise to claims that he confines himself to psychological processes that are very close to consciousness and articulation, or even that in *Ulysses* Joyce (simplistically) identifies thought with articulated language, or attempts to replicate endophasy (i.e., internal speech), which necessarily permits only superficial psychological exploration. But the idea that in *Ulysses* Joyce has regressed from the psychological subtlety of *Portrait* is mistaken primarily because the first-person mode is only one component of the rich and subtle initial style of *Ulysses*. Moreover, the first-person mode in *Ulysses* is by no means so limited as these critics claim. Taken as a whole, the initial style enables a presentation of figural psyche that is not limited to what the character can articulate and that is even more flexible and subtle than the techniques of *Dubliners* or *Portrait*.

Dorrit Cohn, in *Transparent Minds,* raises several questions about the "interior monologue" of *Ulysses*. She calls the mode that is used in *Ulysses* "quoted monologue" (i.e., direct interior monologue presented within a third-person context; see *TM*, 12–13, 15–16), in contrast to "narrated monologue" (i.e., what most critics call *style indirect libre* or *erlebte rede,* or free indirect discourse; 13, 107, 109), employed so extensively in *A Portrait*. Narrated monologue, that is, involves an authorial restatement of the character's thoughts in third person and past tense, in language reflecting that of the character. (This is Cohn's usual characterization [44, 105], but elsewhere she says, "it reproduces verbatim the character's own mental language" [14].) Quoted monologue states the character's thought in first person and present tense, presumably in the character's own words, set within a third-person context: "On the doorstep he felt in his hip pocket for the latchkey. *Not there. In the trousers I left off. Must get it. Potato I have*" (*U*, 4.72; the italicized sentences are quoted monologue — Cohn's example, *TM*, 62).

Cohn sees Joyce's shift from narrated monologue in *Portrait* to quoted monologue in *Ulysses* as a regression both because the first-person mode restricts the author's ability to explore nonverbal and preconscious figural processes, and because it presumably identifies thought with language (79, 86–87, 107). Cohn also makes the questionable assumption that quoted monologue attempts literally to reproduce endophasy — an assumption that gives rise to confusion and inconsistency on her part (cf. esp. 76–98). But interior monologue is a literary technique, a conventional device, that enables novelists to simulate various aspects of human experience. That Joyce (or Faulkner) should use first-person, present-tense constructions in his presentation does not transform him from novelist to psychological scientist, nor does it mean he wishes to *replicate* any aspect of human experience. William Faulkner's use of first-person presentation in the first three sections of *The Sound and the Fury,* for example, is clearly a literary technique, functioning quite differently in each section.

Cohn's presumption that psychological presentation in *Ulysses* is confined to the first-person sentences is implicit in her term "quoted monologue," for while it acknowledges a third-person *context,* the term refers only to the first-person *sentences* of the text. That is, in the passage quoted above from *U*, 4.72, what Cohn sees as the "quoted monologue" is not the passage as a whole, but the italicized portion, which denies any role to the circumambient third-person sentences in presenting figural psyche. This assumption that the third-person material is negligible is shown by Cohn's examples of quoted monologue, in which the third-person element consists simply of throwaway inquit phrases: "(He thought:) I am late (He thought:) I was late (He thought:) I will be late" (*TM*, 104–5). Moreover,

Cohn, after criticizing Erwin R. Steinberg for "disregard[ing] the dovetail-
ing of narration and monologue in presenting his statistics on the quantity
of 'omniscient author's sentences' in 'Proteus' and 'Lestrygonians,'" and
observing that "The haziness of the dividing line between narration and
monologue has been noted in passing by several critics," goes on to say
that "this problem has never been rigorously studied for *Ulysses* as a
whole" (*TM*, 283).

While Cohn is correct that free indirect discourse (narrated monologue) does facilitate exploration of nonverbal, preconscious processes of
individual psychology, Joyce's heavier reliance on the first-person mode in
Ulysses does not mean that he identifies language and thought, nor that he
has lost interest in the penumbra between conscious and unconscious
(*TM*, 103). Rather, it signals his having evolved distinctive literary aims in
Ulysses that are better served by a first-person presentation (in conjunction with other devices) than by "narrated monologue."[17]

Another criticism of interior monologue is that it confines the writer to
a superficial level of the character's consciousness. Since we are dealing
with printed words, it is difficult to demonstrate that some of those words
are verbally articulated by the character, while others simulate mental
images or visceral affects. But if the monologue is presumed to be a literary
convention rather than a transcription, it becomes clear that it does simulate an array of affects.

A number of critics have recognized that the first-person mode can
achieve considerable psychological depth and subtlety. Melvin Friedman
specifically addresses this point, using *Ulysses* as his example:

> The interior monologue may reproduce any area of consciousness;
> it is not limited, as several critics have suggested, to that region clos-
> est to complete awareness. One might glance at the first three epi-
> sodes of *Ulysses* and see the extraordinary area of consciousness the
> mind of Stephen Dedalus traverses, beginning in the earliest chapter
> with a monologue of absolute self-awareness on the margin of atten-
> tion, ending in the third-chapter reverie, which approaches complete
> unconsciousness, with the accompanying metaphors of fantasy (the
> umbilical telephone, the protean linguistic variations). And yet the
> three chapters employ the same technical device, interior mono-
> logue. (*Stream of Consciousness*, 5)

Anthony Burgess discusses at some length a passage in which Bloom
anticipates his breakfast (*U*, 4.43–46), to show that "Joyce is working in
a verbal medium and has to contrive a verbal equivalent for the preverbal

flow" (*Joysprick,* 50). He proposes that Bloom's "O wonder" during his reverie over his experience with Molly on Howth (*U,* 8.904) is "the verbal equivalent of a non-verbal ecstasy" (52).[18]

That Joyce himself saw the first-person mode as capable of considerable psychic depth is shown by his telling Frank Budgen, "I try to give the unspoken, unacted thoughts of people in the way they occur" (*JJMU,* 94), and by his referring Budgen to French novelist and critic Édouard Dujardin, from whom Joyce claimed to have learned of interior monologue. In his monograph *Interior Monologue,* Dujardin cites Valery Larbaud's opinion that interior monologue gets far beneath articulated speech. Quoting Larbaud, Dujardin claims, "Interior monologue . . . is the expression 'of the most intimate, most spontaneous thoughts, those which appear to form unconsciously, prior to organized speech'. Thus it allows one 'to penetrate so deeply the upsurge of thought in the Self and to grasp it so near to its point of conception'" (Dujardin, 103). Dujardin then quotes Edmond Jaloux: "'Its essential characteristic,' says Edmond Jaloux . . . 'is to represent not only interior speech, but intimate thoughts in formation'" (103). A few pages later, Dujardin sums up: "Interior monologue is, like poetry, unheard, unspoken speech, through which a character expresses his most intimate thoughts, closest to the unconscious, prior to all logical organization, that is to say as it comes into being, by means of sentences in direct speech reduced to their syntactic minimum, in order to give the impression of raw experience" (113).

Moreover, the first-person component of the initial style of *Ulysses* varies considerably in syntactic and grammatical coherence, reflecting different levels of awareness and suggesting that the words given on the page are sustained and connected not only by unarticulated words and allusions, but by nonverbal psychic elements—such as images, affects, visceral states, and feeling tone. The first-person, present-tense presentation occurs in passages of varying length and articulateness, from full paragraphs in "Proteus" (*U,* 3.45–54) and "Hades" (*U,* 6.763–75) and "Lestrygonians" (*U,* 8.334–57), to sentences, to elliptical statements or sentence fragments, to single words and even word fragments and exclamations, and it seems clear that these differences in fullness and coherence simulate varying psychic affects and levels of consciousness.

Consider, for example, the following first-person passage from "Lestrygonians," which involves sentences, sentence fragments, elliptical statements, and single words:

All the odd things people pick up for food. Out of shells, periwinkles with a pin, off trees, snails out of the ground the French eat, out of the sea with bait on a hook. Silly fish learn nothing in a thousand years. If you didn't know risky putting anything into your mouth. Poisonous berries. Johnny Magories. Roundness you think good. Gaudy colour warns you off. One fellow told another and so on. Try it on the dog first. Led on by the smell or the look. Tempting fruit. Ice cones. Cream. Instinct. Orangegroves for instance. Need artificial irrigation. Bleibtreustrasse. (*U*, 8.856)

The gist of this passage is clear, but as it proceeds, the "sentences" dwindle into single "words" that it seems unlikely are *spoken* by Bloom, even silently. More likely they exist as images or visceral affects that Joyce simulates in language—Joyce's "verbal equivalent for the preverbal flow," as Burgess puts it—which is much preferable to his importing designated symbols (e.g., % = stomach discomfort, # = angst) into the text!

In order to understand such a passage, we must infer what underlies and connects the words on the page. We must presume, that is, that there are psychic processes going on within Bloom beneath those given by the print on the page, disposing these words in certain associative or emotional or logical relations to one another—which shows that we do not equate Bloom's psychic flow simply with the words given on the page. *Ulysses* contains many such elliptical monologues that require us to reflect on what holds the mental/psychic process together beneath the language presented on the page, and the answer is subliminal, nonlinguistic or preverbal associations, images, affects, memories, feeling tone. Clearly, then, the explicitly given "monologue" of the characters is far from being the whole of their thought.[19]

At several points the first-person presentation becomes incoherent, reflecting the character's emotional turmoil. Steinberg argues at length for the less-than-fully-aware status of many such passages, especially those involving what he calls a "startle pattern," where the words on the page simulate visceral reactions (*SoC&B*, 45–46, 50–51). One that he cites is Bloom's reaction upon wondering whether Boylan might infect Molly with a venereal disease:

That quack doctor for the clap used to be stuck up in all the greenhouses. . . . Just the place too. POST NO BILLS. POST 110 PILLS. Some chap with a dose burning him.
 If he . . . ?
 O!
 Eh?
 No . . . . . . No.

No, no. I don't believe it. He wouldn't surely?
No, no. (*U*, 8.96)

We can readily infer that the thoughts and feelings tormenting Bloom at this time go far beyond the words on the page. Even H. A. Kelly, who argues that Joyce's presentation is confined to a high level of articulation, acknowledges that "on rare occasion in the *Ulysses* monologues the words are meant to be incoherent because the character's thoughts actually are incoherent at that time, due to some emotional disturbance" ("Consciousness," 9), and he cites examples when Bloom is trying to avoid Boylan's eye (*U*, 8.1168) and when he is trying to watch the woman board the carriage in Westland Row (*U*, 5.130).[20]

Before I discuss Joyce's extensive integration of his "interior monologue" with various modes of authorial presentation, it is instructive to compare his first-person mode with that of Édouard Dujardin, from whose *Les Lauriers sont coupés* (1887) Joyce claims to have learned (or stolen) the technique of interior monologue.[21] It is easy to see how utterly different Joyce's mode of presentation is from Dujardin's. The crucial difference is that Dujardin limits himself entirely to a first-person presentation of a character's inner stream of thought—his *monologue intérieur*—and eschews any authorial voice or exposition. This highly restricted use of interior monologue confines the character totally within his "inner world," justifying the criticism that this mode of presentation implies a solipsistic division between inner and outer, private and public—and thus illustrating exactly what Joyce took pains to avoid in *Ulysses*. The restriction to first person makes it very awkward for Dujardin to convey the simplest expository information about where the protagonist, Daniel Prince, is and what he is doing. For example: "Here's the house I have to go into, where I shall find someone; the house; the entrance hall; let's go in" (3); and: "My door; let's open it; the dark; the matches are there; I strike one . . . careful . . . the sitting-room door; in I go; the mantelpiece; the candlestick's on it; I light the candle" (27). By contrast, Joyce's unified mode of presentation achieves a smooth, virtually seamless transition between "inner" and "outer," reconciling the modernist dichotomies that less subtle use of this mode of writing often exacerbate.[22]

The unified nature of the initial style

Having shown that the first-person component of the initial style is neither superficial nor discrete, I want now to show that the work of psychic characterization—of individual characters and the cultural milieu—is not confined to this component, but involves as well the third-person authorial sentences. Moreover, even when we can grammatically distinguish authorial presentation (i.e., third person, past tense) from figural (i.e., first person, present tense), we cannot always tell whether the qualitative and evaluative terms are authorial or figural, and in many paragraphs (or sentences) not even the grammatical distinction between author and character can be sustained. Any paragraph of the initial style in *Ulysses* may involve (in addition to first-person material) authorial exposition, or authorial evaluation, or exposition of the character's mental state (Dorrit Cohn's psychonarration), or a coloring of figural idiom (the Uncle Charles principle), or third-person restatement in the character's language of something he probably could not tell us (free indirect discourse).[23] As a result, virtually every sentence contributes to Joyce's holistic aims and to the subversion of Cartesian dualisms; even authorial sentences that in another novel would simply be exposition or description, within this context contribute to evoking the cultural milieu. The most distinctive feature of Joyce's initial style, then, is his adapting and blending a number of techniques, so as to simulate the inextricable unity of various aspects of reality and of human experience.

I want now to look at an array of passages ranging from single sentences to full paragraphs that illustrate that the initial style cannot be neatly divided into first-person and third-person components, nor into figural and authorial, nor psychological and objective-expository. These passages simultaneously show how this unified style subverts such dichotomies as outer versus inner, or body versus mind, or cultural versus individual, or sensation versus reflection (another species of the outer/inner dichotomy), or description versus evaluation. Consider, for example, the following sentences, which range from "objective" authorial material to qualitative/evaluative statements, to omniscient authorial presentation of character. I venture to describe how these sentences work, often using received categories or labels, but we shall soon see the impossibility of keeping the categories clear and discrete.

- "Stately, plump Buck Mulligan came from the stairhead, bearing a bowl of lather on which a mirror and a razor lay crossed" (*U*, 1.1). Third-person authorial exposition, involving qualitative/evaluative terms—*stately, plump, bearing*—but no figural psychological presentation.
- "Stephen bent forward and peered at the mirror held out to him, cleft by a crooked crack" (*U*, 1.135). Authorial exposition, followed

by Stephen's *perception* of the cracked mirror, in words that probably reflect his perspective.

• "His [Bloom's] heart quopped softly" (*U*, 8.1169). Authorial presentation of Bloom's somatic/affective state.

• "His eyes unhungrily saw shelves of tins: sardines, gaudy lobsters' claws" (*U*, 8.855). Authorial characterization of a bodily state and perceptions, followed by Bloom's unmediated perceptions.

• "Mild fire of wine kindled his veins" (*U*, 8.854). Authorial evocation of a somatic/affective state, and perhaps an associated image in Bloom's mind.

• "Stephen closed his eyes to hear his boots crush crackling wrack and shells" (*U*, 3.10). Authorial exposition, followed by characterization in Stephen's own terms of his sensations.

• "Memories beset his brooding brain" (*U*, 1.265). Authorial characterization of Stephen's psychic state.

• "To serve or to upbraid, whether he could not tell: but scorned to beg her favour" (*U*, 1.406). Authorial characterization—in Stephen's language—of Stephen's aloof response to the milkwoman.

• "Pain, that was not yet the pain of love, fretted his heart" (*U*, 1.102). Authorial characterization of Stephen's psychic state, attitudes.

• "In a dream, silently, she had come to him, her wasted body within its loose graveclothes giving off an odour of wax and rosewood, her breath bent over him with mute secret words, a faint odour of wetted ashes" (*U*, 1.270). Persistently third-person/authorial in form, yet blending Stephen's language with remembered oneric images and sensations.

Both the indeterminacy of the grammatical perspective and the seamless, holistic nature of the experience simulated by these techniques become even more obvious in extended passages. Consider for example this passage from "Lestrygonians," incorporating two of the excerpts quoted above: "Mild fire of wine kindled his veins. I wanted that badly. Felt so off colour. His eyes unhungrily saw shelves of tins: sardines, gaudy lobsters' claws" (*U*, 8.854). The second and third sentences are the first-person mode of presentation that many commentators label interior monologue—though one of them lacks first person and neither sentence is present tense. The first sentence, however, is clearly authorial (third person, past tense) and tells us something about Bloom that he cannot articulate because it is so implicit, somatosensory, preconscious. The use of "fire

. . . kindled" makes us wonder whether the "warming" presents itself to Bloom imagistically as a flame, or exists (perhaps) as a visceral sensation of warmth. The fourth sentence, again authorial, involves a device that Joyce uses frequently—personifying a physical organ, thus suggesting that Bloom's eyes have an experience his mind may not articulate, and leaving us uncertain about the status of the items following the colon—are they semi-articulated words, or images? In this brief passage, then, two sentences of "quoted monologue" occur within a context of visceral, subconscious sensations and (perhaps) images, conveyed in sentences that hover between the categories of narrated monologue and psychonarration.

Or consider this passage from "Lestrygonians": "Wine soaked and softened rolled pith of bread mustard a moment mawkish cheese. Nice wine it is. Taste it better because I'm not thirsty" (*U*, 8.850). We cannot be sure whether the first "sentence" is first person or third, but it seems in context to suggest a series of sensations that are more or less articulated by the succeeding sentences—though "a moment" seems more reflection than sensation. While it is possible that the words of the first "sentence" are articulated by Bloom, it seems more likely that they simulate unverbalized sensations and thoughts. In any event, received technical categories and dualistic conceptions of experience simply cannot do justice to what Joyce is doing in such passages.

Even more complexly unified is the paragraph describing Stephen watching the old milkwoman (I have numbered the sentences for reference):

> [1] He watched her pour into the measure and thence into the jug rich white milk, not hers. [2] Old shrunken paps. [3] She poured again a measureful and a tilly. [4] Old and secret she had entered from a morning world, maybe a messenger. [5] She praised the goodness of the milk, pouring it out. [6] Crouching by a patient cow at daybreak in the lush field, a witch on her toadstool, her wrinkled fingers quick at the squirting dugs. [7] They lowed about her whom they knew, dewsilky cattle. [8] Silk of the kine and poor old woman, names given her in old times. [9] A wandering crone, lowly form of an immortal serving her conqueror and her gay betrayer, their common cuckquean, a messenger from the secret morning. [10] To serve or to upbraid, whether he could not tell: but scorned to beg her favour. (*U*, 1.397)

The paragraph begins with a third-person, past-tense, authorially descriptive sentence—but the closing words of the sentence seem to reflect

Stephen's perspective, especially since they are followed by a three-word fragment (2) that is almost certainly his. So here in this brief span we have a sentence that blends authorial description and a character's perspective, and a fragment that provides no grammatical clue to its status, but that feels figural. Both of these sentences, then, do some psychic characterization, and yet they do not conform to categories such as interior monologue or free indirect discourse.

The third sentence reverts to authorial form (third person, past tense), and we cannot be certain whether its diction reflects Stephen's perspective or the characteristically deft language of the narrator. The next sentence (4) is equally problematic, for its language and thought seem Stephen's, but the form is third person and past tense—but it is possible that Stephen could himself be speaking it that way, though in that case, we would expect *has* rather than *had*. (One reason I judge this sentence Stephen's is that the language and thought here seem too distinctive to be that of this effaced narrator.) The fifth sentence is unambiguously authorial, and then we move into a series of sentences (6–9) that seem entirely Stephen's— virtually "interior monologue." Several of these have no determinate tense, which makes it easier for us to feel them as Stephen's, yet one that seems undeniably his (7) uses the past tenses *lowed* and *knew*, where we might expect *low* and *know*—which may cause us to revisit the *had/has* of sentence 4. The last sentence of the paragraph somewhat surprisingly reverts to third person and past tense, and in its final clause provides a psychological characterization of Stephen that he probably could not—or would not—himself have provided—that is, an authorial perspective on Stephen's psyche.[24]

This paragraph blends quite different perspectives, but unless we are analytically attending to categories of grammar and point of view, we experience it as a unified whole. And that is the point: this "blended" paragraph *is* the style of *Ulysses,* and we misrepresent it if we impose on it discrete categories such as "interior monologue" and "objective narration" and "free indirect discourse." Moreover, this grammatical indeterminacy, and the resulting impossibility of separating authorial from figural perspectives, simulates the symbiosis between the individual and the cultural milieu. This "blend," then, cannot be seen as inadvertent or as a flawed technique; rather, this mode of presentation is pervasive in the initial style and is carefully wrought to achieve Joyce's distinctive literary purposes.[25]

So subtle and persistent is the symbiosis between narrative voice and figural perspective—simulating that between the individual and the cultural milieu—that often we simply cannot distinguish, much less separate, the one from the other. For example, in the "Nestor" episode, we read this description of Sargent: "On his cheek, dull and bloodless, a soft stain of ink lay, dateshaped, recent and damp as a snail's bed" (*U*, 2.126). Occurring in a paragraph of sentences in third person and past tense, this distinctive simile of a "dateshaped" ink stain as a snail's bed appears authorial—and seems to qualify my earlier statement that this effaced authorial persona avoids distinctive figures of speech. But a few lines later, in a passage clearly involving Stephen's perspective, we read: "Ugly and futile: lean neck and tangled hair and a stain of ink, a snail's bed" (*U*, 2.139). We are forced, then, to conclude that the earlier (apparently authorial) simile in fact reflected Stephen's perspective—or if one insists that the first passage is authorial (as does H. A. Kelly, "Consciousness," 5), we must acknowledge an amazing osmosis (or symbiosis) between authorial and figural psyches.

Nor do all such examples of authorial/figural symbiosis occur within a single episode. For example, in the "Telemachus" episode the distinctive word *barbacans* (*U*, 1.316) is used in a paragraph presented entirely in third person and past tense, and thus it seems clearly authorial (the paragraph does involve several qualitative and evaluative terms, but these do not seem to be Stephen's): "Two shafts of soft daylight fell across the flagged floor from the high barbacans . . . ." But in "Proteus" the word occurs, in lines that obviously echo this earlier description of the tower, in a first-person, present-tense reverie of Stephen's: "Through the barbacans the shafts of light are moving ever, slowly ever as my feet are sinking, creeping duskward over the dial floor" (*U*, 3.271). It appears, then, that we were not justified in labeling the earlier instance of the term "clearly authorial," and that in passages such as these it is impossible to discriminate between authorial and figural perspectives. Scrutiny of the initial style with this point in mind will reveal a great many such passages that simply cannot be accommodated to a figural/authorial (or individual/cultural) dichotomy.

The blending (or "mixture") of these materials has been noted by many critics, but remains problematic for most of them. Consider, for example, Karen Lawrence's puzzlement about a passage in "Hades." (She has earlier described the style as "a *combination* of third-person narration, dialogue, free indirect discourse, and the stream-of-consciousness of the character" [*Odyssey*, 49; my emphasis], and has presumed a considerable separation between the characters and an almost personified narrator.) Lawrence says,

Bloom and the narrator carry on a rapid and weird exchange of images:

> The whitesmocked priest came after him, tidying his stole with one hand, balancing with the other a little book against his toad's belly. Who'll read the book? I, said the rook.
> They halted by the bier and the priest began to read out of his book with a fluent croak. (*Odyssey*, 50; *U*, 6.590)

Lawrence attributes "toad's belly" to the narrator, though acknowledging that the following words stem directly from Bloom (both "toad's belly" and "little book," however, sound more like Bloom than the narrator). She then says that the third-person narration resumes in the next sentence — "except for the presence of the word 'croak'" (50), which must stem from Bloom. Lawrence then notes, "Soon after this passage, Bloom looks at the priest and thinks 'Eyes of a toad too,' and the word 'too' must refer to the 'toad's belly' mentioned in the narrator's statement. There is a strange kind of play between narrator and character, almost a parodic form of sympathy between the two. This is a kind of 'sympathy' that reduces the distance between the telling of the story and the story itself, a distance that will be manipulated in increasingly bizarre ways as the book progresses" (50). But rather than seeing what is going on here as "parodic" (of what?), or as involving bizarre narrative manipulation, we can simply note that Joyce's initial style persistently involves an inextricable blending of authorial and figural perspectives — for reasons that are an integral part of his artistic aims in *Ulysses*.

Other critics have remarked on this blended nature of many passages in *Ulysses*, some in admiration, most in consternation. Margaret C. Solomon quotes from the second paragraph of "Proteus": "Stephen closed his eyes to hear his boots crush crackling wrack and shells" (*U*, 3.10). She observes critically, "Separating the voice of the 'narrator' from that of Stephen is often an arbitrary and confusing matter. This particular sentence begins as a statement *about* Stephen; yet it ends by incorporating Stephen's own speech patterns — the words he uses to record his own sense-impressions" ("Character as Linguistic Mode," 130). W. J. Lillyman quotes the following from "Telemachus": "Stephen bent forward and peered at the mirror held out to him, cleft by a crooked crack. Hair on end. As he and others see me. Who chose this face for me? This dogsbody to rid of vermin. It asks me too" (*U*, 1.135). Lillyman comments, "Midway in the [first] sentence, then, Stephen's inner voice wrests control of the narration from the narrator. The next four sentences are also clearly Stephen's interior monologue"

("Interior Monologue," 49). But it seems inappropriate to speak of Stephen "wresting" control here or to invoke the category "interior monologue" for these other sentences, when it obviously applies so poorly to the first. The point is that Joyce's distinctive blending is persistent and pervasive, and our aim should be to understand rather than to admonish.[26]

In other passages in these opening episodes, Joyce subverts the inner/outer, mind/body dichotomy by showing how intricately interrelated are sensation (including visceral affects), perception, and the images, thoughts, and associations of the mind. We think of sensation and perception as stemming from the outer world, and memory and reflection from the inner, but Joyce will show that it is often impossible to draw such a line, or to say which of these most influences the other.

One episode in which this interrelationship among body, mind, sensation, and reflection is obvious and pervasive (and has been pointed out by Joyce) is "Lestrygonians," where Bloom's growing hunger is persistently reflected in his thoughts, images, and turns of speech. Joyce called attention to this technique in his conversations with Frank Budgen: "In my book the body lives in and moves through space and is the home of a full human personality. The words I write are adapted to express first one of its functions and then another. In *Lestrygonians* the stomach dominates and the rhythm of the episode is that of the peristaltic movement" (*JJMU*, 21). In response to Budgen's asking about the characters' minds and thoughts, Joyce replied, "If they had no body they would have no mind. . . . It's all one" (21). As an example of how Bloom's mind is affected by his hunger, Joyce cites his thought that Molly's "legs are out of plumb" (cf. *U*, 8.618), and explains, "At another time of day he might have expressed the same thought without any underthought of food" (21). Michael Groden discusses in detail how Joyce's additions to the text of "Lestrygonians" incorporated a great many instances of such "underthoughts" of food. The examples he cites include such phrases of Bloom's as "buttering themselves," "working tooth and jaw," "crusty old topers," and such clichés as "Bitten off more than he could chew," "Eat drink and be merry," "God made the food, the devil the cooks," "Poached eyes on ghost," "Couldn't swallow it all however," and others (*"Ulysses" in Progress*, 183–85).

Such instances of rapport between mind and body, or mind and milieu, are not confined to "Lestrygonians," or to Bloom. In "Telemachus" there are several passages where Stephen's reflections are strongly influenced by subliminal perceptions of the external scene, or his perceptions are influenced by his reflections. One such instance of melded sensation/reflection (and memory) occurs when Stephen, atop the tower, is thinking of his mother's having appeared to him in a dream: "The ring of bay and skyline held a dull green mass of liquid. A bowl of white china had stood beside her deathbed holding the green sluggish bile which she had torn up from her rotting liver by fits of loud groaning vomiting" (*U*, 1.107). The first sentence is mainly Stephen's perception of the scene from the tower—the ring of bay and skyline—and yet his seeing the sea as a "dull green mass" of liquid, and of the bay as holding it, is certainly influenced by his insuppressible memories of his mother's deathbed scene. The next sentence is mainly reflection, but is influenced by the physical scene before him—especially the similarity of the bay to a bowl. Moreover, it could well be that the bowl image that here serves to link his reverie and his perception was itself occasioned by the shaving bowl in which Stephen watched Mulligan dip his brush (*U*, 1.38). And his subsequently imaging the sea as a "bowl of bitter waters" (*U*, 1.249) is very likely a mental reflection of that same literal bowl that is still sitting where Mulligan left it (*U*, 1.306).

Similarly, the auditory *sensation* of Mulligan's singing "Who Goes with Fergus?" as he descends the stairway (*U*, 1.239) prompts Stephen to recall subsequent lines of the poem that color his *reflections* for the entire next paragraph (*U*, 1.242–47). Stephen's thinking of the line "Shadows of the wood" causes him to see the clouds floating by the tower as "Woodshadows" (literally impossible since no trees shadow the Martello tower). And his thinking of "A hand plucking the harpstrings" may arise from a visual memory of seeing Yeats's song accompanied by a stringed instrument—all of this prompted by the auditory sensations of Mulligan's singing. Joyce's technique here profoundly illustrates the inextricability of body and mind.

Other critics have acknowledged or explored this symbiosis of mind and world. Bernard Benstock notes that in "Proteus" "Stephen's internalized commentary is influenced by his physical surroundings, the sea, sand and water directing word choice and syntactical structures" (*Narrative Con/Texts*, 25–26). Dorrit Cohn acknowledges that "elements of the reported scene . . . activate the associations of Stephen's thoughts" (*TM*, 72). E. R. Steinberg says that passages in *Ulysses* "exemplif[y] the bipolarity of thought, yielding now more to inner needs, now more to external stimuli" (*SoC&B*, 41; 59–60 reiterates the point), and he discusses in detail how Joyce simulates preconscious psychic material, such as sensations, images, perceptions, and memories (esp. 44–61).

Qualitative and evaluative terms that hover
between author and character

We saw earlier in this chapter that the initial style involves many evaluative and qualitative terms that cannot be attributed to any character, in
contravention of modernist strictures against disembodied evaluations. I
want now to consider certain passages, facilitated by Joyce's careful effacement of his narrator, that are especially important to the symbiosis of
the individual and the cultural milieu that the novel is so concerned to
establish. These passages contain qualitative and evaluative terms that we
cannot readily assign either to character or author, or that seem virtually
to hover between them, suggesting that the values that they involve are
simultaneously cultural and individual.

Consider, for example, the complex valuational situation involved in
this ordinary sentence from the opening of the "Lestrygonians" episode:
"A sombre Y. M. C. A. young man, watchful among the warm sweet
fumes of Graham Lemon's, placed a throwaway in a hand of Mr Bloom"
(*U*, 8.5). The basic form of the sentence is clearly authorial—third person,
past tense—and the judgment of the young man as sombre and watchful
appears to be that of the author, since the young man would not describe
himself in that way, and Bloom has not yet noticed him (and would be
unlikely to see him as "watchful" in any event). But "warm sweet fumes"
evokes a sensation that is subjectively experienced by someone, most
likely the young man, though perhaps Bloom as well (as he approaches the
confectioner's). The point is that this simple sentence contains some quali-
tative/evaluative terms reflecting a nonfigural perspective as well as others
that must be figural, and it becomes virtually impossible to separate the
two.

But while this complexity does abrogate modernist shibboleths, this is
not sloppiness or inadvertence on Joyce's part. Rather, Joyce is intentionally employing his narrator in such a way that we cannot discriminate
value judgments between character and author, individual and cultural
context. And if we reflect on it, we know that there is no such thing as a
purely "individual" value judgment made in a vacuum; such judgments
always arise from and reflect the values of a culture. Moreover, in blurring
this margin between individual and cultural, Joyce is also blurring that
between conscious and unconscious, for the valuational responses at work
here are by no means explicitly expressed; they exist not as stated principles but as complex, unarticulated feelings.

This simulation by the initial style of qualities and values that exist in
the cultural milieu can be seen even more clearly in the description of Buck

Mulligan in the opening paragraphs of the novel. On the first page of the novel, an omniscient voice describes Mulligan and his actions in terms that are indubitably qualitative and evaluative—his calling out *coarsely,* blessing the tower *gravely,* his speaking in a *preacher's tone, skipping* off the gunrest, and addressing Stephen *gaily,* for example. These terms clearly stem from, or reflect, the narrator, not Stephen (who has not yet emerged when some of them are used); they seem to involve no bias for or against Mulligan, but simply to be appropriate to his actions and intentions. That is, the evaluative words that the acculturated, Western narrator uses to describe Mulligan's acts are congruous with the intentions behind those actions—perhaps identical with the words that Mulligan would use, or is using (implicitly) to himself. They deftly convey his irony, his irreverence, his mockery. But an unacculturated narrator from an utterly different milieu—such as Thailand, or Mars—might be at a loss as to how to describe these acts by Mulligan, much less to know what evaluation or meaning to ascribe to them. We can appreciate this subtle point more fully if we ask where the qualities and values expressed by these authorial terms reside—for the answer is that they exist within Mulligan himself *and* within the culture—that is, within the audience that would presumably recognize the meanings and implications of these acts.

Leo Bersani makes some relevant observations about these descriptions of Mulligan. He says of such terms as *bearing* (and later of *plump* and *stately*) that "Buck's verbal mannerisms are a necessary part of a *wholly objective* presentation of him" ("Against *Ulysses,*" 7; his emphasis), and then he further says that a sentence such as the opening one "objectifies the point of view which it takes" (8). Bersani calls this a "nonperspectival point of view" essentially similar to that achieved in *Dubliners,* where "Joyce characterizes not only individuals but also a kind of collective consciousness through such objectified subjectivity" (8). Reminding us of Stephen's identification in *Portrait* of the radiance of a thing with the scholastic *quidditas* or whatness, Bersani says of the technique of this episode of *Ulysses,* "It is as if literature could quote being independently of any particular being's point of view. We would, that is, have the point of view of neither a narrator nor a character; rather, we would have the *quidditas* of Buck Mulligan, and even of Dublin" (8). Though his language is different, Bersani is agreeing with my claim that what Joyce achieves here is the simulation of a simultaneously private/public, individual/cultural, subjective/objective psychic milieu.

Once we recognize the subtle dynamics of the initial style, even a brief sentence can be seen to comprehend a whole range of presumed dualisms and dichotomies. An apparently authorial, descriptive sentence that illustrates the complex relations between the individual and the cultural milieu, as well as that between narrator and character, conscious and subliminal, is the sentence from "Proteus": "He turned northeast and crossed the firmer sand towards the Pigeonhouse" (*U*, 3.159). In any other novel this expository sentence would be unremarkable, but, considering it within the context of this episode, we find that it has subtle, inextricable relationships with Stephen's mental processes. The word "northeast" seems purely authorial (and purely expository), for Stephen would hardly think it to himself. (I shall return shortly to the implicit cultural content of this "objective" term.) The words "firmer sand" are interesting, since the firmness of the sand is a quality that is immediately experienced by Stephen, but articulated by the narrative voice, thus effecting an inextricable blending of the two (as well as evoking a preconscious dimension of Stephen's psyche). Interesting also is the authorial orientation "towards the Pigeonhouse" (i.e., the Dublin power plant), without any indication that Stephen even glances at that structure. Yet if we pursue Stephen's thoughts into succeeding sentences, we find that they involve the "pigeon" that impregnated Mary—subtle associative evidence that Stephen did on some level apprehend the Pigeonhouse, whether he named it to himself or not. This again shows how inextricably blended the authorial voice and that of the character have become, as well as the "outer" and "inner," perceptual and reflective, conscious and subliminal dimensions of Stephen's experience.

Having shown the intimate relationship between authorial and figural perspectives in this sentence, I want to revisit *northeast,* which, though not overtly qualitative, is nonetheless highly acculturated, and thus not purely "objective." That is, in its easy resort to compass points to establish the character's orientation, the term invokes a frame of reference that is part and parcel of modern Western culture. The authorial voice in another culture might convey orientation by saying, "toward the rising sun" or "toward the great mountain" or "into the evening wind," rather than invoking something so abstract as compass points. I have already argued that modernist critics betray a lack of philosophical rigor if they do not proscribe qualitative as well as evaluative terms from "disembodied" (i.e., nonfigural) narration; now I propose that many "descriptive" terms implicitly smuggle in cultural predispositions and values, and that those who speak facilely of "objective" description have not reflected on how culturally charged and inherently value-laden any description is that employs natural language. Short of resorting to mathematics or symbolic logic, there is no such a thing as an objective, culturally neutral description. (And of course any use of symbolic logic to describe ordinary experience would itself express the modern Western perspective!)

Let me, then, use this brief, complex example as a basis for summary. First, this typical sentence from "Proteus" involves an authorial voice referring to Stephen in the third person and the past tense, and is thus quite distinct from the character, and this voice provides suprafigural information and exposition—functions that we associate with omniscient narration. Second, some of the most objective-seeming descriptors—such as "northeast"—in fact involve a culturally charged, qualitative perspective of the narrator, and this voice involves other qualitative states that are not articulated by Stephen ("firmer"), but are (subliminally?) experienced by him. Third, it is virtually impossible to separate Stephen's psyche from that of the authorial voice, as shown both by the term "firmer" and by the subsequent effect within Stephen's thoughts of the authorial invocation of the Pigeonhouse.

The Allusive Method: Cultural/Allusive Schemata and the Collective Psyche

A third aspect of Joyce's initial style involves the incorporation into *Ulysses* of hundreds of literary, historical, and cultural allusions and schemata. This pervasive technique enriches the psychic milieu of the novel by invoking the extensive nexus of historical and imaginative accounts—stories, songs, images, rituals—that the members of every culture draw upon in order to understand themselves and to give structure and meaning to their individual and social experience.

Contrary to the modernist presumption that such schemata are given meaning entirely by the individual—that is, are "purely subjective"—Joyce shows that they have a public, "objective" quality, deriving from their existence within the cultural milieu quite independently of any particular individual. Whenever we draw upon such cultural materials, we necessarily invoke an array of structures and meanings that we do not personally create and that we cannot entirely control or even be fully aware of. Though we may presume that any role or myth or schema can be donned or doffed consciously, as we might some item of clothing, we may, to our chagrin, find ourselves ineluctably under the control, or at least under the influence, of the myth.

As we shall see through scrutiny of Stephen's semiconscious awareness of certain literary texts, and more fully by analysis of his discussion of Shakespeare, the myriad narratives and other schemata of our culture affect us subliminally and influence our self-conception, our role-playing, our values—even when we are not thinking consciously about them. Each of us, that is, knows a vast amount of such material that we can easily "call to mind," but that otherwise remains subconscious. Even when it is beneath conscious awareness, this material influences us in profound ways. This is true not only of the canonical narratives and famous historical figures of our culture (e.g., *The Odyssey,* Christ's passion, *Don Giovanni,* or Napoleon or Parnell), but of popular materials as well (e.g., songs, pantomimes, advertising slogans, nursery rhymes, and comic strip figures). Through the allusive method, Joyce shows how such material works upon us, and thus subverts the received dualisms of individual and cultural, conscious and unconscious.

The allusive method enables Joyce to show that the unconscious consists not simply of suppressed personal contents, but that it involves as well a great many cultural contexts and schemata that we constantly draw upon without being aware of it. Thus, conscious and unconscious are not separate and discontinuous, but exist rather in a dynamic relationship that is better understood in terms of Carl Jung's conception of the conscious and subconscious, or Michael Polanyi's distinction between focal and subsidiary awareness, than in terms of the received Freudian conception that involves such strong demarcation (and antagonism) between conscious and unconscious.[27] The pervasive allusiveness of *Ulysses* thus simultaneously simulates the cultural psyche of the novel and evokes a subconscious dimension of the characters' psyches.

Joyce's unobtrusive incorporation of this allusive material into his novel is facilitated by both of the features of the initial style that we have examined—by the effaced narrative voice that simulates the collective psyche and by the subtle blending of first- and third-person modes of psychic presentation. In contrast to *A Portrait of the Artist,* the focus in *Ulysses* is upon not one character, but many, and upon the cultural milieu in which all of the characters subsist. And while the third-person technique of *Portrait* enabled Joyce to tell us more than Stephen himself understood, it focused on the "individual" mind of Stephen Dedalus. As Dorrit Cohn has noted, one strength of the narrated monologue (i.e., free indirect discourse) used in *Portrait* is that it "casts a peculiarly penumbral light on the *figural consciousness,* suspending it on the threshold of verbalization in a manner that cannot be achieved by direct quotation" (*TM,* 103; my emphasis)—but as Cohn's observation suggests, *A Portrait* is concerned mainly with Stephen's personal subconscious. The blending of first- and third-person perspectives in *Ulysses* facilitates Joyce's exploration as well of the penumbral area where the individual's psyche shades off into the collective or cultural psyche. Paradoxically, the first-person mode of presentation used so extensively in *Ulysses,* when mediated by a skillfully effaced omniscient narrator, enables Joyce both to individuate his characters and to evoke their cultural milieu. This is true because the characters' distinctive voices are not filtered through an authorial recasting (as in free indirect discourse), and because the authorial voice in *Ulysses* is the vehicle not just of one personality but of the milieu that sustains them all.[28]

The allusive elements within the novel can originate from either the characters or the author. Allusions introduced through the characters can be conscious, or they can exist more implicitly, on the margin of the character's awareness. For example, when Bloom (thinking of Queen Victoria's numerous progeny) says, "Old woman that lived in a shoe she had so many children" (*U*, 8.379), his invocation of the nursery rhyme seems fully conscious, whereas when a few lines later he thinks, "Old Mrs Thornton was a jolly old soul" (*U*, 8.394), the allusion to Old King Cole may be coming through him rather than from him. (Cf. the claim, later in this chapter, by Erwin R. Steinberg that Bloom's thoughts are affected by the unarticulated presence of "Kubla Khan.")

The fact that we cannot always determine whether such allusive material exists consciously for the character is itself a reflection of how such material exists simultaneously in the individual's mind and in the cultural psyche. Moreover, even allusive material that a character consciously invokes can involve unforeseen, even unwanted, implications, in that events (or the character's own situation) may thrust upon the character a different role within the allusive schema than he intends for himself. For example, at the end of *A Portrait*, Stephen undoubtedly aspires to be Daedalus, but unwittingly casts himself as Icarus when he says, "Old *father,* old artificer, stand me now and ever in good stead" (*PoA*, 253; my emphasis). And when Bloom thinks of the duet from *Don Giovanni,* doubtless he would like to cast himself as the Don (in regard to Martha Clifford), but he is cast by the events of the day and his own complaisance as the bumbling, ineffectual Masetto. A character's "use" of allusion in order to understand his situation can vary greatly in scope and awareness from an educated intellectual like Stephen, to more ordinary persons such as Leopold or Molly. But even the least intellectual person is constantly drawing upon cultural schemata, and even the most reflective cannot fully comprehend and control the implications of allusive schemata that enter his mind.

Allusions in *Ulysses* also originate "authorially"—but not as pronouncements by a persona. In traditional novels, where there is less concern to efface the narrator, allusions are often explicitly stated by the authorial persona. For example, in *Middlemarch* the narrator at one point explicitly compares Dorothea to Santa Barbara looking out from her tower (114). But in *Ulysses* virtually all of the "authorial" allusions arise implicitly, from the structures or situations of the book; as a result, they seem an integral part of the world of the novel, just as such schemata are an implicit part of our cultural world. One pervasive example of this kind of implicit authorial/structural allusive material in *Ulysses* is of course *The Odyssey*, which can be detected in many of the structures and events and analogies within the book, but is not explicitly announced by the primary narrator—except of course in the title of the novel.

Several critics have observed that much of the allusive material in *Ulysses* exists independently of the characters' minds or beyond their awareness. Hugh Kenner asserts, "Stephen does not know he is Telemachus, and Bloom does not know he is Ulysses" (*Joyce's Voices*, 40); Michael Groden says "Without knowing it, the Stephen of *Ulysses* is a Telemachus searching for his father" (*"Ulysses" in Progress*, 26); Marilyn French discusses the assets and liabilities of the characters' partial awareness of such analogies (*Book as World*, 262–63); and William P. Fitzpatrick says that the "mythic analogs which exist in the novel do so independently of the conscious minds of the characters. More specifically, the mythic equations of Bloom/Ulysses, Stephen/Telemachus, or Molly/Penelope exist in the work's structure rather than in fictive consciousness" ("Myth of Creation," 123). While it is doubtless true that the existence of such allusive material does not depend upon the characters, the question of how it exists for them, of how aware of it they are, deserves scrutiny if we are to understand and appreciate what Joyce is doing here.[29]

As an example of how this allusive method subverts the distinction between personal and cultural, or conscious and unconscious, let's consider what Stephen is and is not thinking about during the first hour of this day of *Ulysses*—that is, in the episode that we know as "Telemachus." The question is whether during this time Stephen thinks of himself in comparison with Telemachus in *The Odyssey*. Certainly our own reading of the episode is enriched by our awareness of the ways in which Stephen is like Telemachus, Buck like Antinous, and so forth. But is Stephen thinking in these terms? There is no question that he is familiar with *The Odyssey*, and thus that the story is in some way "in his mind." But even though Buck

Mulligan refers to the common Homeric epithet "*epi oinopa ponton*" (upon the wine-dark sea), and Gifford and Seidman detect some dozen allusions/echoes in this episode to *The Odyssey,* nowhere in this episode does Stephen explicitly think of that work or of any analogy with Telemachus. But does this lack of explicit reference permit us to say that this analogy plays no role whatsoever in Stephen's sense of himself and his situation? I think not.

To complicate (and enrich) matters, there is one place where Stephen may be thinking of Homer's poem—namely, when he sees the old milkwoman as a "messenger from the secret morning" who may have come to serve or to upbraid him—which Gifford and Seidman see as a reference to Athena, who comes to aid Telemachus in the opening books of *The Odyssey.* But Stephen does not call the woman Athena, and there is no textual confirmation that he is thinking of her in that way, or of himself as Telemachus.

This same issue exists even more pointedly in regard to the *Hamlet* material in this episode, since we know from other chapters in *Ulysses* that Stephen's mind is saturated with Shakespeare and *Hamlet,* and there is explicit reference to that material in this very episode by both Haines and Mulligan. But while there are several phrases that are enticing and suggestive, there is no explicit reference by Stephen to *Hamlet* in this episode. It is hard to believe, however, that the comparison does not inform Stephen's sense of himself and his situation.[30]

This issue of the status of material that is undeniably known to the character but is not explicitly (consciously?) articulated arises again at the end of the episode, when Stephen thinks simply, "Usurper" (presumably of Mulligan and/or Haines). Is this articulated word accompanied in his mind by thoughts or images of those usurped princes, Hamlet or Telemachus, whose stories he knows so well? Since Stephen does not explicitly refer to Telemachus or Hamlet, we can only speculate about whether the material exists in his subconscious—or (more precisely) about how close to the surface it comes and what kind of presence or influence it has—for we know it is somewhere in his mind. Furthermore, the idea of usurpation has a Shakespearean association for Stephen, as we know from his saying that the theme of the false or usurping brother is always with Shakespeare (*U,* 9.998).[31]

Kenner is doubtless on safe ground to say that Bloom does not see himself as Ulysses, but as the preceding discussion of Stephen suggests, when it comes to cultural material, we can never be sure what someone is or is not "thinking of," or on what level—conscious, preconscious, subconscious, unconscious—it exists. E. R. Steinberg makes a relevant claim about Bloom's thoughts and images in a passage in "Calypso": "Walk along a strand, strange land . . . dulcimers. I pass" (*U*, 5.86–98). Steinberg argues that these words and images are controlled by the implicit presence of Coleridge's "Kubla Khan," even though that poem is never referred to. He makes the point that the poem is known by virtually everyone, and that in such a passage Joyce is calling forth "in the reader's mind certain images that are probably there *as a result of our common cultural heritage*" (*SoC&B*, 57; my emphasis; interestingly, Gifford and Seidman do not detect any allusion to "Kubla Khan" in this passage). In these ways Joyce's techniques simulate the conscious/unconscious penumbra constituted by schemata that form a part of our cultural milieu, making it impossible for us to draw a line between conscious and unconscious, private and public.

Our very difficulty in pinning down what Stephen or Bloom is "thinking about" illustrates that cultural context exists as a liminal substrate that is always available, but that may or may not be consciously reflected upon or explicitly articulated. And the further point in all of this is that Joyce has taken great care to develop various techniques of presentation that enable him to show the seamless inextricability of human experience in regard to what we call the categories of personal/cultural and conscious/unconscious. This is not to say (as some critics have) that the individual is simply a conjunction of cultural vectors, but it is to acknowledge how impossible it is to draw a clear line between the individual and the world.

Within such a richly represented psychic context, recurrent motifs and themes of the novel, whether allusive or not, carry cultural contents. In traditional omniscient novels, themes or motifs are often articulated explicitly by the author/narrator, so that they seem to exist as a part of the narrator's perspective on the novel, rather than as an implicit part of the world of the book. That is, Forster's "Only connect" in *Howards End* or Woolf's Proportion and Conversion in *Mrs. Dalloway* feel like themes proposed by the author, rather than issues within the world of the novel. But in *Ulysses* themes are not articulated by "the author"; every theme arises from characters or events or structures, and thus feels like a part of the world of the book. All such themes are, of course, "authorial" in that Joyce is ultimately responsible for them, and he skillfully weaves them through the narrative, but not in the sense that they are voiced directly by a persona. Such themes, then, simulate the personal/cultural response we have to the common objects and ideas of our culture, which we necessarily react to both personally and socially.

The themes and motifs of *Ulysses* (e.g., the key or money or many others listed in William M. Schutte's *Index of Recurrent Elements in James Joyce's "Ulysses"*) usually arise within an individual character's experience, but they ramify in the novel in ways beyond the ken of any single character. The motif of money, for example, has considerable importance for both Stephen and Bloom (as well as for Mr. Deasy, the Dignam family, the one-legged sailor, Dilly Dedalus, Bella Cohen, Corley, and others), but the meaning of the motif varies radically among these characters. For Stephen, money is emblematic of his various rivalries with and indebtedness to others, of his sense that he is not paying his way, and yet his disdain of the frugal mentality. For Bloom, money often serves as one means of occupying his mind with petty calculations and schemes, sometimes in evasion of things he does not want to face up to, such as his defection from his Jewish heritage or the situation between Molly and Boylan (cf. *U*, 4.191–99 for his thoughts about "investing" in the Holy Land). What enables money to function so variably in the novel is its public existence as something whereby various kinds of relationships and exchanges are negotiated in this culture. Rather than being a motif defined by the author, money is a component of the cultural milieu of the book. And the same is true for scores of other motifs and themes in the novel.

Having laid such emphasis on Joyce's extensive cultural simulation in *Ulysses*, I must reiterate that it is just that—a highly selective and conventional literary *simulation* that operates on a number of levels, mimetic and diegetic, in conjunction with other novelistic aims and techniques. Joyce never loses sight of the conventional nature of his novel, and he reminds us of this by various devices (e.g., the many metarealistic links or parallels among characters) lest we become so caught up in detail and verisimilitude that we treat his rich novel as merely a documentary slice of life.

Stephen's uses of Shakespeare

As an extended illustration of how *Ulysses* blends individual and cultural, conscious and unconscious, by means of allusive contexts, I want to discuss one particular (mythic) schema that pervades the novel and that is explored by Stephen in some depth—the Shakespearean material, and especially the ideas about Shakespeare that Stephen presents in "Scylla and Charybdis."

In developing a theory about Shakespeare and his literary works, Stephen expresses a deep-rooted proclivity of his personality. In *A Portrait* young Stephen comes to understand himself partly through identifying with various literary characters or historical figures—Baby Tuckoo,

Edmond Dantes, Napoleon, Jesus, Daedalus/Icarus. In each case the young boy naively projects an identification between himself and the literary or historical figure—an identification that he believes he understands and controls. He also presumes that such identifications are utterly his own—something indulged in only by himself. Doubtless he would be chagrined to learn that the aspirations of innumerable late-nineteenth-century adolescents were shaped by their identifying with Edmond Dantes or Napoleon—to learn, in other words, that there is something public and generic about his own individuation process.

Young Stephen's unawareness that his imaginative forays may invoke unexpected dimensions of these narratives is shown in his attempted identification with Daedalus. For us there is an inevitable irony in seeing Stephen at the end of chapter 4 of *A Portrait* treat his newly discovered identity with Daedalus so personally, especially since Joyce has signaled this mythic context for the novel through the epigraph. Stephen regards the Daedalus story largely as a function of himself, as a vehicle of his conscious self-understanding. We, seeing the myth from above Stephen's perspective, know that it has a public existence and that it is in various ways influencing his development. To vary a phrase of Robert Frost's, we see that Stephen was the myth's before the myth was Stephen's.

This is shown by the allusion in the final sentence of *A Portrait of the Artist*, written by Stephen into his diary as he prepares to leave Ireland for the European mainland: "Old father, old artificer, stand me now and ever in good stead." Stephen does not realize this invocation of the myth casts him in a different role than he intends—the role not of the experienced father, Daedalus, but of the naive, irrepressible son, Icarus: "Old *father*. . . ." This reading is confirmed by the passage in *Ulysses* where Stephen, after his anticlimactic return from Paris, reflects with chagrin on this very scene of his earlier departure from Dublin, recognizing that in fact he was then Icarus rather than Daedalus. During his presentation of his theory about Shakespeare, Stephen thinks, "Fabulous artificer. The hawklike man. You flew. Whereto? Newhaven-Dieppe, steerage passenger. Paris and back. Lapwing. Icarus. *Pater, ait.* [Father, he cries.] Seabedabbled, fallen, weltering. Lapwing you are. Lapwing be" (*U*, 9.952). Here a more sober and chastened Stephen acknowledges the naive unreflectiveness of his earlier relation to the myth. In doing so, he understands that the myth enticed him into a role other than the one he had consciously intended to play. In this way Joyce suggests that the various images and allusions Stephen uses in the process of individuation are neither as private nor as consciously controlled as he thinks, but that they have a public, cultural, necessarily "unconscious" aspect deeper and more extensive than Stephen (or any of us) can realize.

My claims about the allusive method can best be illustrated through the allusions to Shakespeare, and especially those surrounding the theory about Shakespeare that Stephen proposes in "Scylla and Charybdis." Allusions to the life and works of Shakespeare are truly pervasive in *Ulysses;* there are more than 500 in the novel. Shakespearean allusions are invoked more or less consciously by many of the characters, but they stem from the authorial (i.e., the novelistic) perspective as well, in the structures and relationships undergirding the novel. And Joyce uses these pervasive Shakespearean allusions to generate a complex matrix of relationships connecting several of the novel's characters.

Stephen's theory about Shakespeare is his most extensive and systematic attempt in *A Portrait* or *Ulysses* to understand himself by identification with a mythic/historic figure, and so it provides some important insights into how such allusive material functions within Stephen's psyche and in the fictive world of *Ulysses.* Through his Shakespeare theory Stephen is trying to understand how a writer's works can arise out of traumatic personal experiences without being mechanically "caused by" those experiences. How, that is, can works that grow out of a writer's unarticulated life-problems be anything more than mere purgation? And can such works achieve transcendence of their origins? Stephen is deeply concerned about whatever experiences in his own life may hold him in thrall, and he hopes to come to a better understanding of them by exploring the life and works of Shakespeare.[32]

Stephen's dilemma as to whether art is merely a reflex physiological reaction to the writer's experience or whether it is transcendent of its biographical origins is one mode of the metaphorical Scylla and Charybdis that he is navigating in this episode, with Buck Mulligan espousing the materialistic position on this issue, and A.E. the idealistic one. (Philosophically, the polarity within the episode is not—as has been claimed— Plato versus Aristotle, but rather A.E.'s Platonic idealism versus Mulligan's materialism, with Aristotelianism representing a via media. The complementariness of these two figures is hinted by A.E.'s departing about one-third of the way through the episode, Mulligan's arriving with about one-third still to go, with Stephen trying to strike a course between them.) A.E. idealistically proclaims that art is about formless spiritual essences, and that if we have *King Lear,* what is it to us how the poet lived (*U,* 9.49, 9.185)? As he says, quoting from Villers de l'Isle Adam's *Axël,* "As for living our servants can do that for us" (*U,* 9.186). Mulligan, on the other hand, is a materialist and cynic, for whom a writer's art has essentially the same status as some symptom the doctor diagnoses; for him, all art is purgative—more precisely, masturbatory, as the little drama he composes suggests. But Stephen cannot be satisfied with either of these positions, for he hopes to understand how a writer's works might grow out of, comprehend, perhaps transcend his experiences, rather than be physiologically determined by them.

Stephen's theory focuses on what the writing of *Hamlet* meant to Shakespeare. He claims that through writing that play Shakespeare was able to articulate (and exorcise?) deep-seated doubts about his failures as a man. According to Stephen, writing *Hamlet* enabled Shakespeare to understand that he was not responsible for the death of his only son, Hamnet, and that most of his troubles could be traced to Anne Hathaway, the older woman who seduced him and drew him into an enforced marriage, thus killing his own belief in himself. Needless to say, this view of *Hamlet* and of Anne Hathaway represents sheer speculation on Stephen's part, based on meager biographical data. Most relevant for my present purposes, though, is how Stephen's interpretation of Shakespeare reflects his own situation, and what his "use" of the Shakespearean material reveals about the relationship between the individual self and the various myths and schemata of our culture that we presume to appropriate.

In contrast to his simple, proprietary stance toward the mythic material in *Portrait,* here in *Ulysses* Stephen has achieved sufficient perspective to twit himself about his unwitting identification with Icarus as he left Dublin—which he does, appropriately, here in the midst of his Shakespeare theory. He has begun to realize that his experience, his identity, is not as simple or as solipsistic as he had believed, and that the meanings and structures he finds in literary or historical narratives are not entirely of his own conscious contriving—that, on the contrary, such public narratives have subtle, unforeseen implications, and that by reflecting on those implications, he can gain valuable insights into the nature and workings of his own psyche and his relationships with the world.

He has also begun to realize that certain dimensions of his own experience are not as radically separate as he had thought—inner and outer, or private and public. Appropriately, Stephen articulates his glimpse of this insight at the end of his presentation, when he says of the mature Shakespeare, "He found in the world without as actual what was in his world within as possible. Maeterlinck says: *If Socrates leave his house today he will find the sage seated on his doorstep. If Judas go forth tonight it is to Judas his steps will tend.* Every life is many days, day after day. We walk through ourselves, meeting robbers, ghosts, giants, old men, young men, wives, widows, brothers-in-love, but always meeting ourselves" (*U*, 9.1041). In other words, what each of us is capable of discovering in the public, outer world is a reflection of what exists in our private, inner world—so profoundly complementary are the two. This is not to say that Stephen yet fully understands the implications or enjoys the benefits of this insight, but he does glimpse the idea, and in terms of his movement out of adolescence and toward maturity, this is very promising. And because Stephen has sensed what can be learned from such narratives, he approaches the Shakespearean material with some openness and flexibility, playing over the relationships and perspectives that it provides, at times from the point of view of Shakespeare, at times from that of Hamlet, at times from that of old King Hamlet, in order to glean from the ramifications of the narrative as much as he can.

To clarify how the Shakespearean material functions in *Ulysses* as a simulation of the cultural milieu, conscious and unconscious, I must distinguish four levels of Stephen's theory of Shakespeare, which I shall call the public conscious level, the private conscious level, the private unconscious level, and the public unconscious level. The fullness and detail of Stephen's engagement with the Shakespearean material enables illustration of each of these levels; I presume that these same dimensions exist in all of the other less extensive cultural schemata the novel involves. And while discriminating these four levels helps us to understand how this material works, they are inextricably intertwined within Stephen's presentation.

First, the *public conscious* aspect of Stephen's interpretation of Shakespeare involves those aspects of his theory that both he and his listeners are consciously aware of. For example, Stephen argues that Shakespeare's playing the role of the Ghost of King Hamlet was instrumental in his coming to a new understanding of himself. The opportunity to speak these words of his own composition to a surrogate of his son Hamnet provided the poet a new perspective upon the earlier events of his life, with liberating effects for Shakespeare. Whether or not we agree with this claim, both Stephen and his auditors fully understand what it involves. For our purposes, this conscious, public dimension of his theory is the least important of the four modes.

The second category is *private conscious* material. In the course of developing his theory, Stephen quite wittingly weaves certain details from his own situation or his private experience into his presentation—details that none of his hearers can possibly be aware of. For example, discussing the original staging of *Hamlet,* in which Shakespeare himself played the role of the Ghost of King Hamlet, Stephen describes actor Shakespeare's entry onto the stage as follows: "The play begins. A player comes on under the shadow, made up in the castoff mail of a court buck . . ." (*U*, 9.164). In this last phrase Stephen weaves in a covert link between himself and Shakespeare: Shakespeare's wearing "the castoff mail of a court buck" echoes the fact that Stephen himself is presently wearing the castoff shoes of his antagonist, Buck Mulligan. We readers know this because earlier in the novel we were told that Stephen "brooded on his broadtoed boots, a buck's castoffs" (*U*, 3.446)—but Stephen's hearers cannot know this. Other examples of private material that Stephen consciously incorporates into his story include the links within Stephen's mind between the prostitutes of London and those of Paris (*U*, 9.641), and (in a different vein) his unspoken allusion to pouring his theory into the ears of his hearers (*U*, 9.465).

Why Stephen incorporates such private details into his theory is not entirely clear; perhaps he sees this as a way of engaging the myth more fully and thus encouraging its effects within his own psyche. In any event, he seems to get a certain frisson out of having a relationship with this Shakespearean material that none of his hearers can share or even be aware of. Joyce himself, of course, frequently incorporated personal material into his art, in scores of ways that we have been able to document, and doubtless in hundreds that we have not. For example, he included in "The Dead" phrases drawn from his personal letters to Nora—material that might easily have been destroyed or have gone undetected by critics. And according to Fritz Senn, he did the same in weaving some of the details, turns of phrase, and so forth of his correspondence with and "courtship" of Martha Fleischmann into the "Nausicaa" episode.[33]

The necessary incompleteness of Stephen's comprehension of Shakespeare is shown by the other two levels of material present within his theory—the private unconscious and the public unconscious aspects. While Stephen consciously inserts some of his personal experiences into his interpretation of Shakespeare, other aspects of his theory embody aspects of himself that he is unaware of.[34] One example of this *private unconscious* aspect of Stephen's interpretation is the crucial (and negative) role that his interpretation assigns to women. According to Stephen, Shakespeare's problems originate in his having been seduced by Anne Hathaway when he was a lad of eighteen, but Shakespeare himself long remains less than fully aware of the dire effects that episode had upon him. Furthermore, Stephen argues that Shakespeare comes to realize this fact only through his writing (and playing) of *Hamlet.* When, playing the role of the Ghost in *Hamlet,* actor-Shakespeare explains to Hamlet that the source of their problems is his mother, Gertrude the queen, it reflects Shakespeare's own newfound realization that Anne Hathaway is the source of his problems. (Stephen develops this point in *U,* 9.164–80, esp. 9.174–80.)

In proposing this misogynistic theory, Stephen is unwittingly projecting an aspect of his own psyche into the material—namely, his implicit belief that women, and especially his mother, are the source of his problems. (On the association in Stephen's mind between Anne Hathaway and his mother, May Dedalus, see W. Schutte, *Joyce and Shakespeare,* 107–9.) Misogyny is very much an aspect of Stephen's personality, expressing itself in various ways in the novel. Consider, for example, Stephen's identification of himself with St. Columbanus, who, in order to carry out his mission to Europe, had to stride across the prostrate body of his mother (*U,* 2.143). And in a more immediate sense, the repeated and disturbing vision of the ghost of his mother is one of Stephen's main stumbling blocks. Stephen's unwitting projection of his misogyny into his theory of Shakespeare illustrates how someone's interpretation of such complex material reveals as much about the interpreter as it does about the text.[35] Thus, Joyce shows that the myth Stephen is currently attempting to use remains larger than he is, and his interpretation of Shakespeare's situation reflects unconscious aspects of his own self.

The *public unconscious* aspect of Stephen's theory is most important for our purposes, since through it Joyce shows how a complex mythic schema can form an important part of the collective psyche, involving all of us in a matrix beyond what we can comprehend. This aspect of Stephen's theory involves elements that neither he nor his hearers are aware of, that constitute links between the Shakespearean material and the fictive world that Stephen himself inhabits.

Before examining some of these, we should recognize that there is a large array of such links that originate "authorially," consisting of correspondences between Shakespeare's world and the fictive world of *Ulysses.* Consider, for example, some of the enticing authorially contrived parallels between the situations of Shakespeare and Bloom. Both Shakespeare and Bloom were "seduced" by women who later became their wives, and in both cases the consummation occurred before marriage and resulted in the birth of a daughter—Susanna Shakespeare and Milly Bloom. More important, Bloom's only son, Rudy, whose death has been a major trauma for Bloom, died at eleven days old, and had he lived, he would now be eleven years old; Shakespeare's only son, Hamnet, whose death Stephen claims was a major trauma for Shakespeare, died at the age of eleven years.[36] Evidence that Joyce was thinking in terms of such parallels is provided by the notes that he assembled for his Shakespeare lectures in Trieste; one of these notes is "*Hamlet* 1602 (38 years old)" (Quillian, "Shakespeare in Trieste," 26), which means that Bloom at thirty-eight is the same age Shakespeare was when he wrote and performed in this crucial play—and as Joyce while writing *Ulysses*.

As to points of comparison between Shakespeare and Bloom unwittingly introduced by Stephen's interpretation, we might consider two—the first rather slight, the second more complex and more interesting. First, when Stephen says that his youthful seduction by Anne Hathaway "unmanned" Shakespeare, he goes on to say that no "assumed dongiovannism" will redeem his manhood (*U*, 9.458). The attentive reader must recall that one of Bloom's devices for suppressing his thoughts of Molly's adultery (which "unmans" Bloom) is thinking of himself as Don Giovanni, though we of course know that the role that he better approximates in this schema is that of the pathetic Masetto, husband of Zerlina—another example both of overlapping of myths and of a myth's assigning a role different than the one consciously aspired to by the character.

Another parallel unwittingly hinted at by Stephen involves some subtle details of his interpretation of Shakespeare and of Bloom's personal situation. Even though Shakespeare had two daughters, Stephen suggests that the death of his *son* at eleven years old affected him profoundly, reflected in Stephen's implication that Shakespeare would not have written *Hamlet* had he not suffered the trauma of his son's death (*U*, 9.171). But Stephen goes on to claim that Shakespeare was surprised by joy at the birth of his first grandchild, his elder daughter Susanna's child, Elizabeth, in 1608, which resulted in the renewed optimism and vitality of the more positive plays that culminate Shakespeare's career—especially *Pericles, The Winter's Tale,* and *The Tempest* (*U*, 9.403, 9.421–24).

Though Stephen cannot know of it, an enticing analogy exists with the familial situation of Leopold Bloom. There is no doubt that the death of Leopold's only son Rudy at eleven days old is a blow from which Bloom has never recovered. But Bloom also has a daughter, Milly—who like Shakespeare's daughter Susanna was conceived prior to wedlock. Now fifteen years old and having recently left home to take a job in Mullingar, Milly writes to Bloom about a young man that she has recently met, causing Bloom some consternation over her possible sexuality and pregnancy (cf. *U*, 4.428–32, 6.88–90, 13.927–28, 17.890–91). If Milly should bear

Bloom a grandchild, might that child revivify Bloom, as Shakespeare's granddaughter Elizabeth revivified him? We find enticement to this analogy when we note that (according to Joyce's own Shakespeare chronology) Shakespeare's granddaughter Elizabeth was born in 1608, twelve years after the death of Shakespeare's son Hamnet in 1596. If Milly were now pregnant, her child would be born in the twelfth year after Rudy's death.[37]

While this connection is admittedly speculative, such speculation is encouraged by the extensive array of analogies that exist between the Shakespeare myth and the situations of various characters in the novel. It is consistent with Joyce's use of Shakespeare's life and works as a comprehensive myth, a compendium of the innumerable links existing among all of us, and recalling Alexandre Dumas's judgment (cited by John Eglinton during Stephen's presentation) that "After God Shakespeare has created most" (*U*, 9.1028).[38]

All of these parallels between Shakespeare's situation and those of the novel's characters, whether unwittingly articulated by Stephen or implicit in the novel's situation, are of course Joyce's doing, and for all the complexity of the details, his point can be stated quite simply: whatever myths we draw upon to give structure to our lives—and we all use them, all the time—these cultural schemata are far more extensive and more comprehensive than we can ever realize. This is true because our response to any complex literary or historical or mythic schema always involves projections of hidden, unconscious aspects of our own self. But it is true even more because such myths are public, cultural entities, providing the basis of an intersubjectivity that intricately links us to others and to the world. Since we can read and discuss and reflect on these schemata, they are in part conscious, but in view of their number, their complexity, and the ways in which we internalize them, they are unconscious as well, showing once again the impossibility of separating private from public, conscious from unconscious.

This illustration of how Joyce simulates the cultural psyche through allusive schemata in *Ulysses* has drawn upon the Shakespearean material, but the point could be made through scrutiny of any of the more pervasive allusive strands in *Ulysses*. In addition to the Odyssean parallel suggested by the title, the novel makes extensive use of Christ's passion and of other biblical narratives and figures such as Moses, Elijah, and Satan, of Faust, of Don Giovanni, and an endless array of more popular material. Moreover, these mythic strands overlap, intersect, qualify one another in ways beyond our comprehension. And for all the many allusive parallels Joyce incorporates into *Ulysses,* there are other such contexts that he could have invoked and still others that he was himself only vaguely aware of; though it may appear comprehensive, his novel in this regard is necessarily very selective. In his dramatization of how such schemata work in the lives of his characters, and presumably in the life of each of us as well, Joyce shows us that the division between inner and outer, subjective and objective, private and public is not nearly so deep as the modernist mentality is wont to think.

Finally I would invoke a passage from Thomas Mann's lecture "Freud and the Future," in which, drawing upon psychoanalysis and upon his own aims in *Joseph and His Brothers,* he discusses the relationship between the individual and the mythic in terms that are singularly appropriate to what Joyce is doing in *Ulysses.* (It is noteworthy that in this statement Mann views the unconscious as something positive—something that sustains our individuality and gives value to our experience; this is an important counterbalance to the Freudian view that—as we shall see—Joyce rejects in "Circe.") According to Mann:

> . . . while in the life of the human race the mythical is an early and primitive stage, in the life of the individual it is a late and mature one. What is gained [as the individual develops] is a . . . knowledge of the schema in which and according to which the supposed individual lives, unaware, in his naive belief in himself as unique . . . of the extent to which his life is but formula and repetition and his path marked out for him by those who trod it before him. [The individual's] character is a mythical role which the actor just emerged from the depths to the light plays in the illusion that it is his own and unique, that he, as it were, has invented it all himself . . . . Actually, if [a person's] existence consisted merely in the unique and the present, he would not know how to conduct himself at all: he would be confused, helpless, unstable in his own self-regard, [he] would not know which foot to put foremost or what sort of face to put on. His dignity and security lie all unconsciously in the fact that with him something timeless has once more emerged into the light and become present; it is a mythical value added to the otherwise poor and valueless single character; it is native worth, because its origin lies in the unconscious. ("Freud and the Future," 31–32)

5

Voices and Values in the Later Episodes of *Ulysses*

In chapters 5 and 6 I will argue that the obtrusive narrative voices of each of the later episodes of *Ulysses* represent styles and values that Joyce does not sanction—in fact, that he wishes to expose as insufficient or distorting. This is not a new idea; some version of it has been suggested by a number of critics over the past several decades.[1] But it is fair to say that this remains a minority opinion, and that the main current of Joyce criticism on this issue runs in the opposite direction.

In the view of most present-day critics, Joyce's aim in presenting this array of styles in *Ulysses* is to show the relativism, the arbitrariness, the equal insufficiency, of all styles—even the initial style of the opening episodes. One influential book in this line of argument is Karen Lawrence's *The Odyssey of Style in "Ulysses"* (1981). A major thesis of Lawrence's book is the relativism of all styles: "As the narrative norm is abandoned during the course of [*Ulysses*] and is replaced by a series of styles, we see the arbitrariness of all styles. We see styles as different but not definitive ways of filtering and ordering experience" (*Odyssey of Style*, 9; see also 121, 122). Similarly, Marilyn French says of "Sirens," "By using language that is for the most part recognizable English and recognizable syntactic units, yet arranging those units so that they make no sense at all, Joyce is again thrusting in the reader's face the arbitrariness of language, the void at its core" (*Book as World*, 127–28).

Moreover, both Lawrence and French argue that Joyce's development from *Dubliners* to *Ulysses* involves his coming to understand that there is no such thing as objective reality, much less a form of language that presents reality veridically, and they see this relativism itself as one of the major points of *Ulysses*. Lawrence asserts, "In *Dubliners*, these voices [i.e., styles] were still consistent with a belief that language could capture reality: each voice of Dublin revealed the precise quality of the life story it told. It is not until *Ulysses* that parody is no longer attached to a specific character and begins to undermine the notion of style as an 'absolute manner of seeing things'" (*Odyssey*, 33).[2]

I disagree with these claims, both because they involve certain confusions in regard to language and reality and to form and content, and because they seem to me mistaken about Joyce's underlying life-attitudes and literary purposes.

One recurrent theme of Joyce's work, from *Dubliners* and *A Portrait* through *Ulysses*, is his concern to reveal the dangers of various ideas, institutions, and modes of discourse that have the capacity to frustrate the potential of his fellow citizens. Joyce lived in a time when an increasing array of voices and media and modes of discourse—nationalistic, religious, commercial, journalistic—arose to assert a claim on people's lives. He subsumed some of these modes and voices into his works in order to take their measure, to display for his readers their baneful effects. Joyce devoted so much time and energy to developing this array of styles in *Ulysses* not because he was a relativist, but in order to expose for his readers certain modes of language and received ideas and attitudes that would inhibit their lives.

Joyce's willingness to make judgments among various modes of language, then, proceeds from his profound concern for the potential of every individual and his wish to expose and subvert certain ideas, institutions, and modes of discourse that would inhibit or distort that potential. I have argued for both of these points in *The Antimodernism of Joyce's "Portrait"* (see esp. 42–45 and 110–18), and they underlie my claims about the secondary narrative voices in *Ulysses*. But linguistic and ethical relativism has such authority in the modernist critical milieu that the view of Joyce as a stylistic relativist is much more popular, and the burden of proof falls on those of us who would argue for a continuity in Joyce's "normative" attitudes in regard to language.

Even critics who proclaim stylistic relativism in *Ulysses* acknowledge that *Dubliners* and *Portrait* involve critiques of various kinds of language, various modes of discourse, that can paralyze or frustrate the potential of the characters. The tragedy of many of the *Dubliners* characters is rooted in the limiting, paralyzing language through which they conceive themselves and their world—for example, Eveline, Little Chandler, James Duffy. One persistent theme of *A Portrait* is the various voices that assail Stephen, each with its own agenda for his future (see especially *PoA*, 83.29–84.13). If he is to escape some form of Dublin paralysis and fulfill his own distinctive potential, Stephen must recognize and circumvent those voices.

Joyce concerns himself with various styles or voices, then, because of his keen awareness of the power of language for good and for ill, and his wish to reveal the dangers of certain modes of discourse to his readers. Such a concern is reflected repeatedly in his correspondence with Grant

Richards about the *Dubliners* stories—for example, in his assertion that failing to publish *Dubliners* would retard the course of civilization in Ireland (letter of 23 June 1906; *Sel Lts,* 90). Perhaps this perennial concern to display various abuses of language is one thing he had in mind when in 1930 he stressed to Adolf Hoffmeister the continuity of his work, saying, "my work is a whole and cannot be divided by book titles," and "My work, from *Dubliners* on, goes in a straight line of development. It is almost indivisible, only the scale of expressiveness and writing technique rises somewhat steeply" (W. Potts, *Portraits of the Artist,* 129, 131). (In a letter to H. L. Mencken, 7 July 1915, Joyce said, "I . . . am engaged on a novel which is a continuation of *A Portrait of the Artist* and also of *Dubliners*" [*Lts,* 1:83].) Most writers, because they do respect the power of language, are concerned about the abuses that are involved in political or religious rhetoric, or journalism, or sentimental romance, or bureaucratic jargon. Joyce is no different, except in the scope of his concern and the brilliant means by which he exposes these abuses and dangers.

In contrast to Yeats and Eliot and Lawrence, who produced impressive volumes of literary and cultural criticism, Joyce incorporates his "commentaries" dramatically into his works of art. We see this tactic, for example, in the inclusion of a journalistic passage in "A Painful Case" and his evocation of the "Celtic Twilight" in "A Little Cloud," as well as his incorporation of Jesuit sermon rhetoric and of aesthetic theory into *Portrait,* and issues of the relationship between life and art into Stephen's theory of Shakespeare in *Ulysses,* and the parody of scholarship in the scrutiny of ALP's mamafesta from a variety of critical perspectives in *Finnegans Wake,* I, 5. Joyce expressed his concern about the effects of various styles and theories that proliferated around him not by (for example) writing an essay challenging Pater's claims that all art approaches the condition of music, or attacking the theory of imitative form, or the false ideal of authorial "objectivity," or penning a diatribe against journalese or sentimental literature, but by incorporating his critiques of these theories and discourses into his literary texts, in the styles and agendas of the later episodes of *Ulysses.* In this substantial sense the latter half of *Ulysses* is about style, about language—though in saying this, I mean something quite different from those critics who describe the book as "self-referential."

Form/Content

In order to understand Joyce's critique of the secondary styles in *Ulysses*, we must think carefully about the relationship between form and content. Current thinking holds that there is no possibility of separating content from form, both because we cannot conceive of any content that has no form, and because a change in form inevitably alters the content. Therefore we cannot (we are told) speak of one linguistic rendering of experience as more veridical than another—they are simply different, and thus incomparable. In keeping with these ideas, Brook Thomas, for example, argues that "Joyce's multiplicity of styles creates the conditions necessary to produce an illusion that an external reality to be portrayed exists independently of the styles themselves. . . . Joyce, by successfully creating this illusion of an independent reality, leads critics to talk about the inadequacy of a certain style to capture the essence of Bloom or to talk about a style screening us from the book's action or to search after the real identity of M'Intosh. But the point remains that there is no action independent of the book's styles. Joyce's supreme achievement is creating the illusion of a subject matter that does not exist" (Thomas, *JJ's "Ulysses,"* 126). This line of thought, though currently popular, is nevertheless confused and misleading.[3]

It is of course true that in this mundane world we never encounter a subject *an sich*—a subject that is not embodied in some form. But in *Ulysses* Joyce shows that while it may not be possible to "produce a subject that exists apart from the words" (Kenner, *Joyce's Voices,* 52), it is quite possible to *distinguish between* a subject and the language in which it is presented, and consequently to say that some modes of language present a given subject more appropriately than others. (This is of course what a composition teacher does whenever she tells a student that he has a good idea but has presented it poorly.) For example, the initial style of *Ulysses* is a more appropriate vehicle for presenting the personalities of Stephen and Bloom and the total fictive world of *Ulysses,* and thus for effecting Joyce's carefully conceived literary aims of evoking a cultural milieu and subverting modernist dualisms, than is the style of "Sirens" or of "Nausicaa" or of "Oxen of the Sun." We know this, both because the initial style fulfills Joyce's purposes so effectively, and because in those later episodes we experience various distortions of the story and the characters through the secondary styles.

Karen Lawrence's argument for the relativism of all style involves the straw man of denying that any style can be "absolute," or can "capture reality." But to describe styles as "different but not definitive" sidesteps the more important issue of whether some are more or less adequate, whether some styles (or writers) present reality more sufficiently or more richly than others—or conversely, whether some styles are less clear, or more distorting, than others. To proclaim that no language can "capture reality" (*exhaust* reality? *contain* reality?) is to ignore the fact that some writers, some works, some styles do convey reality more fully or more richly (or with less obfuscation) than others. This is implied by the fact that virtually every serious writer has pilloried or parodied styles that he or she saw as clichéd or sentimental or somehow inferior. This difference in richness is why we readers and critics have devoted far more loving attention to the works of Shakespeare than to the more voluminous, but less rewarding, works of Barbara Cartland. Critical claims that language is inherently flawed and that all styles are equally incapable of engaging reality are currently in vogue, but they involve a certain intellectual disingenuousness or double standard. In the metaphor of George Steiner, critics who talk this way, and who of course presume to be understood and perhaps even believe their works to be more perspicacious and better written than those of other critics, are duplicitously drawing upon a value bank in which they are not willing to make deposits (*George Steiner: A Reader,* 21).

Joyce understood that we human beings have no unmediated access to the *ding an sich* and thus no "absolute" view of "reality"; we always apprehend the world through our language and through cultural constructs. He understood as well that there is no style, not even the "objective plain style" or the initial style of *Ulysses,* that can present "reality" directly, without mediation, much less one that can exhaust reality. But I differ with these critics about how Joyce responded to this understanding, and, consequently, about what he is doing in *Ulysses.* For in *Ulysses* we *do* have a firm substrate of *novelistic reality* available to us in the events and the personalities of the characters, and this novelistic reality *is* far better mediated by some of the book's styles than by others. This, and not the equal arbitrariness of all styles, is the point of Joyce's beginning with the normative initial style and only later invoking the various distortive styles that force us to peer through them to the bedrock of character and event that persists throughout the book.

It is worth noting that virtually every critic of *Ulysses,* even those who proclaim its stylistic relativism, is shown by his or her own practice to believe that in the later episodes of the novel the reader is trying to see *through* the styles to what is "going on." Yet these critics fail to grasp the implications of this assumption—namely, that *Ulysses does* have a content, a subject matter, as well as a form, and that these later styles are less appropriate vehicles of the subject matter of *Ulysses* than is the carefully crafted initial style.[4] This is not to say that Joyce naively regarded this initial style as either objective or transparent or as "capturing reality" (whatever that might mean); but it is to say that he developed this distinctive style intentionally, carefully, in the belief that it was the most appropriate vehicle for his subject matter and his literary aims. Finding himself in the ineluctable human predicament of having no unmediated access to "absolute reality," Joyce chose to set his book in Dublin, not in u-topia, and to commit himself to certain characters and events and to certain basic modes and techniques of presenting them. Moreover, in presenting these characters and events as he does, he takes a valuational as well as a stylistic stand, for in the book he reveals his preference for *caritas* over selfishness or chauvinism, for responsiveness and engagement over solipsism and self-centeredness, for honest self-assessment over sentimental self-indulgence.

In order to dramatize the insufficiency of these styles and theories within his novel, Joyce needed a firm substrate of character, plot, structure, and technique that we subsequently try to discern *through* the kaleidoscope of less appropriate, even distortive, styles.[5] We come to understand the insufficiency of these later styles in *Ulysses* by recognizing how ill-suited they are to convey the characters and events and milieu of the novel, much less to carry out Joyce's subtle and distinctive literary aims. We see this insufficiency all the more clearly if we ask ourselves why the entire novel might not appropriately be presented in the style of "Sirens" or "Oxen of the Sun" or "Eumaeus"—or even in the sheer interior monologue of "Penelope." Reflecting on this question reveals both the great appropriateness of the initial style to Joyce's underlying aims, and the inadequacy of any of the secondary voices as the possible base style of the novel.

> I am doing it, as Aristotle would say, by different means in different parts.
> (Joyce, on *Ulysses*, to Ezra Pound, 9 April 1917; *Lts*, 1:101)

> Parts constitute a whole as far as they have a common end.
> (Joyce, "The Paris Notebook," *CW*, 145)

Ulysses is not eighteen separate pieces; it is one coherent narrative, about characters who have continuity and integrity, presented through a number of voices. Even in those later episodes that are consigned to some anomalous voice—that is, the secondary narrator or presenter—the events of the novel unfold and the characters develop and interrelate just as they would if all of the episodes were presented through the mode of "Nestor" or "Lestrygonians." Beneath the stylistic veneer of the second-level narrative voices of the later chapters, we do not have a half-dozen new stories, but a continuation of the one that was begun in "Telemachus" and "Calypso"; we do not have new characters that happen to be called "Stephen," "Bloom," and so on, but the unfolding and development of the ones we came to know earlier.[6] Some unified purpose, some complex act of authorial intention, lies behind the whole of the work, and it makes little difference whether we call that unifying mind the "implied author," or "James Joyce," or the "*Ulysses*-source."

Let me venture a profile of the secondary narrative voices of the later episodes: (1) each voice represents some style or theory that Joyce satirizes; (2) the style of each is distinctive and characterizable and is localized in one episode; (3) each secondary narrative voice has knowledge of the whole novel, including the events and language of earlier episodes, the minds of the characters, and so forth; (4) the voice has authority over the mode of presentation of the material (style, or genre), but not over the plot events or the thoughts or feelings of the characters (some narrators do recast the characters' dialogue—e.g., in "Oxen of the Sun" and "Ithaca"—but to recast their thoughts would of course create new characters); (5) in some episodes the voice intensifies as the chapter proceeds, or loses control and parodies itself; (6) the sufficiency of each style, or the validity of the presenter's agenda, is revealed as deficient by the techniques and values of the novel as a whole.

In contrast to the highly effaced primary narrator, the secondary narrative voice of each episode assumes a more tangible presence and distinctive attitude toward its material, often emerging as a persona who is enamored of a certain theory or style or literary mode. That is, "Ithaca" is presented by a speaker who aspires to be objective and "scientific"; "Eumaeus" is spoken by a palpable voice in a distinctive, flaccid style; the "Sirens" episode is narrated by a persona who is enamored of his auditory and rhythmical devices and obsessed with the Pateresque idea of literature emulating music. This is not to say that the secondary narrator is a character of the novel, on the level of Stephen or Bloom or the nameless "I" of "Cyclops"; it is simply to acknowledge a more palpable narrative "persona" in the secondary voice than in the primary narrator. Seeing the secondary narrative voice as a personalized agent makes it easier to recognize the self-indulgent overextensions or apparent defections from the style or agenda (point 5 above).[7]

Finally, having talked so seriously about Joyce's subversion of these styles, I must acknowledge a complementary point—that is, since Joyce himself is the source and springhead of each of these (inferior) styles, there is always something for us to admire and enjoy about their very badness, as with any skillful parody of a bad work. The principle here is essentially no different than in Joyce's skillful representation of journalistic prose in the account of Mrs. Sinico's death in "A Painful Case"; Joyce does not admire or sanction that style, though he doubtless took pride and pleasure in his ability to reproduce it so skillfully, and we should enjoy it at the same time that we recognize its badness.

I turn now to illustration of my claims about Joyce's subversion of the secondary voices in each of these episodes. While there undoubtedly is a growing pervasiveness of the secondary voices as we move through "Aeolus," "Scylla and Charybdis," "Wandering Rocks," and "Sirens," I will discuss first those episodes in which it is clearest that Joyce does not sanction or stand behind the style and then move to those where that conclusion is less obvious or more problematic. Chapter 6 is devoted to fuller discussion of three episodes that pose special problems for my thesis—"Wandering Rocks," "Oxen of the Sun," and "Circe."

"Nausicaa"

I begin with "Nausicaa" because it provides the clearest example of a second-level narrative style that Joyce does not sanction. The style of the first half of the episode is obviously sentimental and clichéd; moreover, these qualities are made salient by juxtaposition with the style of the latter half, which is essentially continuous with the initial style of the earlier episodes. Richard Ellmann correctly observes that "the parodically saccharine narrator of the first part is put to rout by Bloom in the second" ("The New *Ulysses*," 550)—which is to say, by the primary narrator of the novel. And we have Joyce's explicit denigration of the style; in a letter to Frank Budgen of 3 January 1920, Joyce said, "*Nausikaa* is written in a namby-pamby jammy marmalady drawersy (alto là!) style with effects of incense, mariolatry, masturbation, stewed cockles, painter's palette, chit-chat, circumlocutions, etc etc" (*Sel Lts*, 246).

Not surprisingly, no critic of *Ulysses* has claimed that Joyce admires or sanctions this style. This is not to deny that the protean style-master took considerable care in effecting this style and some pleasure in his achievement, since it so effectively replicates (and thus satirizes) the sentimental romance style. But neither here nor elsewhere in these later episodes should we confuse the pride Joyce took in his own linguistic skills, or our admiration for or enjoyment of the effects he has wrought, with his sanction of the style. Moreover, our judgment against this sentimental style is quite distinct from our attitude toward Gerty, and our disdain for the style even has its basis in our concern for the pernicious effects it has had on this young woman's psyche.[8]

Critics have been virtually unanimous both in recognizing the style as atrocious and in lamenting its effects on Gerty. Stanley Sultan says the style is "plainly a parody of pretentious sentimental fiction" and that "Gerty has succeeded, by a continual process of sentimentalizing, in turning black into white. Almost nothing she believes is true" (*Argument of "Ulysses,"* 267, 271). Suzette Henke, pointing to Gerty's devotion to the fashion pages of *Lady's Pictorial,* the prose of Victorian sentimental novels, and the advertising pages of the *Irish Times,* notes, "she seems to have internalized the sweet illusions and the sweeter lies of Victorian sexual mythology, and she confuses both with the puritanical teachings of Irish Catholicism" ("Gerty MacDowell," 132). David Fuller argues that "the control of language over experience is so powerful that Gerty remains the victim of her given fictions" (*JJ's "Ulysses,"* 65). And Fritz Senn says, "The first half of the chapter is a novelette conveying the de-formation of Gerty MacDowell: what she is and what made her what she is. The kind of writing here parodied would lead to that kind of thinking" ("Nausicaa," 309). R. B. Kershner speaks of Gerty's "apparent possession . . . by the guiding consciousness of *The Lamplighter* and *The Princess Novelette,*" and says, "like a cut-rate Madame Bovary or Julien Sorel, she has been painfully misled by her reading, indeed lamed by it. And all of the major characters in *Ulysses* have, to greater or lesser extents, been affected by the reading that Joyce painstakingly specifies—the newspapers, magazines, romances, 'self-improvement' guides, and casual works of fiction that lie scattered throughout the text" (*Joyce, Bakhtin, and Popular Literature,* 2).

Gerty's section of "Nausicaa" represents a sentimental style that lures its clientele into a dangerously simplistic and incomplete view of reality. Gerty's mind has come under the influence of the prose style and the implicit view of experience of sentimental romances such as Maria Cummins's *The Lamplighter* (1854), whose heroine, Gerty Flint, is in several respects our Gerty's prototype (Gerty refers to this novel on *U,* 13.633), and as a result her view of the world has been distorted. In effect Gerty's mind has become so saturated with sentimental romance and with evasive, self-deluding moves for re-accoutering the world around her that she does not live in the real world. Her apprehension of the persons and things about her is so colored by the rhetoric and imagery and clichés she has imbibed from sentimental literature and Roman Catholic Mariolatry that she cannot see things in their true light.

Fritz Senn notes that "Gerty's mind is almost incapable of recognizing an identity," and he compares her with the citizen in terms of the fixity of her categories ("Nausicaa," 296); later he speaks of her "inflexible fixedness and her unconscious and tacit acceptance of the several poses of which the styles are the outward and visible form" (308). Senn pinpoints the narcissistic qualities of the style: "the style chosen for Gerty's parts . . . , the cliché and the shopsoiled charms of stereotyped fiction or commercial slickness, is manifestly unable to characterize anything outside itself. It reflects only its own vacuity, it hardly illuminates or communicates, its glitter is narcissistic, its essence is self-gratification" ("Nausicaa," 309).

Since Joyce believed in the power of literature and took his art seriously, it is understandable that he should wish to expose the baneful effects of such bad writing.[9] He had already done something similar in stories such as "Eveline" and "A Little Cloud," where various modes of language, various styles, are shown to have infiltrated and infected the minds of the main characters. Here in "Nausicaa" Joyce wishes to expose and to warn against the effects of sentimental romance—and this underlying purpose on Joyce's part exists regardless of whether we label this style Gerty's own narration, or the voice of some secondary narrator, or simply say that Joyce is here speaking with sustained irony. The point is that the prose medium through which the characters and events are presented in the first half of this episode is shown by its own bad features, and by the larger stylistic and valuational perspective of the novel as a whole, to be pernicious and to distort Gerty's perception of the world around her.

The undeniably inferior quality of this style, then, poses an interpretive problem for critics who would like to see all of the styles of the novel as equally inadequate or merely relative. For example, because Karen Lawrence assumes that Joyce aims to damn all styles (because all are arbitrary), she finds the prose in "Nausica" to involve a double standard on Joyce's part:

> The succession of styles in "Cyclops" and the different styles in the book as a whole imply that all language is, in a sense, inherently stupid, that all styles are arbitrary. But by choosing a member of the "submerged population" as the object of his parody and by allowing

his prose to "formulate her in a phrase," Joyce allowed the reader and the writer to be exempt from the indictment of Gerty. If the book has demonstrated that all styles are, in a sense, equal, the parody here seems to say that some are more equal than others. The kind of obvious stable irony deployed in the narrative of "Nausicaa" narrows the scope of the parody. The trouble with this section of "Nausicaa" is not that it represents a technical reversion but that it suggests an idea about language that the text has already rejected. (*Odyssey,* 122)

More precisely, the trouble is that "Nausicaa" suggests an idea that Lawrence's theory calls for the text to reject. But Joyce has not contradicted himself here, and this episode is not an anomaly—its narrative voice simply involves a more obviously bad example than do the other episodes. Nor, in spite of Lawrence's politicizing implication, is the object of the "indictment" here Gerty herself. Rather, it is the style that Gerty has fallen victim to. And the reader can hardly afford to condescend toward Gerty or to congratulate himself on having escaped scot-free from whatever indictment such prose involves, for there is doubtless some contemporary stylistic equivalent that we may be in danger of succumbing to, such as television soap operas or Barbara Cartland romances.

Two points, then, are worth noting about the critics' responses to this episode: first, they unanimously judge this style as inferior, obviously not regarding it as sanctioned by Joyce; and second, the basis of their judgment is the baneful effect the style has on Gerty's psyche, its inhibition of what this young woman might potentially be. If it is granted even in this one case that Joyce wishes to expose the pernicious, distorting effects of some mode of language, we have seriously breached the defenses of the relativist arguments that Joyce believed in the equal arbitrariness or "stupidity" (Karen Lawrence's term) of all modes of language. We have established that a style in *Ulysses* can exist in order to reveal the deficiencies, even distortion, that language can involve.

"Eumaeus"

I turn next to "Eumaeus" because it rivals "Nausicaa" in the obvious badness of its style. Ridden with clichés, circumlocutions, loose syntax, imprecision, mixed metaphors, meandering repetition, it is the utter opposite of the deft, precise presentation characteristic of the initial style. Once again, this is not to deny that the prose is carefully contrived and cost Joyce himself considerable pains (as Kenner has said, *Joyce's Voices,* 38), or that he is using it for specific artistic and thematic purposes, or that it is often hilarious. The point is that the Eumaean style is bad, and that Joyce has purposefully engendered its poor quality.

It is interesting to note, however, that some early critics did fault Joyce for the poor quality of the prose. Edmund Wilson, in his brilliant essay in *Axel's Castle*, describes this episode (and "Ithaca") as "artistically absolutely indefensible" ("James Joyce," 174). Similarly, Philip Toynbee criticizes Joyce for the style of "Eumaeus," which he calls "anticlimactic" and "flat and savourless" ("A Study of *Ulysses*," 280). Even Walton Litz in 1961 described the episode as indulging the technique of expressive form and as a "failure" (*Art of James Joyce*, 45). Phillip F. Herring expressed negative judgments about Joyce's performance in it in 1972 (*Joyce's "Ulysses" Notesheets*, 49) and 1977 (*Joyce's Notes and Early Drafts*, 191). More recent critics, however, have quite consistently attributed the bad qualities of the prose not to Joyce's having nodded or stumbled, but to a lethargic, fuzzy-minded narrative persona. This pattern of critical response has been repeated in regard to several of the later episodes—presumption by early critics of Joyce's sanction for an inferior style, followed by subsequent acknowledgement that Joyce himself recognizes the inferiority and intends the style parodically.[10]

The fact that the object of the parody in "Eumaeus" is not so obvious as that of "Nausicaa" has caused critics to try to establish a figural source for the style and even to deny the presence of a secondary narrative voice.[11] Much of the critical literature, that is, has dealt with the question of whose perspective the speaking voice of this episode represents, with Bloom being the most frequent nominee. But even if the style in "Eumaeus" were consistently that of Bloom—which it clearly is not—the fact remains that some mode of discourse is here being parodied.

Critics who have attributed the style to Bloom include Hugh Kenner, who says that "Eumaeus" is written as Bloom would have written it (*Joyce's Voices*, 35; "*Ulysses*," 1987, 130), and John Gordon, who says that "Eumaeus" "registers Bloom's mind at its murkiest" ("Obeying the Boss," 241). Leo Bersani similarly argues, "There is even an entire episode—'Emmaeus' [*sic*]—written in the manner of Bloom, that is, in the style he would presumably use were he to try his hand at writing," and he adds that this episode "lets the reader know the character even more intimately than before by turning the narrator into the dummy-double of a ventriloquistic Bloom" ("Against *Ulysses*," 3).

But such specification of a figural source cannot be supported by close attention to the text. Marilyn French cites a variety of evidence to show that "the point of view resides with neither Stephen nor Bloom" (*Book as World*, 208), and she notes that the style lacks Bloom's "acuteness and honesty" and that it "does not do justice to Bloom" (208, 209). Karen Lawrence argues that "this is not the sound of Bloom's mind" and backs up her claim by quoting from a passage in "Lotus Eaters," to show how much more "creative, intelligent, funny" Bloom is (*Odyssey*, 170). Gerald L. Bruns sees here "a mind fabricated out of other minds," "a man unable to speak in his own voice but only in the impoverished language of his tribe" ("Eumaeus," 366, 367). Moreover, Denis Donoghue points out that the voice is "omniscient" and has access to Stephen's thoughts ("Is There a Case Against *Ulysses?*" 32, citing *U*, 16.269–72 and 16.1142–46 as evidence). Derek Attridge argues that the search for so specific a source is mistaken.[12]

The wish to establish Bloom as source reflects (as I have already argued) a modernist disdain for traditional literary conventions and a need to exorcise any nonfigural voice from the novel. But it is obvious that all of the material of the chapter—except the dialogue—undergoes a stylistic recasting that is not simply a third-person mode of Bloom's mentality.[13] Bloom himself is repeatedly referred to in the third person—for example, Mr. Bloom, the elder man, our hero, "all kinds of Utopian plans were flashing through his (B's) busy brain" (*U*, 16.1652)—and portions of the presentation involve Stephen's thoughts and memories and material that Bloom is not privy to—for example, the conversation with Corley (*U*, 16.128–228) and Stephen's having forgotten his handkerchief (*U*, 16.19–20).

John Henry Raleigh sees the style as "a kind of parody of the conventional novel, the male novel to the female novel of 'Nausicaa'" ("On the Way Home to Ithaca," 27). Others have proposed some mode of journalese as the referent of this flaccid prose. Stanislaus Joyce characterizes "Eumaeus" as "flabby Dublin journalese, with its weak effort to be witty" (*Lts*, 3:58; to James, 26 February 1922). Franz Stanzel describes it as the style of "a reporter who is writing for a stylistically ambitious provincial newspaper" (*Narrative Situations*, 135–36), concurring with Philip Toynbee, who calls this the "language of the provincial gossip column" ("A Study of James Joyce's *Ulysses*," 280). Denis Donoghue also sees this as a newspaper style, especially that of letters to the editor ("Is There a Case Against *Ulysses?*" 31). It seems best, then, to see the style of "Eumaeus" as reflecting the loose, clichéd, enervated prose of much contemporary journalism—but whatever its specific referent, the style here is monitory. Joyce wishes us to recognize its failings and to understand that the mind that employs such a style is perpetually enfogged. Here again Joyce exposes the limitations, the inadequacy, of a style.

And here again (as with "Nausicaa"), the obviously inferior quality of the Eumaean style poses a problem for Karen Lawrence's claim that all styles are equally bad, and draws her into inconsistency. Demonstrating that "Eumaeus" is not the sound of Bloom's mind, Lawrence quotes a passage from "Lotus Eaters," arguing, "One has only to compare this passage with a passage of stream-of-consciousness in an earlier chapter to see the *distortion*" (*Odyssey*, 170; my emphasis)—a conception that has no place in her relativistic thesis. In an effort at consistency, she then says that the style of the earlier chapters "purported to present 'reality' directly, either psychological or material 'reality'" (171). But the initial style involves no such simplistic presumption, for Joyce knows that every style interprets and colors the reality it conveys. Moreover, all that is required in order for the initial style of *Ulysses* to be "normative" is that it further Joyce's literary aims better than other styles, not that it be translucent or present reality "directly." Lawrence seems to acknowledge this when she says, "In 'Eumaeus,' Joyce shows us language that is patently inadequate to the task of capturing the subtle nuances of behavior or even the quality of a physical action—a travesty, that is, of the initial style. . . . The linguistic tools available [in "Eumaeus"] are impediments to the capturing of the complexity and subtlety of reality" (171). Here Lawrence not only recognizes that reality (N.B.: without quotation marks) inherently involves "complexity and subtlety," but also that some styles are better vehicles of that complexity and subtlety than others. This acknowledgement provides a basis for evaluative judgments about the various styles of *Ulysses*.

"Aeolus"

I began discussion of the secondary narrators' styles with "Nausicaa" and "Eumaeus," because in those episodes the style is clearly inferior. We turn now to "Aeolus," the seventh episode of *Ulysses*, and the first to involve a secondary narrator. The presence of that narrator is obvious and carefully limited; the sixty-three discrete, typographically signaled headlines provide the first overt manifestation of the secondary narrative voice that reappears in various modes in subsequent episodes. Michael Groden is quite right to recognize the speaker of the headlines as "a voice distinct from that of the characters or of the narrator" (*"Ulysses" in Progress*, 39; also 32)—that is, as a second-level narrator who here makes his first appearance.

This initial appearance of the secondary narrative voice deserves scrutiny, for here certain aspects of the relationship between the initial style and the secondary narrator are clear that later become less obvious. For one, the continuity of this episode with those preceding and following it is evident, both in terms of the characters and events and the persistence of the initial style. The secondary voice who speaks these headlines clearly has no authority over the events or the characters of the episode; it involves only a perspective upon them—that is, a way of looking at them or talking about them. And this distinction should help us to understand that even in subsequent episodes, where the secondary voice becomes more pervasive, it nonetheless remains a perspective, a mode of presentation, only.[14]

Not surprisingly, a number of critics have taken note of this new voice and issued warnings about its implications. Arnold Goldman acknowledges that in this episode the words and techniques of the novel begin to "stand between us and the Dublin action" (*Joyce Paradox,* 83), and he goes on to make an important point that many subsequent critics have failed to keep in mind. He discusses the "symbolist techniques" in *Ulysses:*

> [These techniques] begin in "Aeolus" to gather head, initiating a process by which we are to be progressively *detached* from the mimetic action of the novel, from the primacy of the Dublin scene. But because of the preparation we do not thereby reject the reality of that scene; though the events may come to be described in hallucinatory terms, we do not therefore assume that the dead really walk in the Dublin of 1904. Though a chapter is written entirely in clichés, we do not believe that the characters spoke entirely in clichés. The opening chapters—and there are strategic returns to their styles, to remind us of the *real* Stephen and the *real* Bloom—have predisposed us to assume we are reading about *"an action* at a *real* place and at a *real* time"* [quoting Goldberg, *Classical Temper,* 35], and so we assign the symbolist techniques entirely to the narrative voice. (83)

Goldman's insight that, whatever guises may subsequently be taken by the narrative voices, we are still dealing with real characters and real actions—the rock of Ithaca of this fictive world—is essential to our remaining clear about Joyce's purposes in the subsequent episodes.

Similarly, Richard Ellmann argues, "By whomever composed, the headlines serve as a warning that the view of reality so far presented may not suffice indefinitely, that the world may move less reliably in later chapters than it has so far" (*"Ulysses" on the Liffey,* 73). He later adds, "In

Aeolus the narrative framework was agitated by the strange, unexplained headlines, which seemed almost composed by another author for purposes at variance with Joyce's" (92).

We can easily imagine this episode without the sixty-three headlines, in which case its style would be continuous with that of the preceding six episodes and the following one, involving a highly effaced but undeniably present narrative voice that provides qualitative and evaluative description and exposition of the cultural milieu, along with first-person and authorial accounts of the characters' psychic states, and so on. And we know that in the October 1918 *Little Review* printing of this episode, these headlines did not exist, and in fact were not added until very late in the composition process.[15]

Nor, given the subject matter and setting of the episode, is it hard to see what mode of discourse Joyce is satirizing through these interpolations. Jackson I. Cope describes the source of the headlines as "some newsprint-oriented modern narrator [who] has been interspersing commentary upon each stage of the conversation by means of headlines" (*Joyce's Cities*, 88; note Cope's personification of the narrator). The secondary narrative voice here represents a journalist who stands apart from the characters' conversations and presumes to label their gist so that even those who run may read. He does so with a tongue-in-cheek quality that looks askance at its subject matter, a condescending, pseudo-witty irony. Some of the headlines are mock-formal ("WITH UNFEIGNED REGRET . . ." *U*, 7.77), others laconic ("SAD" *U*, 7.291), but as a series, they evince a smugness and irony that is clearly enamored of its own wittiness. Moreover, obviously pleased with itself, the voice becomes increasingly more flamboyant and satiric as the episode proceeds. Stuart Gilbert has pointed out the progressive modification of the headlines, the first "comparatively dignified," the later ones "reproduc[ing], in all its vulgarity, the slickness of the modern press" (*JJ's "Ulysses,"* 179, note). By the final headlines the secondary narrator seems carried away by his own wittiness and jocularity—an instance of the intensification and virtual self-parody of the secondary voice that I spoke of earlier in this chapter.

Joyce's satiric intent in these interpolations is clear, and the critique of journalese presented here is consistent with the attitude taken in other parts of *Ulysses* and in other of Joyce's works, such as the portrait of the journalist Gallagher in "A Little Cloud." Joyce may regard such journalistic labeling—the encapsulating of the gist of an event in a headline—as a parody or perversion of the artist's necessary selection of essential details in creating a work of art (see the discussion of modes of realism, above, chapter 1). John Gordon argues that the headlines' "way of segmenting and serially encapsulating the discursive narrative reflects both the business of the environment (a newspaper office) and its residents' putting-in-a-nutshell cast of mind (for example *U*, 7.139–44, 196–202, 643–44)" ("Obeying the Boss," 233). In any event, it seems clear that Joyce is here taking the measure of the journalistic mode and mentality.[16]

"Ithaca"

"Ithaca," as "Eumaeus," is presented entirely in the style of the secondary narrator, and perhaps because of this and their contiguity and similar length the two episodes have often been discussed comparatively. But whereas the style of "Eumaeus" is undeniably bad, that of "Ithaca" is less easily categorized and dismissed, largely because of the "agenda" it involves. This agenda, expressed in catechistic format and formal, pseudo-precise language, espouses "objectivity"—an idea that has had considerable authority not only in the physical and social sciences, but in the arts and literature as well, reflected, for example, in the modernist injunction that the novelist should be "objective" and refined out of existence. Nor has it been obvious to critics that Joyce disavows the voice or agenda of this episode. Perhaps this is because of Joyce's having expressed pleasure with the episode, or because the style itself contains some interesting anomalies, or because the modernist temper is more inclined toward this "objective" style than to the flaccid journalese of "Eumaeus."[17]

Several early critics thought the episode a mistake but presumed that Joyce sanctioned it, with the result that it came in for a great deal of criticism—was in fact so severely censured that Philip Toynbee in 1948 noted, "it has become, and not unjustly, the *point de mire* of all hostile critics" ("Study of *Ulysses*," 281). It was, as we have seen, one of the episodes that Edmund Wilson described as "artistically absolutely indefensible" ("James Joyce," 174). And as recently as 1974 so astute a critic as Walton Litz called the episode self-parodying and said that Joyce seems unaware of the grotesque effects he is creating ("Ithaca," 390).

Here again, the voice and mode of presentation are clearly omniscient; the characters and events are described in third person and past tense, the narrator is not confined to any single character's perspective or knowledge, and he is cognizant of events and characters beyond this episode—for example, Taylor's speech in "Aeolus." But the omniscience of the narrator has not been obvious to everyone; as Bernard Benstock's extensive review of the criticism shows, some critics have tried to naturalize the voice by identifying it with a figural perspective, pursuing what Benstock himself regards as "the overwhelming question" posed by Matthew Hodgart: "But who is the catechiser?" (*Narrative Con/Texts,* 94).[18]

As with "Eumaeus," the figural candidate has (necessarily) been Bloom. Benstock states, "The convenient assumption has usually been held that somehow Bloom's mind is responsible for what is being transmitted, and again a chorus of critical voices can be heard echoing the concept" (*Narrative Con/Texts,* 100). But identifying this narrative perspective with any character is inappropriate and untenable. First of all, here as elsewhere, the omniscience of the secondary narrator's voice is shown by its taking us into the mind of Stephen as well as Bloom, and by its telling us facts that no character can know.[19] Second, while Bloom does have an active scientific (or technological) curiosity, the tenor of this narrator's scientism is utterly different from that of Bloom, and to equate the two does violence to the distinctive nature of our hero—as Karen Lawrence has said, above, in rejecting a similar claim about the voice of "Eumaeus."

Benstock once again resolutely resists the idea of an omniscient narrator, or even of an unreliable persona, though he uses terms that stand in for those functions—for example, "the generating text" (*Narrative Con/Texts,* 103). After quoting several critics' references to a narrator in "Ithaca," he claims that positing any narrator under these circumstances is simply a convention and a convenience (98). He puzzles over the fact that *U,* 17.339 echoes Taylor's speech even though Bloom didn't hear it (114), and over the source of the narrator's knowledge of the dormant mourners: "but in the listing of the dormant mourners there is no available 'encyclopaedia' to provide such information, and in the absence of an omniscient narrator who watches over us all in the night, the reader can only surmise that it is the product of Bloom's deliberative supposition" (109). But this Gordian pseudo-problem has a solution: it is far simpler, in view of this narrator's knowledge of the minds of both Bloom and Stephen as well as facts beyond their ken, to acknowledge an omniscient narrator of the episode.

As Benstock's own review of the criticism shows, several recent critics have done just this, recognizing an omniscient (but unreliable) narrator. Avrom Fleishman asserts, "In literary terms, catechism is a close approach to the point of view of an omniscient narrator: the respondent gives the impression of being a memory bank from which can be drawn complete information on any subject" ("Science in 'Ithaca,'" 139). He goes on to claim that the episode suggests a parody of a complacent scientist, adding: "There is no more need to think that Joyce identifies himself with this point of view than there is to think he is any one of his personae" (139). Other critics who have concurred that the narrator is unreliable or has values contrary to those of the novel include Marilyn French (*Book as World,* 239) and David Hayman (*MM,* 1982, 103).

Since this episode totally recasts the fictive material into its own idiom, it enables us to see more clearly that these secondary voices involve simply a perspective upon the characters and events. That is, in no other episode (including "Oxen of the Sun" and "Circe") is there so complete a recasting of the characters' dialogue and thoughts into the stylistic medium of the episode. Yet obviously Stephen and Bloom do converse and reflect, and presumably they do so in language that is of a piece with what they have used all day, rather than in the vocabulary of the catechist.[20] And not surprisingly, even in this totally recast episode, critics have presumed an underlying continuity of character and of plot; Bernard Benstock notes that even if the questions involve some randomness, "there is none the less an obvious time-frame and plot-determinant as in any other chapter of *Ulysses*" (*Narrative Con/Texts,* 93). Karen Lawrence observes that "what *actually happens* in this chapter can be determined" (*Odyssey,* 184; my emphasis). That is to say, the "objective," catechistic language of the episode exists only as a perspective on the characters and events, which continue to develop and unfold here as they have in earlier episodes.[21]

I find no evidence that Stephen's and Bloom's actions, or their words to one another, or their thoughts or feelings in regard to one another, would be one whit different had this episode been narrated by the secondary voice of "Eumaeus" or by the primary voice of the opening episodes. As a matter of fact, this total recasting into the language of the catechist makes us wonder all the more what specific words or thoughts of Bloom and Stephen might possibly have been the basis of the abstract, recondite language of the text. In this speculation we may find satisfaction of sorts in the Notesheets, for as Walton Litz points out, there, mixed in with the scientist language, "are the terse phrases in Bloom's natural idiom which trigger the cosmic correspondences" ("Ithaca," 393).[22]

While critics agree that the voice of this chapter aspires to "objectivity," there have been a variety of opinions about precisely what this "Catechism Impersonal" represents. Several critics have suggested that Joyce is parodying a mechanical-minded literary realism that inundates us with details, but that—in contrast to Defoe's account of the storm, which Joyce praised in his 1912 lecture on Defoe—never "comes alive." S. L. Goldberg argues, "Taken in the total context of the work [the 'scientific' perspective] parodies the method and outlook of naturalistic Realism in order to suggest what lies beyond its grasp," and he maintains that this perspective "only heightens our sense of an imperishable dignity and vitality in the two characters" (*Classical Temper,* 190). (In his discussion Goldberg distinguishes between the "author," who sympathetically understands the two characters, and the "mask" or the "intelligence" or "ironic persona" directing the action [189–90]—i.e., what I call the secondary narrator.) David Fuller suggests that the episode takes the measure of documentary realism, claiming, "the more detail Joyce includes the more we recognize the inexhaustibility of what might be given and the narrowness of the selection that usually is" (*JJ's "Ulysses,"* 81). Walton Litz also sees realism as the issue joined by this style, and he quotes the crucial passage from Joyce's essay on Defoe ("Ithaca," 387–89).

Attending more specifically to the catechistic format, Franz Stanzel says it has "the external form of an examination paper"; he adds, "The authorial medium, which here provides both questions and answers, wears the masks of the pedantic schoolmaster and his overzealous pupil" (*Narrative Situations,* 137). Walton Litz calls this "the self-confident language of Victorian science" ("Ithaca," 395) and says that the format and style derive not only from the Roman Catholic catechism, but from the "catechistical methods of the nineteenth-century schoolroom," and more specifically from Richmal Mangnall's *Historical and Miscellaneous Questions*—a standard nineteenth-century textbook referred to by Stephen in *Portrait* (*PoA,* 53; "Ithaca," 394).

Whatever the specific stylistic or generic target, the formal question-and-answer format, the technical, pseudo-precise nature of the diction, and the penchant for figures, dates, and calculations all show that this voice aspires to be objective and quantitative. Using the "traditional" catechistic mode for a modern scientistic perspective, Joyce suggests that scientism and the objective attitude have supplanted religion as the presumed source of all the answers in our culture, applicable not only to the physics of hydraulics (*U,* 17.164) but to the characters' temperaments as well (*U,* 17.559). As Fleishman argues, "The amplitude and assurance of his answers suggest a parody of the complacent scientist who thinks any question can be resolved by reducing it to its material components" ("Science in 'Ithaca,'" 139).

As Fleishman's invocation of the "complacent scientist" suggests, this narrative voice, rather than representing an abstract mode of knowledge or an institution, has the feel of a person who is striving to appear objective about every aspect of experience—and not always succeeding. Seeing the voice as personalized helps us to understand the several instances in the episode when the persona overextends or defects from his would-be objectivity.

There are three kinds of internal evidence that Joyce does not sanction this style. The first—which we have already considered—is the inappropriateness and insufficiency of this narrator's presentation of these complex characters, and our having to "translate" the narrator's language to know what the characters are feeling and what is happening between them.

Even more salient evidence of the inadequacy of this would-be scientific, objective narrative voice is the presence of a number of factual and arithmetic errors. This aspect of the episode has been recognized by several critics and explored by Patrick A. McCarthy.[23] McCarthy speaks of the "narrative unreliability" in "Ithaca" and says that "error is itself a major motif in the chapter" ("Joyce's Unreliable Catechist," 606). He acknowledges that some of the errors might be inadvertent, or Joyce's own, but adds, "Yet the sheer number of errors in a chapter where we are led to expect factual accuracy makes it all but certain that some of the mistakes are intentional" (606). He then points out a number of factual and computational errors, such as roman numeral MXMIV for the year 1904; the wrong date for the birth of Queen Victoria; Bloom's impossible physical measurements, making his calf larger than his thigh; errors in computing the time since Bloom and Molly last had intercourse; the claim that absolute zero is *thousands* of degrees below the freezing point of water (which sounds like layman's hyperbole); errors of several sorts in computing Stephen's and Bloom's relative ages; and so forth.[24] McCarthy concludes that "in 'Ithaca' Joyce uses the language of science and mathematics to develop the illusion of objective reliability," which is then shattered by the errors and inconsistencies of the text (616)—which I take as clear evidence that Joyce does not sanction this narrative persona.

Quite apart from explicit errors, the language of the episode is not as accurate or precise as it purports to be. The persona affects a vocabulary that sounds technical and impressive, but in fact it often involves awkward or jargonish coinages or words used in an unusual or archaic sense. Consider, for example, the ambiguity of "games of hazard" (*U*, 17.571), which seems in context to mean games involving risk to the children—that is, "hazardous games"—whereas this phrase usually means games of chance. Bloom's uncovering and recovering Molly's rump is described as "a tentative revelation" followed by "a tentative velation" (*U*, 17.2238, 17.2245); the word "lecture" is twice used to mean reading (*U*, 17.1600, 17.1882); "inconsiderate" for "unconsidering" (*U*, 17.1691); the titles of

Bloom's books are said to be "scintillating" (*U*, 17.1359); "*ritirando*" is used for "*ritardando*" (*U*, 17.1310); "auditive" for "auditory" (*U*, 17.776); "reparation" for "repair" (*U*, 17.374); and other pseudo-technical words, many of them coinages, include "terribility" (*U*, 17.1166), "lattiginous" (*U*, 17.1043), and "repristination" (*U*, 17.518, 17.1724). Presumably the narrator's aim is to impress by *appearing* precise and technical, but the result often comes closer to the vague and approximate language of "Eumaeus."

A third mode of evidence of the fallibility of this perspective is the occasional defection of this voice from its own objective agenda. For example, Dermot Kelly quotes *U*, 17.893–908 — the comparison of Milly and the cat — and argues, "As an imitation of a scientific or legal document this description is imperfect: the traces of human feeling it bears are unmistakable. It is more like a journal entry made by a writer who has scrupulously checked his emotions because of the possibility of publication" (*Narrative Strategies*, 82). I noted earlier in this chapter that several of the secondary voices alter or intensify during the episode in a way that suggests a loss of authorial control, amounting to self-parody (e.g., the changing tenor of the headlines of "Aeolus," or the debacles of dramatic format in "Scylla and Charybdis"). "Ithaca" includes several such anomalous passages.

Consider, for example, the following passage in response to the question "What advantages attended shaving by night?": "A softer beard: a softer brush if intentionally allowed to remain from shave to shave in its agglutinated lather . . . a cleaner sensation when awaking after a fresher sleep since matutinal noises, premonitions and perturbations, a clattered milkcan, a postman's double knock, a paper read, reread while lathering, relathering the same spot, a shock, a shoot, with thought of aught he sought though fraught with nought might cause a faster rate of shaving and a nick on which incision plaster with precision cut and humected and applied adhered . . ." (*U*, 17.277). This passage exhibits a strange loss of control, in which the objective language is ousted by something more akin to the rhythms and echoisms of "Sirens." Or consider the following question: "Which example did he adduce to induce Stephen to deduce that originality, though producing its own reward, does not invariably conduce to success?" (*U*, 17.606). Clearly the objective narrator here has temporarily lost control of his medium. (Other similar examples occur on *U*, 17.866 in the imitation of the baby and *U*, 17.1226 in the rhythmic description of the church bells.)

In several places, the style temporarily takes on an undeniably human, even poetic, quality, as when the spectacle Bloom and Stephen see when they step into the garden is described as "The heaventree of stars hung with humid nightblue fruit" (*U,* 17.1039), or the question as Stephen departs down the lane: "Of what did bellchime and handtouch and foot-step and lonechill remind him [Bloom]" (*U,* 17.1249; cf. also the answer to the query about what Bloom remembered from having watched a dawn some years before, *U,* 17.1265). Such passages are clearly anomalous, and it is not sufficient to say that they reflect Bloom's (or Stephen's) perspective, for that simply defers the underlying question—which is, why does the narrator permit these few responses to be cast in such subjective and poetic form? It may be that the narrator himself tires of the austerity of his objective, formalized perspective, or even is overwhelmed by the beauty of the heavens and reverts (temporarily) to a markedly anthropomorphic and poetic perspective.

In any event, these lines would be appealing for their metaphorical quality and beauty in any context, but they are all the more striking, coming as they do in the midst of these formal, objective exchanges. The presence of such phrases in the midst of the episode shocks us into a keener awareness of the limitations—even distortions, when applied to a human subject matter—of the style.[25] These and other similar passages—and there are a good many of them—suggest that while the speaking voice here strives to maintain a formal scientistic demeanor, it cannot totally suppress a human, subjective perspective.

"Sirens"

The striking narrational mode of the "Sirens" episode involves not just a distinctive style, but a specific theory—namely, the claim of Walter Pater that all art approaches the condition of music. And in contrast to "Nausicaa" or "Eumaeus," where it is obvious that Joyce is undercutting or satirizing the secondary narrative voice, a number of critics have presumed that Joyce stands behind this experiment in rendering literature in terms of musical form. But over the years there has been some development of critical opinion on this question. Most of the early critics, that is, assumed that Joyce stands firmly behind this musical agenda, some of them praising him for it, others (though admirers of *Ulysses*) faulting him for his failure to see the wrongheadedness of the project. Only later did critics dissociate Joyce from the agenda of the episode, and propose (sometimes tentatively) that his intention is in fact to undercut the theory that earlier critics had presumed him to be sanctioning.

It is clear that the "Sirens" episode pursues the analogy between musical form and literary form; the schema designates the science or art of the episode as Music, and the technic as "Fuga per Canonem," and Joyce himself was quite explicit, in letters and in conversation, as to what is going on.[26] My contention is that this attempt is not Joyce's but that of the secondary narrator, the presenter, who, in his determination to make literature emulate music, fails to understand the qualitative differences between these two modes of art and is oblivious to the contradictions that such a program entails.[27] Joyce felt the need to carry out this tour de force precisely because many of his contemporaries were confused about the possibilities of such a "compromise."

The secondary narrative voice presents the episode in a style that emulates musical qualities and forms and devices, epitomizing Walter Pater's influential dictum in "The School of Giorgione" in *The Renaissance* that *"All art constantly aspires towards the condition of music"* (106). This was an idea with great appeal in the fin de siècle climate of opinion—in his famous 1897 preface to *The Nigger of the 'Narcissus,'* Conrad refers in passing to music as "the art of arts" (xlix).[28] In the less-quoted first paragraph of his essay, however, Pater makes exactly the point I shall insist on later: "Each art, therefore, having its own peculiar and untranslatable sensuous charm, has its own special mode of reaching the imagination, its own responsibilities to its material. One of the functions of aesthetic criticism is to define these limitations; to estimate the degree in which a given work of art fulfills its responsibilities to its special material" (*The Renaissance,* 102). But when Pater comes to what this special material and responsibility involve for literature, he says blandly that it is "to define in a poem that true poetical quality, which is neither descriptive nor meditative merely, but comes of an inventive handling of rhythmical language, the elements of song in the singing" (103).

Interestingly, the presumption of several early commentators on "Sirens" was that Joyce agreed with Pater and sanctioned such an exercise. Stuart Gilbert takes the tour de force seriously and consistently praises the episode: "both in structure and in diction [it] goes far beyond all previous experiments in the adaptation of musical technique and timbre to a work of literature" (*JJ's "Ulysses,"* 1930, 242). Gilbert does, however, quote the crucial part of Ernst Robert Curtius's critique of the episode, in which he says that "Joyce has deliberately ignored [an] essential difference between sounds and words, and, for this reason, his experiment is of questionable value" (qtd. on 243; see Curtius, *Essays on European Literature,* 348–52).

Curtius's judgment was typical of a number of critics—many of them admirers of *Ulysses*—who were convinced both that the experiment was seriously carried out by Joyce, and that it was a regrettable failure. Harry Levin assumes that the stylistic agenda in "Sirens" is Joyce's, and that it is mistaken: "Joyce's premise, that any given physical effect can be exactly duplicated by means of language, lures him into a confusing *mélange des genres*" (*James Joyce*, 98). Melvin Friedman is convinced both of "the impossibility of reproducing musical devices in fiction," and of Joyce's seriousness in this attempt: "Joyce's failure in the Sirens episode is probably due to his unwillingness to compromise with his medium. He was apparently determined to build up a structure dependent on music in every way, even in the essential aspects where music differs from literature. . . . unfortunately, he attempted to reproduce their [musical devices'] actual effects on the page, by his own unhappy use of word-clusters and by his frequent insertion of overtones which never seem musical at all" (*Stream of Consciousness*, 121, 131–32; chap. 5, "The Analogy with Music," discusses the issue at length).

Commenting on responses to this episode, Jackson I. Cope notes, "Even Joyce's most ardent supporters were puzzled and alarmed," and he cites the reactions of Ezra Pound and Harriet Shaw Weaver ("Sirens," 218–19). A. Walton Litz, however, tries to vindicate what he presumes to be Joyce's intention (*Art of JJ*, 64), but Litz acknowledges that Curtius's objections "cannot be dismissed": "In trying to atone musical and literary forms, Joyce weakened the rational structure of his prose, exalting secondary qualities ('suggestion' and 'sound-imitation') at the expense of full communication. The Sirens episode demonstrates the weaknesses of a compromise between the two arts" (70).[29]

Perhaps the most perspicacious of the early critics was Frank Budgen, who appreciated and enjoyed the amazing tour de force of the episode's style, and yet was quite clear about Joyce's unwillingness to make literature subservient to music. Speaking of the inherent differences between the two mediums, Budgen argues, "The poet is bound to sense, and if he followed the musician here he would leave sense behind, and then farewell to poesie. . . . The beauty of *The Sirens* episode lies in this: that Joyce has mimicked all the musician's mannerisms and rhythmical devices with so much fantastical humor, at the same time carrying his own narrative a most important step forward. It was a field-day for the virtuoso in Joyce" (*JJMU*, 136). Budgen goes on to say that "Joyce's brilliant burlesques of the more banal tiddleypom aspects of music pleased him, and all of us who heard him read them, immensely" (141). He cites two examples, the first the lines beginning, "Miss Douce withdrew her satiny arm" (*U*, 11.813), and the second, "Bald Pat who is bothered mitred the napkins" (*U*, 11.915).

More recently several critics have recognized that Joyce looks askance at or disavows this experiment. Richard Ellmann asserts, "For [Joyce] all music aspires to the condition of language, and being brought to that condition in the *Sirens* episode, reveals itself as less than supreme" (*"Ulysses" on the Liffey*, 104). And Karen Lawrence qualifies her claim that Joyce is showing all styles to be equally relative when she says, "A crucial component of the chapter's irony is its revelation of the way in which writing is *not* music" (*Odyssey*, 92).

There is both biographical and textual evidence that Joyce regarded deference to musical and aural qualities of sound and rhythm as inappropriate and distorting for literature. In the letter to Harriet Shaw Weaver of 6 August 1919, Joyce followed his musical description of the episode by saying, "I did not know in what other way to describe *the seductions of music* beyond which Ulysses travels" (*Sel Lts*, 242; my emphasis). In a letter to her two weeks earlier, he said, "Since I wrote the *Sirens* I find it impossible to listen to music of any kind" (20 July 1919; *Sel Lts*, 241). In his conversation with Georges Borach, Joyce, after detailing the musical devices of the episode, states: "Since exploring them in this chapter, I haven't cared for music any more. I, the great friend of music, can no longer listen to it. I see through all the tricks and can't enjoy it any more" (qtd. in W. Potts, *Portraits of the Artist*, 72). Several years earlier, in his 1912 lecture on Daniel Defoe, Joyce had praised Defoe's realism by saying that it "defies and transcends the magical swindles of music" ("Daniel Defoe," 22; editor/translator Joseph Prescott gives this as the "magical beguilements of music," but the word *frodi* seems better translated as "swindles" or "cheats").[30]

The distinctive techniques of this narrative voice require us to think carefully about the relationship between sound and sense in literature and in music. While sound and rhythm are indispensable, inextricable aspects of literature, they are nonetheless accessories of meaning, and this is what distinguishes literature from music and makes it for Joyce the paramount art. (In *Portrait* Stephen, contrasting literature with the "inferior" art of sculpture, describes it as the "highest and most spiritual art" [*PoA*, 214]). Music, for all its beauty and emotive power, cannot vie with literature in terms of the modes and specificity of meaning it can convey, and so we cannot take the distinctive qualities of music as normative for literature.

But the key to understanding virtually all of the distinctive techniques of this episode is that for this narrator, sheer sound and rhythm can at any moment displace sense as the organizing principle of what is going on. The narrator's obsession with sounds and rhythms per se is obvious from a number of devices within this chapter. These include the introductory "motifs" (*U*, 11.1–63), as well as many passages in which aural and rhythmic effects pervade the presentation and replace meaning as the basis of associative links and literary structures. For the reader virtually all of these sounds are "words" or "syllables"—that is, they carry meaning— but for this narrator they are not so much morphemes or phonemes as sounds. Given our penchant for meaning and our knowledge of the characters and events of the novel, we readers can "make sense" of virtually all of these fragmentary words and syllables—even those where no sense may be intended by the secondary narrator. But we can do this only because the entire novel is not presented in this musical mode, and because the secondary narrator does not have total leeway even in this episode, having to work within parameters given by the characters and events of the novel as a whole. (Here again critics have read assiduously in order to determine "what really happens" in the episode; see esp. Blamires and van Caspel.)

Some of the narrator's adaptations of language to music exemplify the objections of Yeats, above—for example, "Her wavyavyeavyheavyeav-yevyevyhair un comb:'d" (*U*, 11.809), "Lugugugubrious" (*U*, 11.1005), "Waaaaaaalk" (*U*, 11.1125). The narrator's treating of words as if they were musical notes is shown also in the great many sheer repetitions: "by by" (*U*, 11.86), "in in" (*U*, 11.147), "inexquisite contrast, contrast inexquisite" (*U*, 11.464), "mashed mashed" (*U*, 11.553), and so forth. This technique is reflected as well, as Charles Peake has argued, in the three sets of monosyllabic words that occur when the narrator wishes to imitate the effects of a piano student's doing scales: "Bald deaf Pat brought quite flat pad ink. Pat set with ink pen quite flat pad. Pat took plate dish knife fork. Pat went" (*U*, 11.847; Peake, *JJ: Citizen and Artist*, 221).

To appreciate fully the effects of this agenda, we must recognize that for most of this episode (about *U*, 11.320 through 11.1141) some music is being played, sung, whistled—sometimes more than one piece at a time— and the words and rhythms of these works affect the narrative voice and the interior monologue of Bloom. Charles Peake has illustrated this idea that "musical performances . . . influence the words and rhythms of the narrative and the monologues" (*JJ: Citizen and Artist*, 215), and Paul van Caspel has provided further examples of how the rhythms of the melodies being performed affect the quality of the prose—for example, the letter

Bloom is writing, and the passage reflecting scales (*Bloomers*, 169–71). But the undercurrent of melody throughout the episode doubtless affects the exposition or interior monologue in other ways as well.

There are also many passages, some of paragraph length, in which the aural qualities become paramount and impede our attempts to glean sense from the passage. Examples include: "All most too new call is lost in all" (*U*, 11.634); "Where? Here there try there here all try where. Somewhere" (*U*, 11.739); "Yrfmstbyes. Blmstup" (*U*, 11.1126). As a more extended example, consider one of the passages specified by Budgen: "Bald Pat who is bothered mitred the napkins. Pat is a waiter hard of his hearing. Pat is a waiter who waits while you wait. Hee hee hee hee. He waits while you wait. Hee hee. A waiter is he. Hee hee hee hee. He waits while you wait. While you wait if you wait he will wait while you wait. Hee hee hee hee. Hoh. Wait while you wait" (*U*, 11.915). We can of course "make sense" of most of this, but I suspect that much of this is included (by the narrator) for reasons of sound, not sense. For example, I am doubtful that we are to read these "hee hee's" as expressions of amusement or humor; they are primarily if not solely an aural motif.

If we force meaning on such material, we are likely to see it as making fun of the characters or events—as "ironic"—which is highly questionable. Consider, for example, the paragraph describing the arrival of the blind stripling at the Ormond: "Tip. An unseeing stripling stood in the door. He saw not bronze. He saw not gold. Nor Ben nor Bob nor Tom nor Si nor George nor tanks nor Richie nor Pat. Hee hee hee hee. He did not see" (*U*, 11.1281). Is the narrator here laughing at the blind boy? Are we to see this as "ironic"? I very much doubt it. More likely the "hee hee" motif originates for the narrator in the "He . . . He . . ." of the preceding sentences. Unfortunately, when readers are frustrated in their attempts to "make sense" of some passage, they may invoke "irony" as the explanation. (Paul van Caspel, e.g., repeatedly sees the "whimsical narrator" or commentator as ironic or derisive; *Bloomers*, 158, 161, 162, 162, etc.) But we probably presume irony when the narrator is simply playing with aural motifs.

This narrator also has other traits or quirks that grow out of his aural/ rhythmic obsession. For example, verbal motifs are often inserted from elsewhere in this episode, or even beyond it, into a context where they have no meaning. Often such insertion is occasioned by some aural association, but at other times it is virtually impossible to see what the rationale is. The most problematic insertions are those that obtrude directly into Bloom's flow of thought. Bloom's interior monologue while writing his letter to Martha, for example, involves two such insertions: "Jingle, have you the?" and "You must believe. Believe. The tank" (*U*, 11.869, 872). In the latter, it is apparently Bloom's writing of "You must believe" that causes the narrator to insert "Believe. The tank," echoing the conversation among Miss Douce, Lidwell, and the gentlemen with the tankards (*U*, 11.813 ff.). We have no way of knowing whether Bloom "thinks" these last three words, or whether they exist solely as a verbal insertion into the text. Later, as Bloom is thinking of the noise made by an organ, we find in his monologue: "(want to have wadding or something in his no don't she cried)" (*U*, 11.1201), in which the last four words reiterate a statement of Miss Kennedy's before Bloom ever entered the Ormond; again, we cannot say whether they form part of his stream of thought. (Other such examples of insertions into Bloom's monologue occur on *U*, 11.1047, 11.1110, 11.1240, and 11.1254.)

As the comments he made to Harriet Shaw Weaver and Georges Borach indicate, Joyce in this episode presents the allurements of music as consisting largely of soft, self-indulgent emotions that are to be resisted. This is suggested first of all by Ulysses' having to resist the Sirens' song, but also in various ways by the psychological context of the episode and specifically by some of Bloom's comments and observations that are critical of the effects of music. Listening to Simon's singing, Bloom thinks, "Words? Music? No: it's what's behind" (*U*, 11.703). Soon after, reflecting on the second postscript of his letter, Bloom says, "Too poetical that about the sad. Music did that. Music hath charms" (*U*, 11.904). Thinking of the effect of music on Cowley, Bloom reflects in a way that seems pointedly critical of many of the effects this narrator strives for: "Cowley, he stuns himself with it: kind of drunkenness. Better give way only half way the way of a man with a maid. Instance enthusiasts. All ears. Not lose a demisemiquaver. Eyes shut. Head nodding in time. Dotty. You daren't budge. Thinking strictly prohibited" (*U*, 11.1191). Other passages in which our prudent hero expresses what could be regarded as critiques of the effects of music include "Rhapsodies about damn all" (*U*, 11.626), "music hath jaws" (*U*, 11.1055), and "Music. Gets on your nerves" (*U*, 11.1182). As Budgen says, "Music moves Bloom, but does not carry him away. He arms his nerves against its seductions in the same way that he protects his intelligence against the mass suggestions of religion" (*JJMU*, 145).

There is, then, ample evidence, internal and external, that although Joyce devoted a great deal of energy and genius to this tour de force—and it represents the most extensive example we have of musical structures and effects within a literary text—Joyce does not concur in Pater's judgment that music is the normative art, and this episode was written to illustrate the dire effects that result when the distinctive qualities of literature are made subservient to those of music.

"Cyclops"

"Cyclops" is the only episode other than "Penelope" that is narrated in the first person by a character of the novel. Here the unnamed first-person narrator is a character, not a secondary narrator. His distinctive personality emerges as the episode proceeds, and the only style he is responsible for is that of his own individual voice; he has no narrative scope or authority comparable to that of the secondary narrators of the other later episodes—that is, no access to the minds of the characters or to the events or language of earlier episodes of the novel. Virtually all commentators have accepted this presentation as traditional first-person point of view, whose conventions permit the narrator to address his words directly to the reader, and to convey veridically the dialogue of other characters in the scene.[31] Because of his personal biases, this narrator is "unreliable" when he is describing other characters (Bloom, the citizen), but is utterly reliable in his (conventionalized) role as a vehicle of the novel's events and dialogue.

One reason that Joyce includes this mode of narration in his comprehensive novel is to illustrate its limitations. For all its immediacy and appeal, first-person point of view simply cannot compare with the initial style of *Ulysses* for the fullness and subtlety of what it can achieve. It cannot delve into the subliminal or subconscious reaches of the speaker's own psyche, much less evoke the circumambient cultural milieu as the initial style of *Ulysses* can. Moreover, in a carefully wrought first-person narrative, the question of the reliability of the narrator dominates our interest, and while that issue may be intriguing, it is constricting. Conrad's *Heart of Darkness* (1899, 1902) and Fitzgerald's *The Great Gatsby* (1925) are brilliant works. But analysis of those works necessarily turns largely on the personality of the narrator and of how capable Marlow or Nick Carraway is of understanding what he is conveying to us. For Joyce's purposes in *Ulysses*, such a technical focus is too restrictive, and so for all the skill with which the first-person technique is used here in "Cyclops," we see how much better for Joyce's purposes is the initial style of *Ulysses*.

Given Joyce's epic ambitions for this novel—his wish to evoke a cultural milieu and to subvert modernist dichotomies—we cannot imagine *Ulysses* presented entirely as a first-person narrative.

The episode does, however, also involve a secondary narrator comparable to those of the other later episodes of the novel, and this narrator is responsible for the interpolated parodic passages that punctuate the episode. Clearly these interpolations represent a distinct narrative voice, utterly beyond the mental and verbal capacities of the I-narrator. But, to consider the reverse possibility, there is no basis for claiming that this secondary narrator of the interpolations is himself the source of the entire episode and has "ventriloquized" the first-person passages. Thus, in "Cyclops" we have two distinct voices, neither of which subsumes the other: the unnamed character who is the first-person narrator, and the secondary narrator who is the parodic interpolator. The situation is analogous to that in "Aeolus," which has the main body of the episode and interjected headlines—with the difference that some of these interpolations in "Cyclops" convey, rather than simply comment upon, the action of this episode. (In his list of interpolations, Hayman marks eleven that "contain information about the main action" ["Cyclops," 274–75].) The question before us is what style or agenda this secondary narrator represents, for Joyce to take the measure of.

The most salient feature of the secondary narrative voice—virtually its identifying trait—is its parodic, satiric penchant, and I propose that it is this pervasive, undiscriminating stance of satire—or, more accurately, of mockery—that Joyce critiques in this episode. One problem with this claim, of course, is that satire is a device long honored in the tradition of Irish and Anglo-Irish literature, and one that Joyce himself uses and values—some would even say that satire is the generic mode of *Ulysses*.

But there are certain troubling characteristics of this parodic voice in "Cyclops." First is the omnivorous, undiscriminating quality of its satire that often makes it hard for us to know what the object of the parody is, much less what purpose lies behind it. Paul van Caspel acknowledges this quality, saying of the interpolations that "their parodistic nature . . . is not always evident in the sense that it may not be clear in each case what exactly it is that is supposed to be parodied" (*Bloomers,* 187). The pleasure that we derive from satire or parody is rooted in seeing something or someone get its deserved riposte—seeing some pompous style deflated via exaggeration, or some hypocritical attitude exposed. At some points in "Cyclops," the parodic object is clear and appropriate, and then we enjoy the parody—for example, the citizen's clichéd and reactionary Irishness evokes an epic description of him as an Irish hero in the vein of the romantic late-nineteenth-century translations of the early Irish tales; his concern with who does and does not pass muster as Irish evokes an ultra-chauvinistic list of those claimed as Hibernian; and the citizen's talking to the dog (in Irish tags) occasions the delightful account of the dog's amazing capacities in reciting highly recondite traditional Celtic verse.

But the parodist's barbs can also be occasioned by the most inoffensive, ordinary events or statements, and his parodic shafts seem to be directed toward virtually everything, indiscriminately, so that we are sometimes puzzled about the object or justification of the parody. For example, why should Bloom, who has just been referred to by Joe Hynes as "the prudent member" (*U*, 12.211), be made fun of for his hardihood or his prudence, or why should his admirable and endearing curiosity about natural phenomena subject him to mockery as a meticulous German scientist (*U*, 12.468)? Admittedly, these parodies are entertaining, some of them hilarious, but they trouble us by their inappropriateness, and we soon realize that the parodist is more interested in displaying his own wit and showing his capacity to mock anything and everything, than—in the time-honored tradition of Swift or Fielding—exposing pomposity or pretense. Especially disconcerting is the mockery that ensues after Bloom has disavowed violence and spoken up (admittedly not very articulately) for love, the opposite of hatred: "Love loves to love love. Nurse loves the new chemist. . . . You love a certain person. And this person loves that other person because everybody loves somebody but God loves everybody" (*U*, 12.1493). Neither witty nor probing, this is simply banal.

The parody here, that is, is deracinated from the evaluative ground that this mode customarily grows out of, and it becomes parody for its own sake, or to illustrate the parodist's disdain for any values or commitment, or to give him something to hide behind. A *Ulysses* seminar a few years ago recognized this penchant for indiscriminate parody by dubbing this voice the "mad parodist." (A similar judgment of the parodist by David Hayman is indirectly suggested when he describes the "Eumaeus" narrator as "a supercilious mocker similar to the persona behind the masks in 'Cyclops'" ["Cyclops," 270], and says, "Each aside is locked securely in its own particular mode of mockery" ["Cyclops," 269].) What Joyce is critiquing in this indiscriminately mocking voice, then, is not satire per se; rather, it is an unbridled penchant for parody and undercutting that values its own wit and exuberance more than the appropriateness of its objects, and that preens itself on mocking virtually everything, all the while unwilling to commit itself to any values—what Yeats refers to as "safety in derision" ("The Apparitions").

These are, of course, qualities that we have already seen in one of the novel's characters—Buck Mulligan. Intelligent, witty, articulate, Mulligan obviously has literary skill, as we see from his Ballad of Joking Jesus in "Telemachus" and his *Everyman His Own Wife* in "Scylla and Charybdis." But though initially appealing, Mulligan soon wears thin, for we find that his metier is mockery. His intelligence and talent, that is, are devoted to derision and undercutting, and to projecting his own carefully contrived image.

Moreover, certain aspects of this episode suggest that Joyce sees this penchant for indiscriminate and destructive mockery as a characteristically Irish proclivity. "Cyclops" is in some respects the novel's most Irish episode. Certainly the issue of who qualifies as Irish or who "represents" Ireland comes into sharper focus and gets fuller treatment here than anywhere else in the novel, bringing to the forefront the themes of xenophobia and chauvinism. And Joyce's use of the pub setting here is wonderfully appropriate, for this Irish institution often involves a facade of conviviality and verbal banter, concealing corrosive caustic humor at someone's expense, where the speakers are concerned for the wittiness of their comments or the image they are projecting, and seriousness or reflectiveness seems forbidden. Nowhere does Bloom appear more out of place than in this setting, where the last thing that the habitués want to do is carry on a conversation about serious issues. (One of Ireland's finest living poets has spoken of his inability to tolerate the pub scene, with its veneer of conviviality over a hard grain of pettiness or viciousness.) The Irish capacity for mimicry, for the deflating barb, for parody or mockery, is nowhere better displayed than in such a milieu.[32]

So while the citizen obviously epitomizes an Irish type (signaled by the Gaelic tags that he frequently drops), and our first-person narrator may represent another, the same can be said of this secondary narrator who is totally devoted to mockery and undercutting and is more concerned for the impression he is making on his audience than for the accuracy or fairness of his witticisms.[33] And George Bernard Shaw concurs when, in his preface to his novel *Immaturity*, he comments: "James Joyce in his *Ulysses* has described, with a fidelity so ruthless that the book is hardly bearable, the life that Dublin offers to its young men, or, if you prefer to put it the other way, that its young men offer to Dublin. . . . A certain flippant futile derision and belittlement that confuses the noble and serious with the base and ludicrous seems to me peculiar to Dublin."[34]

The object of Joyce's critique of this secondary narrative voice, then, is a localized Irish version of a type that has become all too common in Western culture in the past two hundred years—the ironist who insulates himself from everything via parody or derision. Not that this attitude is the special prerogative of the Irish; it seems to be a perennial risk for writers and for intellectuals generally. According to Henry James, Flaubert's two refuges from the need to look at humanity squarely are the exotic and irony. Wayne Booth quotes James as saying of Flaubert: "'when all was said and done was he absolutely and exclusively condemned to irony?' Might he 'not after all have fought out his case a little more on the spot?'" Booth comments, "Coming from James, this is a powerful question. One cannot help feeling, as one reads many of the 'objective' yet corrosive portraits that have been given us since James, that the author is using irony to protect himself rather than to reveal his subject. If the author's characters reveal themselves as fools and knaves when we cast a cold eye upon them, how about the author himself? How would he look if his true opinions were served up cold? Or does he have no opinions?" (*Rhetoric of Fiction*, 85). These questions could appropriately be asked of our mad Irish parodist.

The purpose, then, of Joyce's allowing this mad parodist his freewheeling caustic attacks is to take the measure of yet another pernicious literary/temperamental perspective—one less doctrinaire than imitative form or Pater's ideas on literature and music, but perhaps a more serious threat to Joyce's fellow artists or fellow Irishmen. The object of Joyce's critique is the cynic (or Pyrrhonist) who finds everywhere something to mock or deride, but has himself no point d'appui, no place to stand—a person, that is, very like Buck Mulligan, for whom literature itself is essentially a vehicle of parody and mockery, rather than (in Stephen's phrase) an "eternal affirmation of the spirit of man" (*U*, 17.30). Undoubtedly, satire and parody have in the hands of Irish writers such as Brian Merriman or Swift or Wilde been effective instruments for social criticism and for the exposure of various human follies and hypocrisies. But for the secondary narrator of this episode, parody is not a powerful weapon to be wielded against hypocrites and sycophants, but a means of self-display and self-defense.

"Scylla and Charybdis"

The ninth episode of the novel, this is only the second (after "Aeolus") where the secondary narrator is in evidence, and the first in which that voice is not confined to discrete interpolations (i.e., the headlines of "Aeolus"). Still, this secondary narrator does not totally recast the episode into a distinctive stylistic idiom (as in "Eumaeus" or "Ithaca"), and much of this chapter uses techniques of presentation essentially congruent with the initial style of the opening chapters. The characters, including Stephen, are referred to in the third person, and there is considerable authorial exposition and characterization, as well as a great deal of first-person material, from Stephen's point of view. But it is undeniable that something other than the initial style is present here, as we see from the persistently ironic tone, from certain anomalous stylistic traits, and from some striking passages where the material is presented in blank verse that decays into gibberish (*U*, 9.684 ff.), or in a dramatic format (*U*, 9.893 ff.). Erwin R. Steinberg concurs that something is different here, finding in "Scylla and Charybdis" "the omniscient author's sentences calling attention to themselves in a way that they did not in Proteus," and finding as well "a display of virtuosity that reminds us that the author, who seemed to have all but refined himself out of existence, is back there behind his characters after all" (*SoC&B*, 279). But because the narrator's presence is neither discretely confined (as in the "Aeolus" headlines), nor pervasive (as in "Eumaeus" or "Ithaca"), it is more difficult to pinpoint this narrator's stylistic mode or his "agenda."

Some critics have attempted to account for the distinctive features of the episode by attributing them to Stephen, as the voices of "Eumaeus" and "Ithaca" have been ascribed to Bloom. They would attribute to him the ironic tone and the echoic verbs and modifiers, and even the anomalous format.[35] But while the episode is presented from Stephen's point of view, in the sense that we are constantly in his presence and his is the only mind we enter, this does not provide an explanation for the distinctive qualities of the presentation. First of all, this episode is presented in third person, including many references to "Stephen" (*U*, 9.16, 9.56, 9.76, and others), so that there is undeniably an authorial voice that mediates the presentation. Joyce could have cast the episode in first person (like "Cyclops" and "Penelope"), or he could have presented it dramatically (like "Circe"), but he chose not to do so, probably because he would have had to forgo certain distinctive assets of the initial style.

Second, "Telemachus," "Nestor," and "Proteus" are indubitably "Stephen episodes," but they do not involve the ironic tone or the coyly echoic terms or the anomalous format features that we find here. Moreover (as Paul van Caspel points out), the narrator's echoic inquits can precede a character's utterance:

> The benign forehead of the quaker librarian enkindled rosily with hope.
> —I hope Mr Dedalus will work out his theory for the enlightenment of the public. (*U,* 9.436; *Bloomers,* 139; for other such proleptic inquits, see *U,* 9.387 and 9.240)

This technique shows that an omniscient narrator, not Stephen, is responsible for the echoic tags. And Charles Peake says pointedly that "the sustained theatricality of 'Scylla and Charybdis' cannot plausibly be attributed to Stephen" (*JJ: Citizen and Artist,* 208).

Especially in view of the clear emergence of a "presenter" in subsequent episodes, it seems best to see "Scylla and Charybdis" as involving a secondary narrator who simply has more limited authority (or a less sharply defined role) than later ones will have. Thomas Jackson Rice sensibly says that in this chapter, "the reader confronts a mixture of the 'initial style' and the same antic sensibility, quite separate from Stephen's, that plays with the reader and the text in the earlier episode 'Aeolus' (in its headlines) and throughout the second half of the novel" ("The (Tom) Swiftean Comedy," 122). Rice points out that "the Tom Swiftie jokes work at the level of the episode's narration, quite independently of Stephen's speech or thought" (121).

One important difference between this narrator and the more overt, pervasive narrators of the later episodes is that this one aspires to effacement—though (as Steinberg has pointed out) does not achieve it nearly as well as the primary narrator does in the initial style. The reason for this relative failure is that this secondary narrator aims at effacement by the specious principle of letting the natural or "inherent" qualities of the subject matter, scene, situation, and characters dictate the mode of presentation—much as some critics have claimed that *Ulysses* "writes itself" out of the events of this June day in Dublin.

The episode tends toward a dramatic format, then, both because this narrator believes the dramatic mode to be the most fully effaced, and because the subject matter and situation of the episode tend "naturally" toward that mode. Not only is the topic of the discussion Shakespeare's dramas and his own performing in them, Stephen himself is in effect undertaking a dramatic performance of his theory for an audience, and the sharply controlled setting of the scene in the assistant librarian's office, with a small cast of characters and clearly marked entrances and exits, is conducive to a dramatic mode of presentation. The dramatic quality of the presentation, the narrator presumes, arises out of the scenic and dialogic qualities of the material. That this narrator aspires to let the subject matter dictate the form—good modernist doctrine—provides a rationale for the various echoic phrases; that is, in saying "'Piper!' Mr Best piped" (*U*, 9.274), the self-effacing narrator presumes to let the act describe itself.[36]

There is, however, evidence within the episode that this narrator in various ways botches the job of achieving both effacement and "objectivity." The most obvious examples are the repeated failed attempts to cast the material into dramatic format or blank verse, reflected in the narrator's resorting whenever possible to devices of dramatic typographical format for everything from Stephen's interior monologue (*U*, 9.22, 9.32, 9.96, etc., including the final lines of the chapter) to Best's "playbill" (*U*, 9.118), to the Gloria (*U*, 9.499), to the dialogue of Eglinton (*U*, 9.684, cast in blank verse), to the dramatic format (*U*, 9.893), to Mulligan's playbill and cast of characters (*U*, 9.1171). This secondary narrator, that is to say, tends always toward the effaced—that is, the dramatic—mode of presentation, even in terms of format.

More important, if less salient, is the coy, ironic tone that continuously colors the presentation—a far cry from the truly effaced quality of Shakespearean drama, or even of the initial style of *Ulysses*. This satiric tone shows how difficult it is for the narrator to achieve real effacement—which is Joyce's point. I mentioned earlier the careful achievement that is involved in Joyce's effacement, and how easily such an attempt devolves into an ironic tone toward the characters and the material. We see that exemplified in the pseudo-dramatic presentation of this episode.

Finally, however, the material of *Ulysses* is not dramatic, it is narrative, and attempts to impose a dramatic format on it, whether that of blank verse or of inquits and stage directions, are doomed to erode into nonsense. And the narrator of the episode is no Shakespeare (nor even the primary narrator of *Ulysses*), for his attempts to refine himself out of existence leave behind a coy, ironic tone that is often the residue of callow "objectivity." Just as "Sirens" shows us that literature should not approximate the condition of music, this failed attempt at refinement out of existence (or into the material) shows us that fiction should not aspire to be

drama, and that not all narrators are capable of the sympathetic effacement of Shakespeare or Joyce.

"Penelope"

"Penelope" is stylistically unique, even in *Ulysses*. The episode does not
involve any secondary narrative voice whose agenda is undercut, but neither does it employ the third-person omniscient voice of the opening chapters of the novel. On the contrary, in this chapter we have no overt "narrative voice." As Dorrit Cohn says, this is "the only moment of the novel
where a figural voice totally obliterates the authorial narrative voice
throughout an entire chapter" (*TM*, 218). The convention here is that this
monologue is presented to us unmediated, by Molly herself—though the
success of this technique should not cause us to lose sight of the author
who is responsible for every word of the novel.[37]

Earlier I argued against critics' description of the style of the opening
chapters as "interior monologue," demonstrating the essential role of
various third-person and omniscient modes of psychological presentation
in the initial style. But here, in the novel's closing episode, we do have
interior monologue, in the purest form. How, then, does this distinctive
narrative situation fit into the claims that I have been making about
Joyce's various purposes for the initial style, and for all of the secondary
narrators?

Joyce's intention here is to use unmediated interior monologue as skillfully and effectively as it can be used, thereby revealing both its strengths
and its limitations. Joyce does "stand behind" or sanction this style, in the
sense that it is highly appropriate to the dramatic situation of the episode,
and he uses it brilliantly; but he is nonetheless taking the measure of pure
interior monologue, in the sense that he reveals its inherent limitations,
and thus causes us to appreciate all the more fully the appropriateness and
the achievement of the initial style.[38]

What enables Joyce to use the interior monologue mode so successfully
in "Penelope" (in addition to his sheer genius) is that he has created in this
episode the best possible situation for its use.[39] We have seen in Dujardin's
Les Lauriers sont coupés the great awkwardness of unmediated interior
monologue when used to present a character who is moving about in the
public world. The simplest exposition of the character's actions, sensations, or relationships to others becomes problematic—much less achieving any in-depth presentation of the character's feelings, motives, or reflec-

tions.[40] But the "Penelope" episode comes at the end of the novel, when we know a great deal about Molly's situation and her relationships with others; the new information we learn is easily assimilated by virtue of what we already know. Moreover, Joyce creates a highly controlled scenario involving no interchanges with other characters or with the public world, and few perceptions or sensations that are not easily conveyed. And Molly's situation is one in which an extended monologue is most plausible—lying awake in the dark and letting one's mind wander over the events of the day and the reflections and memories spawned by those. His careful contrivance of all of these circumstances enables Joyce to achieve the ultimate in nonnarrated presentation—an unmediated interior monologue that is virtually isochronous with the time it takes us to read it.[41]

Because of the carefully controlled narrative situation, Joyce achieves in this episode as successful an example of this mode as one can imagine. Even so, we are aware of certain limitations on (or problems arising from) such total effacement. For example, the absence of punctuation and typographic markers seems intended to increase the immediacy and verisimilitude of the situation; we are hearing a voice, and obviously that voice does not speak commas, apostrophes, periods. But presumably that voice would involve pauses and rises and falls of inflection—what a structural linguist would mark as various stress, juncture, and pitch patterns. But to suggest that verisimilitude would be increased by incorporating some markers for these qualities would be literal minded and wrongheaded; this is, after all, a literary technique—a simulation, not a replication. (For example, traditional spellings are generally observed, and homonyms are orthographically distinguished as they would not be in speech.) Moreover, it is appropriate to ask whether the authorial effacement might not be smoother and more complete if there were some minimal punctuation, since we find ourselves stumbling over puzzles created by its absence, or even by the ambiguity of the pronoun referents.

Perhaps this is, then, one inherent limitation of the mode—perhaps, paradoxically, such unmediated interior monologue is more obtrusive, and makes us more aware of the mediating presence of the author, than does the skillfully blended mode of the initial style. E. R. Steinberg says of this episode, "Constantly feeling for the ends of sentences as he progresses, the reader is continually aware of the difficulty of the reading and conscious of the fact not only that he is reading but that he is solving a puzzle. This awareness, of course, keeps him aware of the author, who presented the difficulty" (*SoC&B*, 283).

To acknowledge this greatest imaginable absence of a narrative voice here in "Penelope" is not to deny Joyce's continuing, pervasive, authorial control over the presentation. One lesson that the careful reader learns from this tour de force is that even in this most totally effaced of all narrative situations, the author is still very much present and in control, technically and valuationally. Molly is of course Joyce's creation, as are her experiences, her memories, her attitudes and values. Moreover, the episode is intricately linked with the rest of the book, through various characters and events, and more implicitly through the many comparisons and contrasts that we readers are constantly making—for example, with Gerty—and the various themes and motifs that are carried through this episode. Accompanying all of this is our constant admiration at the artistic skill with which this tour de force is achieved. Here at the end of the novel, Joyce reminds us of the undeniable presence of the author by virtue of the total absence of the narrator.[42]

Finally, we can infer from this best of all imaginable uses of this technique the inappropriateness of unmediated interior monologue as the base technique, the initial style, of *Ulysses*. Unmediated interior monologue is incapable of presenting the complexity, the inextricability, of "inner" and "outer," self and society, within human experience; for that Joyce needed the distinctive third-person/first-person meld that he took such pains to create in the initial style. The verdict is that while interior monologue is appropriate and effective within the carefully controlled parameters of this concluding episode, it is not viable for presentation of a full world of characters, objects, events, sensations, and so forth. For that what is required is the initial style of *Ulysses*.[43]

6

"Wandering Rocks," "Oxen of the Sun," and "Circe"

This chapter discusses in detail three of the episodes of *Ulysses* that are presented through a secondary narrative voice—"Wandering Rocks," "Oxen of the Sun," and "Circe." I have chosen these three for scrutiny because the presenter exists in each of them in quite different ways, and because most critics have presumed that Joyce sanctions the techniques and themes of these episodes. In "Wandering Rocks" the presenter manifests himself mainly in the organization of the episode and in a persistent irony, both of which arise out of his naturalistic thesis about the city. In "Oxen of the Sun" the presenter exists most saliently in the daunting succession of styles and only slightly less so in his determination to illustrate the "evolution" or "gestation" of English prose style, grounded in his literal-minded espousal of imitative form. In "Circe" the presenter exists most obviously in the expressionistic dramatic mode, grounded in Freudian psychoanalytic theories about the human psyche. I will show that the techniques and theories in these episodes are not Joyce's own, but reflect the flawed perspectives of the secondary narrators, the presenters, to whom he has relegated the episodes.

"Wandering Rocks"

Inclusion of "Wandering Rocks" among the episodes of *Ulysses* that involve an unreliable secondary narrator may seem questionable, since the mode of presentation in "Wandering Rocks" appears continuous with the initial style of the opening episodes. C. H. Peake specifically says that this chapter "continues the methods already developed to present narration, dialogue and thoughts" (*JJ: Citizen and Artist,* 209), and Patrick McGee notes, "At first glance, the style [of "Wandering Rocks"] seems to be classical, referential, and objective in presenting us with a panoramic view of the labyrinth through which the citizens of Dublin wander" (*Paperspace,* 71). But there is a distinguishable, ironic narrative voice here, as several critics have acknowledged.[1] And there are as well certain distinctive techniques, involving a literary agenda that Joyce wishes to subvert—namely, the realistic/naturalistic depiction of urban life as mechanical and fragmented and dehumanized that was increasingly common in modernist literature. That such a perspective and agenda exist in this episode is not hard to demonstrate; my further aim is to show that Joyce and *Ulysses* do not sanction such a naturalistic view.

First of all, this episode is obviously about the city. The large array of characters, the great variety of scenes and settings, the pains that are taken especially in the opening and closing sections to traverse large areas of the city, the vast number of urban objects and details that the episode involves—all of these confirm that the subject of "Wandering Rocks" is the city. As Frank Budgen notes, "this is peculiarly the episode of Dublin. Not Bloom, not Stephen is here the principal personage, but Dublin itself" (*JJMU*, 125).[2]

The most distinctive technique of the secondary narrator, or presenter, is the division of the episode into discontinuous vignettes—a technique used nowhere else in the novel and one obviously felt by the narrator to be especially appropriate to his conception of the city.[3] The effect is to present the lives of the city's inhabitants in short, unrelated fragments. Even when these vignettes involve presentation of a character's psyche, that presentation is brief and unsympathetic and prevents our knowing the characters in any depth—a point I shall return to shortly.

Another distinctive technical feature of the episode is the interpolations that intrude into the nineteen vignettes. Through these interpolations, which involve unrelated quasi-simultaneous actions occurring elsewhere, the narrator further fractures the presentation, suggesting that a great many events are going on concurrently, but in total separation from one another.[4] These techniques result in a highly fragmented presentation of the city from the ironically privileged overview of the narrator, with the implication that the lives of the city's inhabitants are divided by the time/space parameters of the labyrinth they live in, and that while these life-paths may intersect, the citizens never truly engage one another. As Richard M. Kain asserts, "the counterpoint structure . . . seems to imply that individuals are again submerged by the very size and complexity of an urban population" (*Fabulous Voyager*, 27).

Frank Budgen points out that the perspective constantly changes from close-up to bird's-eye view: "The scale suddenly changes. Bodies become small in relation to the vast space around them. The persons look like moving specks. It is a town seen from the top of a tower. The spiritual attributes of each person remain what they were, but all, as individuals, become small in relation to the city that contains them" (*JJMU*, 126; Kathleen McCormick also says that "the narrator has a bird's-eye view of Dublin" [*"Ulysses," "Wandering Rocks," and the Reader*, 10]). Not surprisingly, since Joyce in the Linati schema described the Technic of the episode as "Labyrinth moving between two banks," the image of the labyrinth has been invoked by a number of scholars in discussing this episode—some of them pursuing the metaphor in great detail, applying it not only to the city but to the episode itself and to the challenge it presents to the reader.[5]

The style of this episode—and especially the descriptions of the characters—is also persistently impersonal, even mechanical. Characters who reappear in the text are spoken of as if we have not met them before. For example, "A onelegged sailor" who appears on *U*, 10.7 is still "A onelegged sailor"—not "The onelegged sailor"—when he reappears on *U*, 10.228. (Similarly, "an elderly female" on *U*, 10.473 and 10.625; "a crumpled throwaway" on *U*, 10.294 and 10.753; "a blind stripling" on *U*, 10.1104 and 10.1270.) Moreover, the narrator repeats himself almost verbatim from one section to another, and many of the characters are described by tags or epithets or set phrases that seem fixed, impersonal, and ironic—for example, "Mr Denis J Maginni, professor of dancing &c," or "Marie Kendall, charming soubrette." Karen Lawrence notes these aspects of the style and argues that they "impart a curiously mechanical quality to the narrative, as if a writing machine, rather than a human imagination, produced it" (*Odyssey*, 85). Of the epithets she notes, "It is as if these linguistic labels exhausted the potential of the characters, as if Thom's Dublin Dictionary were equated with the real life of Dublin" (86).[6]

Another stylistic trait that sets this episode apart from those presented through the initial style is its tone. While the narrator apparently aspires to objectivity or neutrality, there is a persistent irony that pervades this presentation. The opening vignette depicting Father Conmee is the clearest example of condescending irony, though Mr. Kernan is similarly presented in section 12 (*U*, 10.718). It is as if the naturalistic narrator cannot maintain the "objectivity" that he presumes characterizes this literary mode and subject matter, and he resorts to irony or sarcasm to point up the foibles of these paltry, pawn-like figures. (We have considered other episodes in which Joyce demonstrates the perils of authorial objectivity—"Aeolus," "Scylla and Charybdis," and "Ithaca.") Or perhaps Joyce simply gives this secondary narrator sufficient leeway to reveal the ironic attitude that is inherent in even the most thoroughgoing naturalistic pre-

sentations, since naturalism does conceive of its human subjects as passive
and ant-like. In any event, this tone is distinctive, and it does contribute to
the realistic/naturalistic agenda.[7]

Several critics have judged this episode to involve a naturalistic, mechanical view of the city, and John Gordon, for example, says pointedly
that this episode "presents a fragmented environment with a series of
fragments, the random juxtapositions of the text echoing the aimlessness
of the lives depicted" ("Approaching Reality in 'Circe,'" 5). This view of
the city developed during the nineteenth century and reached a culmination in Eliot's *The Waste Land,* published the same year as *Ulysses.* That
poem is the apotheosis of the depictions of the mechanical denizens of the
"unreal city" that had been common from Baudelaire (who is the source
of that phrase in Eliot's poem) through Zola, Oswald Spengler, Ferdinand
Tönnies, Georg Simmel, George Gissing, and others. In a perceptive essay
on the image of the city in Eliot, Pound, and Joyce, Michael Long says of
The Waste Land:

> The Modernist, fragmented city is virtually the poem's protago-
> nist. The city's dirty buildings and polluted river, sweating oil and
> tar, the city's canal, gashouse and rats, those scarcely living roots in
> the winter ground or under the city's stones: all go to make up one of
> the great wilderness images of Modernism. In English this is the
> classic image of the Modernist city, and when it ends with fragments
> shored against ruins the stress is on the fragments and the ruins, not
> on any very successful shoring. . . . The force of Eliot's genius gave
> this image of the city as fragmentation and pain tremendous author-
> ity.[8]

This, then, is the modality, the genre, into which the realistic/naturalis-
tic presentation of the city in "Wandering Rocks" fits—the city as deper-
sonalized, as mechanical, as a social wasteland whose citizens are separated and buffeted by forces beyond their control. As Michael Long says
in the opening paragraph of his essay, "We are used to the idea of Modernism as an art of disintegration; and to the idea that its typical location, the
scene and the cause of the disintegration it records, is the city. An art of
despair and pain; a dissonant, fragmented art that confronts meaningless-
ness; an art bred by the city where the scale of life dwarfs the individual
and where each isolated person lives in bewildering, shifting patterns of
relationship with others, or in no discernible patterns at all: this is probably the most prevalent view of Modernism" (144).

But while "Wandering Rocks" unquestionably involves such a naturalistic, modernist view of the city, it stems from the secondary narrative persona of the episode, not from Joyce, who is no more enamored of such a "realistic" view of human nature than is his antitype D. H. Lawrence. My earlier description of the naturalist's view of the city's citizens as passive and ant-like echoes the language in which Lawrence described and rejected realism:

> Realism is just one of the arbitrary views man takes of man. It sees us all as little ant-like creatures toiling against the odds of circumstance, and doomed to misery. It is a kind of aeroplane view. It became the popular outlook, and so today we actually are, millions of us, little ant-like creatures toiling against the odds of circumstance, and doomed to misery; until we take a different view of ourselves. For man always becomes what he passionately thinks he is; since he is capable of becoming almost anything. ("Introduction to *Mastro-don Gesualdo*," 281)

That Joyce also rejected this view is shown by evidence within the episode and the larger context of the novel, as well as in the temperament of Joyce himself. Consider first the evidence within "Wandering Rocks." While the techniques and tone of the episode imply a naturalistic view of the citizens as mechanical pawns, several critics have pointed to a quite different and more positive thematic strand in the episode, a strand inherent in the characters and the events (which I attribute to Joyce) rather than in the mode of presentation (which I attribute to the secondary narrator). I refer to the many acts of charity and kindness, large and small, that run through the episode. For example, in spite of the narrator's smug irony toward him, Father Conmee is presently engaged in an act of mercy— trying to find a place in the Artane orphanage for one of the children of the recently deceased Paddy Dignam.

Other examples of charity or personal concern abound: the tram conductor pulls the cord and helps an old woman get her basket and marketnet off the tram (*U*, 10.134); Molly flings a coin to the onelegged sailor and an old lady gives him a copper (*U*, 10.238); the nuns have given the Dedalus children pea soup (*U*, 10.278–80); Mulligan helps the waitress unload her tray (*U*, 10.1080); M'Coy pushes a banana peel into the gutter, lest some fellow get a nasty fall (*U*, 10.512); his Italian teacher, Artifoni, gets so caught up in trying to give Stephen good advice that he misses his tram (*U*, 10.338 ff.); and Stephen in turn is profoundly moved and appalled by the plight of his younger siblings (*U*, 10.875). We find that Martin Cunningham has not only written to Father Conmee in behalf of the Dignam family, but he and several friends are actively gathering money in their behalf (*U*, 10.956), and we hear of Tom Rochford's risking his life to save a man who was overcome by gas in a sewer. Regardless of how ironically the narrative voice may present these people, they are not mechanical entities or pawns, but human persons concerned about and trying to help one another.[9]

I noted earlier how the fragmented technique and ironic tone of the episode prevent us from getting a full view even of those characters whose stream of consciousness we enter. It is worth reflecting on what our view of any of the novel's characters would be if we were restricted to the incomplete and ironic picture of them that we are given in this episode—that is, if we had to judge these characters solely on the basis of what this presenter and this mode of presentation involves. In this episode we several times see Stephen and Bloom externally (i.e., as they are seen by others), and we do see them "internally" in two vignettes. If we had to judge them on the basis of these brief passages, our impression would be superficial and simplistic, and we would have no sense of their good qualities that we learn of through the novel as a whole.

Just such a "quick take," however, is all that we are permitted of Father Conmee and Tom Kernan—and we see even less of several others—with the result that we come away with negative impressions of these characters. Conmee appears as pious and mechanically religious and Kernan as concerned only with his appearance and his success as a salesman. But who is to say whether, if we could observe them over the course of an entire day rather than in a brief vignette, we might not discover the underlying motives or extenuating circumstances behind their apparent superficialities and find qualities in them to admire. This is exactly what the whole of the novel enables us to do with Stephen and Bloom, but if we were restricted to what we are given in "Wandering Rocks," our image of them would be paltry indeed. Clive Hart makes a similar point when he says that the negative tone of the episode affects even the passages of interior monologue, making them qualitatively different from those earlier in the novel: "Throughout most of *Ulysses,* up to 'Wandering Rocks,' the interior monologue has served not only to enrich our knowledge of the inner lives of the characters, but also, as a consequence, to increase our compassion for them. Knowledge brings understanding, and understanding, pity. Now [in "Wandering Rocks"], however, the interior monologue is made to serve other, harsher purposes, as it is turned on and off at carefully selected moments" ("Wandering Rocks," 191).[10]

Another relevant feature of this episode is the great many traps that the narrator has laid for unwary or uninformed readers. That such traps exist is obvious—Clive Hart notes, "This is, indeed, a chapter full of traps for everyone, readers and characters alike" ("Wandering Rocks," 188)—though, as we shall see, it is impossible to draw a clear line between those traps and certain confusions or errors of the narrator himself. These traps include misleading descriptions and confusions of identity—such as the Bloom who is a dentist and is utterly unrelated to our hero, the Russell who is a lapidary not a poet, the Dollard who has a printing firm. The number and nature of these traps suggest that they represent part of the narrator's agenda about the city, designed to demonstrate the confusion and loss of identity inherent in the urban environment. Kathleen McCormick recognizes this aim and attributes it specifically to the narrator: "The narrator also appears to do all within his power to confuse the reader by creating jarring juxtapositions and reader traps of various kinds, such as ambiguous names, apparent errors, factual anomalies, false analogies, and a general absence of connections of any kind" (*"Ulysses," "Wandering Rocks," and the Reader,* 26; McCormick cites several critics who have discussed these traps).

That the narrator himself is confused and mistaken is suggested by another interesting and *almost* unique feature of this episode—the several undeniable factual errors or geographical mistakes it contains. I take these to be errors made by the narrator, and see their presence in the episode as one further means by which Joyce takes the measure of the narrator and shows his fallibility. That is, this narrator, who presumes to know Dublin so well and to regard it so "objectively," is himself mistaken about certain important features of the city. That Joyce has intentionally included such errors is hinted by the schema entry under "Symbol," which reads in part: "Errors: Homonyms: Synchronizations: Resemblances."

The most egregious mistakes (all detailed by Clive Hart in his essay) involve errors that Joyce himself could not possibly have made and that seem too blatant (or pointless) for the narrator to try to foist upon his readers, such as describing the statue of Henry Grattan in College Green as being stone, when it is bronze; or saying that the river Poddle emerges from Wood Quay, when it comes out of Wellington Quay; or mistakenly referring to Merrion Hall as Metropolitan Hall; and, worst of all, saying that the Viceregal Cavalcade crosses the Royal Canal in the southern part of the city, rather than the Grand Canal. Hart makes some effort to justify these and other errors, but they are too blatant and too gratuitous for explanation; rather, they serve to undercut the authority of the narrator. And such errors are not unique to this episode, for as we have seen, an even greater number of factual or arithmetic errors exist in the similarly "objective" "Ithaca" episode, where they similarly undermine the authority of the secondary narrator's presentation.

In addition to evidence of various sorts within this chapter itself, the callow naturalism of the episode is exposed by comparison with the much richer and more positive picture of the city and its citizens implicit in the novel as a whole. In his essay on the city in Eliot, Pound, and Joyce, Michael Long shows that, in contrast to the other two modernists, Joyce recognizes and celebrates the virtues of the city: "In the end the result was the creation of a city, Dublin, and a city-dweller, Mr Bloom. They are his [Joyce's] two greatest gifts to our imaginations. They make English Modernism look quite different, taking from Eliot some of his authority as an obvious centre" ("Eliot, Pound, Joyce," 150). Long then demonstrates that "Joyce's Flaubertian patience, his failure to recoil, has been rewarded with a new vision of the city, with at least the authority of Eliot's, in which the variety of people and the separateness and freedom of their comings and goings are superbly caught up in the imitation of their walking styles" (153). Long interestingly discusses Joyce's positive uses of this peripatetic motif for several pages.

Other critics have also seen Joyce's portrayal of the city quite positively. Edward Timms, in the introductory essay to the volume in which Long's essay appears, says of *Ulysses*: "Joyce's novel is a celebration of a city which is irreducibly alive, in a style whose variety and energy mirrors the heterogenous perambulations of Joyce's characters through the streets of Dublin" (*Unreal City*, 9). Christopher Butler similarly claims that Joyce "celebrates the city," as do Jules Romains and Andrei Biely, in contrast to more pessimistic sociologists and novelists ("Joyce, Modernism, and Post-Modernism," 269). And Frank Budgen says of *Ulysses*, "One important personality that emerges out of the contacts of many people is that of the city of Dublin" (*JJMU*, 69). Budgen quotes an exchange he and Joyce had: "And what a city Dublin is!" [Joyce] continued. "I wonder if there is another like it. Everybody has time to hail a friend and start a conversation about a third party, Pat, Barney or Tim. 'Have you seen Barney lately? Is he still off the drink?' 'Ay, sure he is. I saw him last night and he drank nothing but claret'" (69).

Finally, we cannot ignore the evidence that Joyce himself was so much a man of the city. Frank Budgen notes, "He was an urban type. Cities with their streets, people and the noises of people, cafés and the conversation of cafés; these things were what he wanted when he went out of his house door" (*Myselves When Young*, 185); Clive Hart concurs: "Joyce was by temperament an urban man" ("Wandering Rocks," 181). Similarly, Carola Giedion-Welcker stated, "James Joyce had a deep interest in towns, whether large or small, and in their design and history. They appeared to him as collective individuals, history turned into shape and space, large reservoirs of life. He saw them in the past and in the present as manifold units growing with time, as self-determining identities, as living history. Even if only passing through he always tried to penetrate into their special 'nature' and into the secret laws of their complex substance, and to listen to their current and eternal heartbeat" (qtd. in W. Potts, *Portraits of the Artist,* 261). While Joyce was aware of its various liabilities, he knew the virtues of city life and could hardly have lived in any other milieu. The whole of his life was spent in one or another of the great European cities, and the imagination simply boggles at the idea of Joyce residing in bucolic contentment. Bernard Benstock, writing about *Finnegans Wake,* goes so far as to say that the building and rebuilding of the city emerges as Joyce's concept of man's major contribution, and was his reply to Edgar Quinet's statement that art survives the city, but that nature survives both ("Anna Livia and the City Builder," 353).

In the "Wandering Rocks" episode, then, the secondary narrator presents a realistic/naturalistic view of the city as fragmented and mechanical, but his agenda is subverted not only by the qualities of charity manifested in the acts and persons of the episode, but by his own errors, and by the richer and more positive image of the city that we are offered by the novel as a whole.

"Oxen of the Sun"

> . . . he sets his mind to sciences never explored before, and alters the laws of nature.
>
> (Ovid, *Metamorphoses,* VIII, 188–89)

"Oxen of the Sun" has always been one of the most problematic episodes of *Ulysses*—Joyce called it the most difficult episode both to interpret and to execute.[11] Its scant action is obscured by the murky, at times opaque, presentation, which involves a total recasting of the material of the episode—events, dialogue, even the characters' thoughts—into the language of a distinctive narrative voice, a voice so pervasive and distinctive that critics have declined to "naturalize" it by attributing it to any character.[12]

While discerning the characters and action of the chapter requires attention and effort, it is even more difficult to understand the rationale, the purpose, of its mode of presentation. This difficulty stems in part from the complexity and ambiguity of the style itself, but another contributing factor is Joyce's own statement about his aims in this episode, compounded by earlier critics' attempts to vindicate this authorial pronouncement. Joyce's famous statement occurs in a March 1920 letter to Frank Budgen:

> Am working hard at *Oxen of the Sun,* the idea being the crime committed against fecundity by sterilizing the act of coition. Scene, lying-in hospital. Technique: a nineparted episode without divisions introduced by a Sallustian-Tacitean prelude (the unfertilized ovum), then by way of earliest English alliterative and monosyllabic and Anglo-Saxon . . . then by way of Mandeville . . . then Malory's *Morte d'Arthur* . . . then the Elizabethan chronicle style . . . then a passage solemn, as of Milton, Taylor, Hooker, followed by a choppy Latin-gossipy bit, style of Burton-Browne, then a passage Bunyanesque . . . . after a diarystyle bit Pepys-Evelyn . . . and so on through Defoe-Swift and Steele-Addison-Sterne and Landor-Pater-Newman until it ends in a frightful jumble of Pidgin English, nigger English, Cockney, Irish, Bowery slang and broken doggerel. This progression is also linked back at each part subtly with some foregoing episode of the day and, besides this, with the natural stages of development in the embryo and the periods of faunal evolution in general. The double-thudding Anglo-Saxon motive recurs from time to time . . . to give the sense of the hoofs of oxen. Bloom is the spermatozoon, the hospital the womb, the nurse the ovum, Stephen the embryo.
>
> How's that for high?[13]

Each of the claims Joyce makes here has left its mark in critical discussions of this episode. Several critics have attempted to pin down precisely what styles and sources Joyce used, and have debated whether he parodies them. Joyce's explicit statement that the "idea" of the episode is "the crime committed against fecundity by sterilizing the act of coition" understandably caused some critics to read the episode as an attack on contraception. Perhaps most influential and most problematic have been Joyce's suggestions that the structure of the episode is based upon the physical process of fetal gestation and the historical process of faunal evolution. Several early critics assiduously attempted to show how the structure of the episode is grounded in embryology and evolution, but for others these claims of imitative form have posed serious problems. And one persistent effect of Joyce's pronouncement has been the presumption that Joyce does stand behind and sanction the narrative persona or presenter of this episode—a presumption that has been doubted by some critics but has never been seriously challenged.[14]

But if this chapter has had its defenders and its devoted explicators, it has also had its detractors, so much so that Marilyn French calls it "the most censured chapter in *Ulysses*" (*Book as World*, 168), and Jennifer Levine considers it "the episode that readers have been most likely to resist and to resent" ("*Ulysses*," 151). For the most part what the detractors criticized were the same features other critics were laboring to defend— the attempt to portray the "evolution" of English prose, or to provide a literary analogue of gestation. Among the most trenchant early criticisms was that of Harry Levin, who, in 1941, said of this episode:

> By this time [Joyce] has abandoned all pretense of adhering to the coign of vantage of certain characters. . . . The clinical small-talk of Stephen's friends, while Bloom awaits the birth of Mrs. Purefoy's child, is reported in language that recapitulates the evolution of English prose, from a primitive ritual to an American revival meeting, and that obliterates the point of the story—when Stephen gives up his key. These parodies, we are admonished, illustrate the principle of embryonic growth. We cannot take this admonition very seriously. To call in so many irrelevant authors as a middle term between the concept of biology and the needs of the present narrative is to reduce Joyce's cult of imitative form to a final absurdity.[15]

I find Levin's criticism of Joyce's presumed excursion into imitative form, and especially his term *cult*, very perceptive, as my own interpretation will show.

Over the years, there have been three noteworthy developments in critical responses to "Oxen of the Sun." First, the earlier assumptions that Joyce sanctioned the program described in his letter have been replaced by skepticism. J. S. Atherton, in an intelligent essay that does not simply dismiss Joyce's claims, says, "Indeed I find it impossible to reduce Joyce's details to a consistent pattern."[16] Second, critics now look askance at the earlier assumption that the episode presents fertility as sacrosanct—a view taken in 1964 by so astute a critic as Stanley Sultan, in *The Argument of Ulysses* (282–87). Marilyn French, for example, argues, "Religious groups have been maintaining for some years that if God ordered increase, contraception is sin, and that is the premise of this chapter. However, this premise is handled ironically and comically as well as seriously" (*Book as World*, 173).[17]

Third, and perhaps most important, it has been questioned whether the speaking voice, the narrator, of this episode can be identified with Joyce, and whether the aims and values of this narrator are consistent with those throughout *Ulysses*. We have already noted a general questioning of the narrative voice in *Ulysses* by several critics from 1959 on, including Arnold Goldman's claim in 1966: "The theory of the 'organic whole' of style and subject will not work for *Ulysses,* whose symbolic dimension (including its 'styles') wars with its human dimension" (*Joyce Paradox,* 95). Goldman specifically observes that "the styles in 'Oxen of the Sun' are the narrator's" (95); Ben Kimpel characterizes the narrator of this episode as "clearly prejudiced" ("Voices of *Ulysses,*" 311); and Jennifer Levine notes, "The 'author' that seems to speak in 'Oxen of the Sun' is strangely unauthoritative" ("*Ulysses,*" 156).

I concur in these critics' skepticism about the presumed program behind this episode, and I want now to develop a reading of "Oxen of the Sun" that will clarify what the narrator's agenda is and show how the underlying themes of the episode reveal it to be fallacious. In order to do this, we need an interpretation that will incorporate the medical setting, the Homeric parallels, the style (including the narrator's untenable aims), and the main themes of the episode into a coherent unity.

Some critics have ventured broad statements about the themes of this episode, but there is little agreement among them, and their failure to incorporate the style or voice into their interpretations exacerbates the dichotomy between style and substance that commentators on this episode have always run up against.[18] The basic problem is in finding a meaningful connection between the themes of this chapter and its mode of presentation. Not that this problem is unique to "Oxen of the Sun." It is present in every episode from "Wandering Rocks" on, and our general failure to solve this problem should have suggested that there is some fundamental point that we were missing—a point having to do with the status of the narrative voice in each of those episodes. For when we do come to understand the underlying purpose of an episode, that purpose should encompass both style and substance.

The unifying theme of the "Oxen of the Sun" episode is idolatry, in several appropriate senses of that term. While less obvious on the surface than procreation or gestation, this theme is more fundamental and comprehensive, enabling us to see implicit links between subject matter and technique and to understand the relevance of the narrator's dogged devotion to imitative form. In essence, the act of idolatry involves worship of an object or icon, a physical thing, rather than the true God who is spirit.

Idolatry is a serious offense because it reflects the worshiper's confusion about what is real, about the very nature of God. In essence idolatry is present whenever the physical is mistaken for, or given priority over, the spiritual. In terms of the themes of this episode, it involves a misunderstanding of the proper relationship between man, God, and nature. It involves, in George Herbert's apt phrase in "The Pulley," resting in Nature, not the God of Nature.[19]

That the theme of idolatry incorporates the setting and the subject matter of this chapter can be readily shown; and working from that base, we can see that idolatry is also the underlying ontological issue raised by the narrator's stylistic tour de force in the episode—the attempt to ground the development of English prose and the literary structure of this episode in the physical processes of gestation and faunal evolution. Let us turn first to idolatry as unifying the various themes and motifs of the episode.

Apropos of the theme of idolatry, one persistent topic of discussion among those gathered in the maternity hospital is the nature of God, which necessarily entails a number of issues that turn on the relationship between spirit and matter. The young men debate, for example, the precise time when the developing fetus acquires a soul, and, while their tone is mocking, their subject is one that has seriously engaged theologians for centuries. Nor is the subject passé in our day, though we cast the argument in less overtly religious terms, debating with even more vagueness than the schoolmen when the fetus becomes a "person," and consequently whether, or when, abortion is murder. Among the other inherently theological topics broached here are "transubstantiality *oder* consubstantiality" (*U,* 14.308), and the "theological dilemma created in the event of one Siamese twin predeceasing the other" (*U,* 14.1002–3).

The most pervasive theological issue, and the one most relevant to the theme of idolatry, is the recurrent question of the nature of God. The chapter involves, for example, an array of epithets for God, calling attention to the various aspects of God and to our persistent bewilderment about how to characterize him. There are, for instance, references to God the Maker, God the Almighty, God the Wreaker, God the Allruthful, to the Creator, to Bringforth, Phenomenon, Thor, Nobodaddy, Christ, the Author of my Days, the Healer and Herd, the Agenbuyer, Theosophus, and so on. While these obviously reflect mankind's varied and persistent attempts to understand God, the thematic gist of these epithets for this episode (and for the whole of *Ulysses*) becomes clearer when we see that they resolve themselves into three "faces" of God: (1) God as creator—as the source of everything that exists, physical and spiritual; (2) God as prohibitor, curser, and punisher; and (3) God as reconciler and redeemer.

The first aspect of God gets little explicit attention in this episode, but its presence forms a necessary backdrop, for unless we understand that God is the source of the *prima materia* underlying both matter and spirit, we fall into a dualism that denigrates one or the other, and thus we fail to see the inextricable unity of matter and spirit, of nature and imagination, that forms one of Joyce's main themes in *Ulysses*. But we can fully appreciate the importance of God the creator only after having seen how the other two deific aspects work.

The second face of God—that of rule-maker, prohibitor, and punisher of those who defect—is most prominent in this episode. We are told ominously that "the god self was angered" (*U*, 14.411); there is reference to the ambiguous and terrifying "sin against the Holy Ghost" (*U*, 14.226)—usually the sustainer, here the punisher; and we are told that God "was in a very grievous rage that he would presently lift his arm up and spill their souls for their abuses" (*U*, 14.471).

This prohibiting face of God is also prominent in the Odyssean analogue of this episode. The story of the Oxen of the Sun in book XII of *The Odyssey* tells of Zeus's interdict against eating the sacred cattle of Helios and of the failure of Odysseus's crew to heed that prohibition. Gnawed by hunger, they slaughter the cows for food, and for this offense, Zeus destroys their ship with lightning. Several of the most prominent motifs of this episode of *Ulysses* take their meaning from this story, relating in some way to the aspect of God as punisher. Lightning, for example, is seen as the tool of God the Wreaker: "Lo, levin leaping lightens in eyeblink Ireland's westward welkin! Full she drad that God the Wreaker all mankind would fordo with water for his evil sins" (*U*, 14.81).

The omnipresent cow imagery of the episode is more variable and complex, but is always related to some fetish ("sacred cow") or to some pseudo-authority, generally one that acts with purported divine sanction. The Odyssean story is a forcible reminder that many cultures have taken cattle as objects of worship and have idolatrously endowed them with such sanctity that the people would refuse to eat the cattle even though they were starving. The papal "Bull" of Pope Adrian IV is an attempt to intimidate the Irish into accepting as God's will what was in fact this (English) Pope's own wish to see Ireland under the control of England.[20] The cry "*Mort aux vaches*" (*U*, 14.551) involves a challenge to the supposed authority of king as well as priest when we know that it means "Death to the cops."[21]

Another story involving God the prohibitor is an important source of the imagery, motifs, and themes of this episode—the story of the Garden of Eden, references to which include the "penny pippin" for which Eve sold us (*U*, 14.301), the "eating of the tree forbid" (*U*, 14.873), and most notably that "woman should bring forth in pain" (*U*, 14.208–9). The two aspects of Jehovah's Genesis curse that are most relevant to "Oxen of the Sun" are death and woman's bringing forth children in pain. These provide direct thematic links with the medical, specifically obstetric, setting of the episode, and they enable us to see medicine as one of man's attempts to challenge God's threatening second face and thus to challenge the "idolatry" that such curses often involve.

The theme of man's attempts to understand God and to placate his more threatening aspects is also suggested by the several references to religious denominations and cults. There are references to a prophetical charm out of Hindustanish (*U*, 14.524), to Madagascar rituals (*U*, 14.345), and to Egyptian priests (*U*, 14.1169). Of particular thematic relevance are two sorts of cults—those that worship the cow and the phallus. The bovine cults have their paradigm in the Homeric episode, and their essence is the idolatrous veneration of the (presumably sacred) cow, even at the cost of human life. Worship of the phallus or of physical fertility per se is important here as well. Joyce's comment that the idea of the episode was "the crime committed against fecundity by sterilizing the act of coition" has made some critics wary of speaking against the idea of fertility, but if we approach this theme without preconception, the episode shows that worship of physical fertility easily becomes "idolatrous" and humanly destructive—something that Joyce himself had seen in the experience of his own mother.

At best, fertility worship is an acknowledgment of the first face of God, as source and creator of all. But such worship, especially when it venerates a physical object such as a cow or the phallus, undervalues and betrays the distinctively imaginative, spiritual aspect of the creation and distorts man's proper respect for sexual creativity into sheer idolatry. *Ulysses* does not ask us to worship "yerd our Lord" (*U*, 14.1527), or to approve of the fertilization scheme by which Mulligan will proclaim himself "*Fertilizer and Incubator*" and "devote himself to the noblest task for which our bodily organism has been framed" (*U*, 14.663). The values Mulligan espouses are consistent with the simplistic, materialistic stance he represents throughout the novel; to take them unironically here would be to invert the underlying values of the novel. In this episode, far from espousing or worshipping sheer physical fertility, Joyce suggests that such veneration is naive to the point of destructiveness. Furthermore, such idolatry draws us into regarding physical nature as something fixed and absolute, as if it were fully and finally created at one point in time by God, static and sacrosanct. And such an attitude leads naturally to seeing any attempt on our part to modify or improve upon nature as sacrilege, inviting the wrath of God the prohibitor and punisher.

But if the face of God most prominent in this episode (and perhaps in Judeo-Christian history as well) is that of the prohibitor, there is another more beneficent visage. Following the lead of William Blake (whose Nobodaddy is one avatar of God the prohibitor in this episode, *U*, 14.419), Joyce suggests that, if we have the hope and the imagination, God can also be seen as reconciler and redeemer, significantly qualifying his darker and more threatening aspect. This third face of God is suggested in "Oxen of the Sun" in several ways, among them Stephen's allusion to Christ as "our Agenbuyer" (*U*, 14.295), the reference to Jesus as "our alther liege lord" (*U*, 14.168), or the suggested power of Christ's rood to placate God the Wreaker (*U*, 14.83). Redemption is also suggested by the several references to rain, which, "please God" (*U*, 14.475) comes after hard drought.

The more receptive stance toward physical nature on the part of God the redeemer is shown as well in the dual role attributed to woman in this episode. As Eve she is the "source" of the curse; but as Mary she is the means of its melioration: "she [Mary] is the second Eve and she won us . . . whereas that other, our grandam, which we are linked up with by successive anastomosis of navelcords sold us all, seed, breed and generation, for a penny pippin" (*U*, 14.298). God's willingness to turn to a second woman, Mary—herself a part of the natural creation—as the vehicle of his redeemer aspect, is a sign of his wish to reconcile himself with his creation and to invite mankind to join in its extension.

As it is presented in this episode, this theme suggests that mankind, made in the image of God, is an agent of God's continuing creation. Nature is not, then (as the prohibitor/Jehovah aspect of God would suggest) static and sacrosanct, but is an array of potentialities to be given still undiscovered forms. As Stephen puts it, "In woman's womb word is made flesh but in the spirit of the maker all flesh that passes becomes the word that shall not pass away. This is the postcreation" (*U*, 14.292). The implication is that by virtue of our spiritual, imaginative aspect—our image of God—we are obligated to question and to challenge what may appear to be the prohibitions of Jove or Jehovah, and to participate in the continuing creation.[22]

In one sense, then, just as this episode is about the nature of God, it is also about the nature of Nature. One of the many ways this theme surfaces is in the motif of the *lusus naturae*, the freak of nature. In the present context this is a particularly important motif, because the very existence of the freak reveals that the "nature" that God the prohibitor would (presumably) have us revere is imperfect and capable of miscarrying. One section of "Oxen of the Sun" is a veritable catalogue of nature's errors, with particular attention drawn to deformed or monstrous births—miscarriages, acardiac *foetus in foetu*, agnathia, *Sturzgeburt*, "multiseminal, twikindled and monstrous births," harelip, supernumerary digits, swineheaded and doghaired infants (*U*, 14.961–88). These freaks are relevant here because they show that nature is fallible and should not be left entirely to its own devices; certain aspects of nature need complementing and correcting through the agency of human intelligence, which (we should not forget) also comes from God. For God the creator is responsible not only for the material cosmos but for the human mind as well, which is itself a part of "Nature."

In "Oxen of the Sun" the two main modes of mankind's extending or remaking of nature—that is, of the "postcreation"—are medicine and literature, the first suggested by the episode's action and setting, the second by its succession of styles, and beneath that by aspiring artist Stephen (who believes in "the eternal affirmation of the spirit of man in literature," *U*, 17.30), and by the very text of *Ulysses* itself. Especially in this maternity hospital setting, medicine presents a direct challenge to the curse of God the prohibitor in Genesis—through alleviating the pain and danger that Jehovah said childbirth must involve. What medicine attempts to do, then, is in a sense "unnatural," in that it refuses to accept idolatrously the status quo of nature—such as woman's pain in childbearing, or the *lusus naturae*—as something immutable or sacrosanct. Instead of accepting pain, deformity, and death as parts of some deifically fixed scheme of things, medicine audaciously, imaginatively, presumes to ameliorate and correct them. And in thus modifying and extending the creation, medicine challenges the prohibitor aspect of God and affirms the redeemer aspect.

Approaching the episode through these themes enables us to see the appropriateness, even the brilliance, of Joyce's use of medicine and the setting of the maternity hospital in this episode. Medicine has throughout its history been accused of impiety and unnaturalness in its methods and in its audacious aims. Consider, for example, the resistance to the study of anatomy through the dissection of human corpses (medicine dared to ask, Is man made for the corpse or the corpse for man?), and today medicine continues to present us with trenchant questions about what is and is not "natural" for us to do. The issues of abortion, the mechanical prolongation of life, in vitro fertilization, and genetic engineering and cloning are some of the most complex current examples. When we debate such issues, whether or not we regard them as theological, we go to the very core of our species' inclination to alter or extend God's natural creation.

Medicine, then, as Joyce saw, is a perfect subject through which to dramatize the issue of idolatry—that is, the proper relation between matter and spirit—in that it continually involves us in the question of whether any of the "givens" of physical nature are inviolable and sacrosanct. Joyce, it appears, is sympathetic with young Dr. Dixon's description of medicine as "an ennobling profession which, *saving the reverence due to the Deity,* is the greatest power for happiness upon the earth" (*U,* 14.824; my emphasis). Seen in this light, medicine becomes one of mankind's most noble efforts, and one that materialist Mulligan neither comprehends nor is worthy of.

But if medicine is an important example of our remaking and extending of nature, language and the literature expressed through it are for the purposes of this episode (and this novel) even more important. God the creator is the source of nature and of "human nature"—that is, of the human mind and imagination—which means that he is the source of language and of all those things expressed and achieved through it. A. N. Whitehead acknowledges this idea when he claims, "it is not going too far to say that the souls of men are the gift from language to mankind. The account of the sixth day should be written, He gave them speech, and they became souls" (*Modes of Thought,* 41). But the uses or misuses we make of language, this most powerful of all tools, while indirectly attributable to God, are ultimately a matter of human judgment and human imagination.

Language, then, as the underlying themes of this episode and the whole of *Ulysses* suggest, is our most powerful means for continuing and extending the creation, for "redeeming" it from sheer materiality and randomness. This is true both in the sense that all distinctively human enterprises (including medicine) are made possible by language, and in the sense suggested by Whitehead, that the human spirit, the soul, is dependent upon language for its emergence. The powerful capacities latent in language can, however, be abused or perverted. Language is a tool, and, like fire or atomic energy or genetic engineering, its power for good if used wisely and responsibly is matched by its power for harm if used foolishly or irresponsibly. And this observation recalls a point about *Ulysses* insisted upon throughout this book—that in the stylistic excursions in the later episodes of the novel, *Ulysses* critiques certain misunderstandings and misuses of language and of literature that our age is subject to.

Within the context of these claims about Joyce's aims and the episode's themes, I wish to reemphasize two points about the style of "Oxen of the Sun." First, the secondary narrative voice that presents this episode does not reflect Joyce's own attitudes toward language, especially in its attempts to ground the structure of the episode on gestation or evolution. Undeniably, such an agenda does exist here, but it is not Joyce's own. Second, underlying this secondary narrator's imitative tour de force is a theory about literary form that can properly be called idolatrous—a theory that is thus the appropriate stylistic counterpart of the themes we have just examined.

The intention of the presenter of this episode is to depict the "evolution" of English prose, based on an analogy with "faunal evolution" and with the development of the fetus in the womb. But there are several reasons to doubt that this program expresses Joyce's own perspective. For one, the style of the relevant passages is frequently turgid and opaque, and does not involve skillful representations of the various writers and periods, though Joyce could certainly have produced them. Rather, there is a simplistic, almost parodic, tendency on the narrator's part to signal a style through tags, excesses, and superficial traits. David Hayman notes these qualities when he speaks of the "rigidly stylized prose pastiches" (*MM*, 1982, 100).[23]

Another problem that more seriously undermines the presumed agenda of the episode is the difficulty, perhaps impossibility, of following with any precision the purported analogies with fetal development and with evolution, and the greater difficulty of seeing what these analogies are supposed to mean. If it can be established that references to Alec Bannon's "cut bob" (*U*, 14.497) and to Mrs. Purefoy's biting off "her last chick's nails" (*U*, 14.516) correspond to the fifth month of fetal development, when hair and nails first appear, what is the meaning of having this occur in a passage reflecting the style of Defoe? What is the connection between Defoe's "stage" of English, or that of the eighteenth century generally, and the fifth month of fetal development?

More pointedly, if we are to take the purported gestative form of the episode seriously, we must ask where the culminating event of birth occurs and why: When was English style "born"? Critics who have faced this question have come up with differing answers, which is itself remarkable, considering how specific and tangible an event birth is. J. S. Atherton says that the birth has begun by *U*, 14.1026, when we find the phrase "his head appeared," and it is still in progress on *U*, 14.1380. But what an intolerable gestative disproportion is involved in devoting ten pages of the episode's forty-five to the parturition! And even then Atherton has to distinguish between birth "on the literary level," and the birth of Mrs. Purefoy's child ("Oxen of the Sun," 328–33), and he makes apologetic claims for the idea that "English prose has apparently reached its full growth with the style of Ruskin" (333). Even allowing for the significant difference between "birth" and Atherton's term "full growth," it seems unbelievable that Joyce felt any such statement could be made about English prose style. On reflection, we know that while the literary style of any culture may be said to "develop," in that writers are influenced by what has gone before, we simply cannot use such terms as "birth" or "full growth," or even "evolution" to describe literary style.[24]

On the basis of my own critical efforts and those I have read, I conclude that anyone who attempts to vindicate this secondary narrator's evolutionary or gestative agenda is doomed to failure. The reason for this failure is crucial to the underlying point of this episode—that language and the literature cast in it are rooted in meaning, and their "structures" are psychological and spiritual, while gestation and "faunal evolution" are physical processes, and because of their very different natures, no attempt to ground literary form upon a physical process can succeed. When applied to literary style, such physically grounded analogies are necessarily metaphorical, and to lose sight of their metaphorical nature is to invite chaos, or, in the terms of this episode, to indulge in idolatry.[25]

Kenneth Burke has made an axiomatic point:

Language, to be used properly, must be "discounted." We must remind ourselves that, whatever *correspondence* there is between a *word* and the *thing* it names, the word is *not* the thing. The *word* "tree" is *not* a tree. And just as effects that can be got with the thing can't be got with the word, so effects that can be got with the word can't be got with the thing. But because these two realms coincide so usefully at certain points, we tend to overlook the areas where they radically diverge. We gravitate spontaneously toward naive verbal realism.[26]

The narrator of this episode evinces an attitude toward language that involves "naive verbal realism," and that is a stylistic equivalent to the simplistic totemism of cow worship or phallus worship; and Joyce is here taking the measure of the theory of imitative form, as he did in "Sirens" of the idea that literature should approach the condition of music. For all his attempts—often amazingly successful attempts—to suggest or evoke nonverbal entities through the written word, Joyce knew that literature has its own nature and its own forms, and for any writer literally to take a physical process as a basis for literary form would reveal his deep confusion about the nature of literature.

The point is that literature has a "nature" of its own, quite different from the nature of music or painting or of the growth of a fetus or a tree. Literary form is inextricably linked with tone and mood, with character and theme, with meaning; its proper inherent forms are psychological and aesthetic and spiritual rather than physical. Earlier I said that physical fertility may serve as a metaphor for imaginative fertility—but we must not regard physical fertility as our appropriate *telos,* or as sacrosanct. Similarly, critics and writers may use metaphors from the physical world to suggest literary form, but if they lose sight of the fact that these are metaphors, and begin to expect literature to imitate physical structures, they commit a failure of discrimination tantamount to idolatry.

J. S. Atherton in the opening sentence of his essay on this episode puts his finger on an essential point—a point adumbrated years earlier by Harry Levin. Atherton states, "This chapter is an exercise in imitative form. Joyce is trying to make words reproduce objects and processes" ("Oxen of the Sun," 313). I agree with Atherton, but I attribute this intention not to Joyce, but to the secondary narrator, the presenter, of the episode. On one level Joyce is of course responsible for this, but just as in "Nausicaa" or "Sirens" or "Eumaeus," Joyce is presenting a mode of language that he does not sanction, so here he dramatizes imitative form, but he does not stand behind it. Why do it then? Because *Ulysses* takes seriously the powers and responsibilities of language, and Joyce wished to incorporate into his novel some of the major current misconceptions about this soul-giving, reality-creating medium. Joyce was aware of attempts to translate one art into another, or to see literature as imitating music or painting, or to use some physical object or event as the basis for literary structure. But for Joyce all such theorizing was mistaken in its failure to recognize the distinctive nature of literary form.

"Circe"

In each of the later episodes of *Ulysses,* a secondary narrator or presenter has authority over the stylistic disposition of the material, but not over such basic elements of the novel as the plot events or the characters' personality traits or their acts or thoughts. In several episodes such as "Sirens," "Oxen of the Sun," "Eumaeus," and "Ithaca," we have seen the dialogue and even the thoughts of Stephen or Bloom recast into the sometimes opaque idiom of the presenter, leaving us to infer as best we can their actual conversations or reflections, and even the events of the novel. (On the objection that there are no "actual" thoughts, dialogue, or events, see chapter 5, above.)

I reiterate this point about the limitations of the secondary narrator's authority because failure to recognize the presenter's pervasive but none-theless limited role in this episode has caused some critics to regard the "Circe" episode as qualitatively different from the others, and as involving unique and intractable "ontological" problems—that is, problems about the mode of reality that the episode involves. Arnold Goldman, for ex-ample, calls it "the most complex chapter in *Ulysses ontologically*" (*Joyce Paradox*, 96; my emphasis), and his puzzlement over the "reality" of the episode has been echoed by others. Hugh Kenner argues, "Nothing, in 'Circe,' distinguishes 'real' from 'hallucinatory,' nor any part of the epi-sode from any other," and subsequently he declares, "Deprived of reliable criteria for 'reality,' we have no recourse save to read the text as though everything in it were equally real" ("*Ulysses*," 1987, 123, 126). Bernard Benstock proclaims "Circe" "different from all other chapters in *Ulysses*" (*Narrative Con/Texts*, 130) and asserts, "Attempts to achieve a finite sepa-ration of that which is 'reality' from that which is presumably someone's 'hallucination' have been relatively unsuccessful, and readers should be-come suspicious of anything taking place in 'Circe' that cannot be proven retrospectively—and then to continue to question that 'proof'" (133).

That the problems in "Circe" are not so categorical or unique as these critics claim is shown by the practice of virtually every reader of the epi-sode, including Kenner and Benstock. Kenner's sweeping assertion that all events in "Circe" are equally real—that is, that we cannot distinguish the real from the hallucinatory—cannot be credited, any more than can Ben-stock's insistence on retrospective proof. Surely a number of "actual" events do happen between the time the characters leave Burke's pub at the end of the "Oxen of the Sun" and the arrival of Bloom and Stephen at the Butt Bridge cabman's shelter in "Eumaeus," and we can determine many of those events through scrutiny of the "Circe" episode, as we did in "Si-rens" or "Oxen of the Sun." For example, reading this episode within the context of the novel, we ascribe a different level of reality to Stephen's striking the lamp chimney and to Bloom's rescuing him from arrest, than we do to Bloom's fantasy about Mrs. Mervyn Talboys (*U*, 15.1057), or to the coming of the End of the World (*U*, 15.2177), or to the navvy's walk-ing away with the flaming street lamp on his shoulder (*U*, 15.136).

Kenner himself subsequently admits, "Common sense will abstract from this reading certain things it is confident must have 'really hap-

pened'" ("*Ulysses*," 1987, 127). Moreover, Benstock cannot remain consistent in his skepticism; at one point he seems to question whether Bloom
even goes to Bella's house (*Narrative Con/Texts*, 135), but at another he
presents a realistic reading of the opening of the episode (138 ff.). And a
great many critics base their interpretations of *Ulysses* upon certain important events in this episode, such as Bloom's following Stephen into
Nighttown, or his confronting Bella, or his taking Stephen in tow and
preventing his arrest. If these plot events cannot be relied upon, many
interpretations of *Ulysses* collapse.[27]

Despite some critics' claims and the admittedly daunting nature of the
episode, the challenges presented by "Circe" are not categorically different from those of the other chapters. Here as elsewhere the difficulties are
not a matter of ontology, but of style and of literary genre—that is, they
arise from the distinctive literary and psychological agendas of the presenter to whom the episode has been delegated. In "Circe" that presenter
is an expressionistic dramatist who has a Freudian view of human nature
and especially of the unconscious, and those literary and psychological
agendas control the presentation of everything in the episode.

What has misled some critics into thinking that this episode involves
radical discontinuity with the rest of the text is that the expressionistic/
Freudian mode of presentation here is total and pervasive. In no other
episode is there so extensive a transformation of the "raw material" of the
novel by the secondary narrator, nor does any other episode involve such
liberties in re-presenting the thoughts of the characters. In "Circe" the
presentation is given over from first line to last to the conventions and
techniques of expressionistic drama, so that the exaggerations and distortions are not confined to the characters' "hallucinations," but exist
throughout the episode—for example, in the phantasmagoric opening
scene. Furthermore, the dramatic form in "Circe" is used (as expressionism often has been) as a vehicle of the Freudian view of psychological
dynamics and especially of the unconscious, and much of the exaggeration
and distortion within the episode reflect that psychological agenda.
Though recognizing the literary genre and psychoanalytical bias of this
presenter does not enable us to draw a distinct line between the real and
the hallucinatory in "Circe," it does enable us to understand that the episode is ontologically no more radical than "Sirens" or "Oxen of the
Sun."[28]

If certain inherent qualities of expressionistic drama and Freudian psychology render the line between "content" and "mode of presentation"
harder to discern in "Circe" than elsewhere in *Ulysses*, the presenter's

prerogatives and Joyce's purpose in employing him nonetheless remain the same in this episode as in the others. The presenter can only *recast* events and persons in ways that reflect his agenda, and Joyce permits the presenter of this episode to recast the characters and events of "Circe" as he does in order to take the measure of something—in this case, the Freudian view of human nature, especially the unconscious, and the limitations of the expressionistic dramatic mode. The difference between "Circe" and the other later episodes, then, is one of degree, not of kind. This means that in this episode as in all others we can talk meaningfully about the underlying characters and events, and we can also make informed judgments about the coloring or distortion that this agenda imparts to the content of the episode.

The dramatic format and the extensive stage directions make it obvious that "Circe" does involve a narrator, a presenter. The voice presenting this drama and speaking these directions is not that of any character in the novel; it is obviously authorial and shares the basic traits of the presenter in other episodes, including total access to the characters' minds and the events of the novel.[29] One result of the distinctive presence of the dramatist/narrator in "Circe" is that critics have fretted less in "Circe" than in several other episodes about whether this narrator can be identified with the perspective of a character—that is, with "naturalizing" the narrative voice.

Expressionism/Freudianism in "Circe"

That "Circe" is presented in an expressionist mode has been noted by a number of critics. Perhaps the first to invoke the genre was Ernest Boyd, who said that the method of *Ulysses* "recalls that of Jules Romains and the *Unanimistes*. But its form is more akin to that of the German Expressionists" (*Ireland's Literary Renaissance*, 1922, 409). He also argues, "In its bewildering juxtaposition of the real and the imaginary, of the commonplace and the fantastic, Joyce's work obviously declares its kinship with the Expressionists, with Walter Hasenclever or Georg Kaiser" (411). Other critics over the decades have concurred in this generic designation, with the fullest discussion of the expressionistic sources and analogues of "Circe" being Ira B. Nadel's "Joyce and Expressionism."[30] Nadel documents in impressive detail Joyce's interest in expressionistic writers and painters, showing the availability of many of these in Zurich during Joyce's days there, and he highlights a number of expressionistic techniques within the episode.

Sherrill Grace has written perceptively about the uses of expressionism within the episode, contrasting Lowry's serious use of the mode in *Under the Volcano* with Joyce's parodic use of it in "Circe." Grace finds Nadel's claims of Joyce's awareness of expressionism conclusive, but adds, "Nevertheless, it is important to remember that James Joyce was no expressionist. If he used expressionism, he did so in the form of parody—parody that served his larger, and different, purposes" ("Midsummer Madness," 12). Grace acknowledges that "Circe" "stages, in a heightened and exaggerated form—even for expressionism—almost all the features of expressionist plays" (13–14), listing a number of these. But Grace stresses that Joyce's aim is "a mockery of expressionism and the expressionist protagonist" (15), and that in "Circe" Joyce "has exposed the 'expressive fallacy,' with its metaphysics of presence and its privileging of the inner, subjective reality as Truth, and in so exposing it he ridicules, debunks, and defuses the central expressionist paradox and dilemma" (16). Grace's argument, then, supports my own that Joyce relegates this episode to an expressionistic presenter in order to display certain limitations and weaknesses of the mode.

That the expressionism of "Circe" specifically involves a Freudian view of the psyche and the unconscious has also been recognized by a number of critics. R. M. Kain says that the style is "that of expressionistic drama," and the characters are "menaced from within by the seething desires of the libido" (*Fabulous Voyager,* 31). Mark Shechner describes the techniques of "Circe" in distinctly Freudian terms: "Boundaries evaporate; inner and outer interpenetrate, and identity becomes a flux of interlocking possibilities. . . . The logic of this reality follows the canons of dreamwork: condensation, displacement, and symbolization" (*Joyce in Nighttown,* 120). L. H. Platt describes the expressionistic opening scene, with its stunted men and women and its "Rows of grimy houses with gaping doors" as "Freudian dream imagery" and refers more generally to the "heavily signalled Freudian symbolism" of the opening pages of the episode ("*Ulysses* 15," 36–37). Jeffrey Perl's extensive reading of the episode in Freudian terms presumes Joyce's concurrence in the theory; he argues that taking Nighttown as the Freudian unconscious clarifies via psychoanalytical terms much that is otherwise inexplicable, and he claims that in "Circe" Joyce "brings us face to face, as Freud does, with the single, psychic root of our fictions and truths" (*Tradition of Return,* 201, 210).

The most important aspect of Freudian psychology incorporated by the expressionistic presenter/dramatist is its conception of the unconscious. According to Freud, the unconscious consists of repressed personal contents, mainly sexual contents, that we are fearful or ashamed to acknowledge. Freud presumes as well a considerable discontinuity, even antagonism, between the conscious and unconscious domains of the psyche, a gap generated by the threat that the repressed material within the unconscious poses to the individual and to society, and that can be bridged in real life only by psychoanalysis. Significantly, the presenter also shares the Freudian assumption that these repressed contents reveal far more about who we really are—that is, reveal our inherent (bestial) nature—than do our conscious, public acts. As Austin Briggs says, "'Circe' promises the truth in its foray into the red light district, a place where reality can be seen unveiled and without disguise—the 'raw, naked truth,' as film posters put such matters" ("'Roll Away the Reel World,'" 151).

In his own presentation of these ideas, Freud often uses the rhetorical ploy of claiming that while we of course do not want to admit what he has discovered about our nature—and he takes our reluctance or denial as further evidence of its truth—we must be rigorous enough, brave enough, to face these unpleasant facts about ourselves. In so doing, Freud invokes what Paul Ricoeur calls a hermeneutic of suspicion that would intimidate us by claiming that those things we least wish to admit are therefore the most true, and that it is our lack of tough-mindedness that prevents our acknowledging this (I discussed this idea briefly in chapter 1). The brothel district setting and the Odyssean parallel with Circe's transforming men into swine are especially appropriate for displaying this unflattering, intimidating view of human nature.

While the expressionistic Freudianism of "Circe" is perhaps most obvious in the "hallucinations" of Bloom and Stephen, it is by no means confined to those scenes. It pervades the chapter, coloring and distorting every aspect of the presentation, including the persistent depiction of the Nighttown milieu and inhabitants as grotesque and bestial. For example, the opening scene that occurs before Stephen or Bloom enter the action involves grotesque figures: stunted men and women, a deafmute idiot, a pigmy woman swinging on a rope between two railings, a gnome. It is unlikely, however, either that such grotesques are actually present in Mabbot street on this June night, or that the dramatist has utterly fabricated these characters (which would overstep the presenter's prerogatives). Rather, this depiction is presumably a Freudian/expressionistic representation of the motley crew of men and women who are milling about at the entrance to Nighttown, with the grotesque descriptions reflecting this presenter's sense of the "true nature" of these persons. L. H. Platt describes the opening scene as involving "transformation of urban people and urban objects into strange and unfamiliar figures" ("*Ulysses* 15," 37), and David Hayman concurs, arguing that the "creatures whom we are *fooled into seeing as grotesques* discomfort us as part of an *unnatural landscape* into which we are drawn by a *web of illusion*" (*MM*, 1982, 91; my emphases).[31]

The Freudian expressionist's recasting of personages and events in "Circe," then, pervades the episode, but undoubtedly the most salient such technique in "Circe" is "hallucination," through which the dramatist specifically displays the repressed guilts and fears of Bloom and Stephen, and thus brings to the surface the "hidden truth" about them.[32] For example, Bloom's hallucinations depict him as someone engrossed in sexual fantasies and debilitated by masochistic fears. At the nadir of one of these hallucinations, just after he has been assailed by "The Sins of the Past," Bloom is challenged by Bello with a quintessentially Freudian question: "Say! What was the most revolting piece of obscenity in all your career of crime? Go the whole hog. Puke it out! Be candid for once" (*U*, 15.3042)—to which Bloom cannot answer coherently, whether because his deed is too revolting to utter, or because he cannot come up with anything sordid enough to satisfy Bello, we cannot be sure.

Critical Response to "Circe"

The presenter's Freudian expressionism is, then, the agenda that Joyce is subverting in this episode. But, not surprisingly, there have been critics who have applauded the technique or endorsed the view of human nature, presuming them to be Joyce's own. Some, accepting the Freudianism of the episode, have argued that these hallucinations reveal the truth about Stephen and Bloom, or that these characters achieve psychoanalytical catharsis of their suppressed problems. But here as with other episodes, there has been some development of critical opinion, and several recent critics have expressed misgivings about how well the agenda of the episode aligns with Joyce's own thinking or with the view of the unconscious implicit in the rest of the novel.

Perhaps some early readers admired this episode (and presumed Joyce sanctioned its technique and ideology) because of the audacity and brilliance of the dramatic/stylistic tour de force it involves, and because of the contemporary authority of Freudian psychoanalysis—that is, the presumption that Freudianism involved an undeniable (if unsavory) truth about human nature and that modernist, avant-garde Joyce would concur with modernist, avant-garde Freud. R. M. Kain, for example, calls "Circe" "Possibly the most brilliant dramatization of Freudian psychology in literature" (*Fabulous Voyager*, 31). And Edward Brandabur says explicitly, "The Joycean version of unconscious repression resembled that of Freud, for whom much of the unconscious was a malign realm, echoing with childhood injunctions long since barred from consciousness"; then, after quoting Freud's claim that repressed instincts grow "like a fungus in the dark," he notes, "When Joyce comes to depict repressions explicitly emerging in *Ulysses,* he displays a similar sense of the unconscious as a moldy cellar" (*Scrupulous Meanness,* 165).

Some critics have accepted the episode's agenda at least to the extent that they believe that these hallucinations reveal truths about the characters that have been veiled from us during the day. Harry Blamires, for example, seems to feel this in regard to Bloom (cf. *New Bloomsday Book,* 166, 169, and esp. 182), and Zack Bowen pointedly says that "in 'Circe' we get to know more about the inner workings of Bloom's and Stephen's minds than in all the stream-of-consciousness thoughts thus far in the novel" ("*Ulysses,*" 518). Other critics have suggested that the episode involves a compressed process of psychoanalysis, and that through these experiences, Stephen and Bloom confront and master their worst repressions and achieve a kind of psychoanalytic catharsis (Henke, *Joyce's Moraculous Sindbook,* 181; Maddox, *Joyce's "Ulysses" and the Assault upon Character,* 142; Kenner, "*Ulysses,*" 1987, 127).

But several critics have denied that these hallucinations reveal the truth about these characters, and others make the important point that while what these fantasies depict may not be lies about Bloom—that is, they have some basis in his personality—they greatly exaggerate minor elements of his psyche. Richard Ellmann asserts that "Bloom's peccadillos are magnified out of all recognition in the *Circe* episode" (*JJII,* 509) and that "Circe" "portray[s] the suppressed desires of Bloom and Stephen in vaudeville form, psychoanalysis turned into a vehicle of comedy" (495). Paul van Caspel warns that we are not to believe all the perverse and shameful things that Bloom is accused of in the trial scene; these accusations, he says, "point to certain tendencies in his nature: He may not really have written indecent letters to society ladies, but he may very well have felt vague yearnings to do so" (*Bloomers,* 220). James H. Maddox, Jr., concurs: "Bloom's masochism is a tendency, not a definition of his whole self" (*Assault upon Character,* 123). Even Frederick J. Hoffman (who seems to assume that the chapter endorses Freudian ideas) notes that "such trivial matters as the cake of soap and the evangelist are endowed with an absurdly high importance, out of proportion to their trivial place in the events of the day" ("Infroyce," 138, n. 43).

Austin Briggs makes the cogent point that "Bloom appears in 'Circe' in a myriad of costumes and roles, yet we have no trouble recognizing him even when he is sex-changed or transformed into a drooling Mongolian idiot. As in the cinema, the theater of 'Circe' presents a place where individuality triumphs over all other roles" ("'Roll Away the Reel World,'" 151). (Briggs cites a letter from Joyce to Budgen, 29 September 1920: "I want to make *Circe* a costume episode also. Bloom for instance appears in five or six different suits. What a book!" [*Lts*, 1:148].)

These critics' defense of Bloom, and their insistence on the continuity and integrity of his character even through the distortions of this episode, support my contention that the secondary narrators have no license to foist upon the characters traits contrary to those manifested in the novel as a whole. It is indubitably *Bloom* who appears in these different guises and is subjected to these calumnies. Nor, technically speaking, is the presenter's elaboration of a character's flitting thoughts or fears through hallucination essentially different from the total recasting of dialogue and thoughts that takes place in "Oxen of the Sun" or "Ithaca." In those episodes we must try to discern what Bloom and Stephen have actually said or thought, beneath the stylistic veneer; here we must similarly discount the hyperbole and distortion of the Freudian expressionism.

Several critics have rejected the idea that any catharsis or abreaction occurs for Bloom or Stephen by virtue of these hallucinatory episodes, pointing to flaws and slippages in such a claim. Karen Lawrence rightly says that since we cannot be sure how much of this hallucinatory material Stephen or Bloom knows, or how large it looms in their minds, it is questionable how effective the psychoanalytic process under such conditions could be (*Odyssey,* 164). She asks, "How can 'moments' like the vision of Rudy, or Bloom looking through the keyhole at Boylan and Molly, really be decisive when we are uncertain of the degree to which they represent the character's experience?" (161). I agree with Lawrence that to attribute profound transformative power to feelings or "experiences" that may never rise to awareness is to invoke an almost magical process, utterly out of keeping with the realistic premises of the rest of the novel. (Stephen is, after all, quite drunk during the episode.)

Fritz Senn, in an approach that complements my own, challenges the entire modus operandi of the episode. Senn argues that the episode is persistently characterized by "provection"—that is, by distorting, hypertrophic development of the novel's material. He presents "Circe" as a "distortive escalation of all preceding Joycean texts" ("'Circe' as Harking Back," 66–67), and says that "'Circe' mirrors all that precedes it and *distorts it out of shape*" (75; my emphasis). Senn suggests that the events of "Circe" may not be as important as they seem:

> Above all, the most sensational occurrences have next to no effect. The end of the world comes and is forgotten. "*Time's livid final flame*" with the "*ruin of all space*" (*U*, 15.4244) amounts to the "Pwfungg" of a gasjet (*U*, 15.4247). The damage is minimal, "not sixpenceworth" (*U*, 15.4290–91). "*Pandemonium*" (*U*, 15.4662), all these disasters come and go without leaving a trace behind. A minor mischance, signalled by a feeble "Bip" that is almost lost in discordant Circean noises, is one of the few consequential events. In the reasserted reality of "Eumaeus," we find Bloom handicapped as "one of the back buttons of his trousers had . . . gone the way of all buttons" (*U*, 16.36). A single absent button, carefully recorded again in "Ithaca" ("six minus one braced trouser buttons," *U*, 17.1444) outlives coronations and serial cataclysms. (87)

Senn's cogent objections challenge the reliability of the entire mode of presentation, as well as the view of the psyche that underlies this episode.

One crucial question, then, raised by this Freudian/expressionistic depiction of Stephen and Bloom is whether it does present (in Briggs's words) the "raw, naked truth" about them, or whether it represents a hyperbolic exaggeration of their fears and defensiveness and is thus a distortion of their natures. The issue here goes to the heart of Joyce's artistic method and view of life—that is, whether we put most stock in those dark and furtive things that Freud has relegated to the cellar of the psyche and that he claims reveal our true nature, or in those more ordinary acts and events that constitute our everyday intercourse with one another.

I believe that this elaborate and dramatic hallucinatory material, while grounded in flitting thoughts or shivers of insecurity or guilt within Bloom and Stephen, does not supersede what we learn about them from their public acts and their reflections throughout *Ulysses*. Though not total fabrications—the secondary narrator is not permitted that latitude—none of these hallucinations counts for nearly as much as the Freudian/expressionistic presenter would have us believe. Having accompanied Bloom through Dublin all day, we know that, while he does have his foibles and flaws, he is essentially a man of great sympathy and charity, as reflected, for example, in his kindness to the blind stripling, his concern for Mina Purefoy in labor, and perhaps most of all in the acts that he carries out in regard to Stephen within this very episode.

If some change is going to take place within Stephen or Bloom, or between them, will it be because of the bogeymen they may have faced—perhaps totally unawares—in their hallucinations, or because of what happens between them during and after their stay at Bella Cohen's whorehouse? Karen Lawrence, questioning Kenner's and Maddox's claims that some psychoanalytic process has been effected in Bloom, argues, "Bloom does act like a father in 'Circe,' from his entrance into Nighttown to search for Stephen, 'the best of the lot,' to his defense of him and his literal 'rescue' at the end of the chapter. But it is impossible to pinpoint the relationship between the expressionistic dialogues and these naturalistic events. . . . More importantly, Maddox overlooks the fact that Bloom's confrontation with his own worthlessness is a process that occurs *continually*, all day long" (*Odyssey,* 162). I concur in Lawrence's judgment that the public acts of Bloom express far more of his real character than do these exaggerated fantasies. The important events here—the ones that leave some residue in succeeding episodes (and beyond?)—are not the hyperbolic or apocalyptic ones within the Freudian unconscious, but the more ordinary events that compose the public plot of the episode. Again Frank Budgen shows great insight about this episode: "It is steeped in the atmosphere and governed by the logic of hallucination, but its dominant theme is the fatherly love and care of Bloom for Stephen Dedalus" (*JJMU,* 231).

Joyce on Freud

There is both biographical and textual evidence that Joyce did not subscribe to the Freudian psychological agenda. In an interview with Djuna Barnes in April 1922, Joyce spoke critically of Freudians: "as for psychoanalysis . . . it's neither more nor less than blackmail" ("James Joyce," in *Djuna Barnes: Interviews,* 293). Ellmann's biography contains a number of similar judgments reflecting Joyce's suspicion of Freud and his schema. Joyce once shocked his friend Ettore Schmitz by "dismissing his interest in psychoanalysis with the comment, 'Well, if we need it, let us keep to confession'" (*JJII,* 472), and he "brushed [psychoanalysis] aside as absurd, saying that its symbolism was mechanical, a house being a womb, a fire a phallus" (*JJII,* 382). Ellmann also quotes Joyce as saying, "People want to put me out of the church to which I don't belong. I have nothing to do with psychoanalysis" (*JJII,* 628). Ellmann tells us that Joyce's friend Ottocaro Weiss "had a knowledge of psychoanalysis which Joyce disparaged but found useful" (*JJII,* 393), and that Joyce differed with Weiss about Freud's theory that humor was a means of relief for some repressed feeling (*JJII*, 398).

Many critics have concluded that Joyce was no Freudian. In *The Consciousness of Joyce,* Ellmann explores Joyce's rejection of the Freud/Jones Oedipal theory of *Hamlet* (56–57). Ronald Thomas argues, "Like Jung, Joyce learned from and reacted against what he perceived to be the exclusively scientific and mechanistic aspects of Freudian dream theory and sought to return some authenticity and authority to the manifest content of the dream" (*Dreams of Authority,* 257). Kenner asserts, "Whatever insights he may have owed to Freud, Joyce was fundamentally unconvinced by Viennese sexual determinism" ("Circe," 360). Tim Cribb also distances Joyce from Freud, noting that "unlike Freud, Joyce's prime material is not the pathological but the healthy." He argues, "There is no evidence, however, that [Joyce] represents human behavior according to any single system, whether the elaborately hypothesized sexual system of the early, nor the more mythical speculations of the later Freud" ("The Unconscious and the Cognitive Epiphany," 70–71).[33] And both Ellmann and F. J. Hoffman point to various passages in *Finnegans Wake* that seem derisive of psychoanalysis (*JJII*, 466, 472; "Infroyce," 124).

The anti-Freudian evidence within *Ulysses* is even more compelling. Not only does the Freudian/expressionist agenda of this episode involve a distorted picture of Stephen and Bloom, the Freudian conception of the unconscious as consisting of personal repressions and sharply divided from the conscious domain is quite different from the understanding of the unconscious that informs the rest of the novel. One of my main points about the initial style, developed in preceding chapters, is that the style of the opening episodes has been carefully crafted by Joyce specifically to show the inextricability of conscious and unconscious, inner and outer, private and public. Joyce's distinctive mode of psychic presentation in the initial style involves a subtle blend of sensation, perception, reflection, memory, somatic state, and apprehension that simultaneously involves elements that are conscious and "focal" in the characters' experience, and those that are preconscious or "subsidiary" in it (see chapter 4, above, on these terms from Michael Polanyi)—enabling a simulation of experience that is far more interwoven and holistic than that sanctioned by the Freudian schema or depicted through expressionistic devices.

Another aspect of the initial style by which *Ulysses* illustrates the pervasiveness and immediacy of the "unconscious" in our experience is Joyce's allusive method. Through this technique Joyce illustrates how various cultural narratives and cultural schemata—such as songs, stories, plays, historical accounts—are continuously present in the characters' psyches, sometimes consciously, but more often on a preconscious or unconscious level. These cultural schemata, these narratives that the characters wittingly and unwittingly invoke in structuring their experience, represent modes of the "unconscious," simultaneously personal and collective, that we draw upon at all times. This is the view of the psyche that is sanctioned by the novel as a whole, as over against the more limited, if dramatic, one offered in "Circe." Joyce himself suggested this when he said to Frank Budgen, "Why all this fuss and bother about the mystery of the unconscious? . . . What about the mystery of the conscious? What do they know about that?" (*JJII*, 436). He told Djuna Barnes, "In *Ulysses* I have recorded, simultaneously, what a man says, sees, thinks, and what such seeing, thinking, saying, does to what you Freudians call the subconscious" ("James Joyce," in *Djuna Barnes: Interviews,* 293).

Thus, while the Freudian conception of the unconscious as a sharply demarcated repository of suppressed and threatening personal content reigns in "Circe," the unconscious at work in *Ulysses* as a whole is very different. It involves a much more permeable and dynamic relationship between conscious and unconscious, a view espoused by William James and more fully developed by Carl Jung.

In *Varieties of Religious Experience* (1902), James invokes the emerging idea of a "field of consciousness": "The important fact which this 'field' formula commemorates is the indetermination of the margin. . . . Our whole past store of memories floats beyond this margin, ready at a touch to come in; and the entire mass of residual powers, impulses, and knowledges that constitute our empirical self stretches continuously beyond it. So vaguely drawn are the outlines between what is actual and what is only potential at any moment of our conscious life, that it is always hard to say of certain mental elements whether we are conscious of them or not" (227). James goes on in subsequent paragraphs to emphasize the importance of the discovery of "memories, thoughts, and feelings which are extra-marginal and outside of the primary consciousness altogether, but yet must be classed as conscious facts of some sort"—"a consciousness existing beyond the field, or subliminally" (228).

Such a permeable and dynamic conception of the relation between conscious and preconscious, expressed tentatively by James, becomes an integral part of Carl Jung's thinking. In a section of "On the Nature of the Psyche" entitled "Conscious and Unconscious," Jung says that the unconscious involves "an extremely fluid state of affairs: everything of which I know, but of which I am not at the moment thinking; everything of which I was once conscious but have now forgotten; everything perceived by my senses, but not noted by my conscious mind; everything which, involuntarily and without paying attention to it, I feel, think, remember, want, and do; all the future things that are taking shape in me and will sometime come to consciousness: all this is the content of the unconscious" (185). After developing these ideas for several pages, Jung insists, "We must . . . accustom ourselves to the thought that conscious and unconscious have no clear demarcations, the one beginning where the other leaves off. It is rather the case that the psyche is a conscious-unconscious whole" (200). This is precisely the conception of the unconscious that Joyce has dramatized through the various techniques of the initial style—and it stands in direct opposition to the Freudian view that maintains in "Circe."

Moreover, speaking specifically of the difference between the views of Jung and Freud, Jungian scholar Jolanda Jacobi asserts: "The widely accepted idea of the collective unconscious as a 'stratum' situated *below* the conscious mind is . . . unfounded and misleading. This widespread tendency, particularly frequent among those trained in philosophy and theology, to identify the unconscious with something negative, unclean, or immoral, and hence to assign it to the lowest level of the psyche, stems from failure to distinguish between the personal and collective unconscious; in line with Freudian theory, the whole unconscious is taken as a mere 'reservoir of repressions'. But the collective unconscious is not made up of individual experience; it is an inner correspondence to the world as a whole" (*Complex/Archetype/Symbol,* 59–60). This last idea is echoed in Stephen's statement that Shakespeare "found in the world without as actual what was in his world within as possible" (*U,* 9.1041).

In *Ulysses* as a whole, this is the view of the unconscious that maintains; only in "Circe" do we have a view that would strongly demarcate conscious from unconscious, would threaten us with the effects of repression, and would claim that the darker and danker the secret is, the closer it is to the truth about us.[34]

In an analysis that concurs substantially with my own, Tim Cribb makes some important distinctions between the thinking of Joyce and Freud. For example, describing the unconscious in *Ulysses* as a whole, Cribb argues, "The unconscious is now united with the conscious mind, and both with the world and the body, through a constantly interacting dynamics that makes any systematic separation between the elements impossible. . . . The unconscious, for example, may be conceived as a set of spatial relations moulding the behavior of individuals or collectivities, or it may act through a person's biological processes, such as digestion and excretion, or it may operate through the system of language itself" ("The Unconscious and the Cognitive Epiphany," 73). As for "the terms in which, since Freud, it [the unconscious] has been conventionally conceived, that is, as repressed sexuality, escaping unawares in sleep, slips, dreams, and fantasy" (73), Cribb says that the place to look for that conception is the "Circe" episode.

Cribb then argues that Bloom is far more than the presentation in "Circe" would suggest. Cribb says of the flamboyant scene in which Bloom is forced to change sex and be humiliated: "It is tempting to construe these [events] as revealing the 'deep' truth about his character, i.e. that he is a masochist" (73). But Cribb maintains that while such indications do exist "back [in] the earlier chapters when his character is being established in the daylight world" (73), there are also "other truths about Bloom, perhaps inconsistent, but co-existent rather than contradictory" (74), and that the existence of these means that "the scene is by no means as terrible as some commentators insist" (74). He adds, "It is also important to remember that Ulysses comes through Circe's enchantments unscathed and so does Bloom" (75). For Cribb, then, the conception of the unconscious informing "Circe" is not consistent with Joyce's own view or with that of the novel as a whole.

Joyce versus Expressionistic Drama

Having argued at some length that Joyce rejects the Freudian ideology in "Circe," I want to return to the claim that this episode also takes the measure of expressionistic drama. Expressionism is one of several literary modes or techniques that developed in the early twentieth century to simulate and interpret psychological processes and the relationship between the individual mind and the world, and for that reason we might expect Joyce to admire it. But I suspect that its limitations and deficiencies in this regard are precisely why he did not admire it, and came to regard it instead as simplistic and distortive.

In my discussion of interior monologue in "Penelope," I argued that Joyce's relegation of a style to a single episode, and the implicit comparison of the style to the normative initial style that this invites, can itself involve a critique of the style. That is, once we come to understand how effectively the initial style carries out Joyce's artistic and thematic aims in *Ulysses,* we see that none of the other styles is nearly so subtle and effective in presenting the complex symbiotic relationships between mind and nature, self and society, conscious and unconscious, as the initial style.

We can, then, recognize the serious inherent limitations of expression-ism more fully if we ask why Joyce did not cast the opening episodes of *Ulysses*—or the whole of the novel—in this expressionistic dramatic mode. The answer is that, compared to the subtle, appropriate techniques of narrative presentation developed in the initial style, expressionism is crude and simplistic, that it in effect capitulates to the dualistic view of experience that Joyce is concerned to challenge, and it is vitiated by a negative agenda in regard to human nature. The initial style—involving an effaced narrative voice that simulates a cultural psyche, a blending of fig-ural and authorial perspectives, and implicit use of cultural allusions and schemata—offers a far more subtle and satisfactory means of presenting the fabric of human experience, and of subverting various dichotomies modernism would foist upon us, than something as limited and tenden-tious as expressionistic drama ever could.

For example, instead of showing experience to involve a seamless fabric of conscious/unconscious, inner/outer, expressionism heightens and exag-gerates these differences—what Sherrill Grace describes as "its privileging of the inner, subjective reality as Truth" ("Midsummer Madness," 16). It implies a strong discontinuity and antagonism between conscious and unconscious, and it implies a greater "reification" and importance to cer-tain elements of the unconscious than Joyce could accept. Moreover, even if it is not joined with Freudianism, expressionism involves a view of hu-man nature that has no place for the better qualities of his characters that Joyce wished to depict. Given the inherent biases and limitations of the mode, we cannot imagine how it could convey the charity and open-mindedness of Bloom or the anguished aspirations and idealism of Stephen. Finally, Joyce's charge against expressionistic drama, even when it is not the handmaid of Freudian psychology, is that it implies a simplistic view of the unconscious, an exaggerated view of the importance of the unconscious, and a reductionistic view of human nature.

In the "Circe" episode, then, Freudian psychology and expressionistic drama conspire to present a reductionistic and falsely dramatic sense of the true nature of the characters, raising issues that go to the heart of Joyce's artistic method and view of human experience—that is, what value we ascribe to those ordinary acts and events that make up our everyday relationships with one another—what Wordsworth referred to as those "little, nameless, unremembered, acts / Of kindness and of love" ("Tintern Abbey"). To put the apocalyptic hallucinations of this episode into per-spective, we should remind ourselves of what really happens here—namely, that Bloom, out of concern for Stephen, follows him into

Nighttown, protects him from exploitation by the whoremistress and from incarceration by the police, and then takes him home to minister to him as best he can—charitable acts that reveal far more of his real nature than do his demeaning hallucinations.

I would suggest, then, that the real "rawhead and bloody bones" of this episode is not Bloom's humiliating fantasy of Molly's adultery, or the threats of Bella/Bello, or the ghost of Stephen's mother, or even the *dio boia* or hangman god (*U*, 9.1049); it is the Freudian/expressionistic bogeyman that would intimidate and demean us by claiming that what we really are is a bestial psyche divided against itself and haunted by shameful repressions.

Epilogue

Unlike Stephen Dedalus I feel no need to disavow these ideas now that I have expressed them, but I do need to admit how partial my achievement is. While I believe very much in the ideas I have developed in this book and I hope they provide a way of looking at *Ulysses* that can be clarifying and enriching for readers, my experience with this novel requires that I acknowledge how much my approach does not encompass. One obvious example of this is the novel's playfulness and humor—sources of great pleasure to all readers and yet barely mentioned in this book.

I say this not simply as a general disclaimer that great books always elude our grasp, but in order to make a specific point about my own claims and methodology. Having worked carefully with the narrative voice of this novel for many years, and having developed a complicated thesis about several aspects of that voice, I am all the more convinced that our models for talking about such matters remain inadequate to describe, much less to do justice to, what goes on in any rich, complex literary work. In any given passage of *Ulysses,* there is far more happening, there are far more dimensions at work, than any schema of narrative presentation can comprehend.

In the second chapter of this book, I distinguish between the man James Joyce, the implied author, the primary narrator, and the secondary narrator or presenter—all four of which exist nested within one another in many passages of the later episodes. And within this schema I have had to argue that the primary narrator often takes on the perspective of various characters, and that the secondary narrator (who, though limited in his scope, shares some omniscience with the implied author) sometimes loses control of the agenda he is promoting. But even these complex discriminations say nothing of whether these voices are speaking seriously or tongue in cheek or humorously or ironically. When we allow for the permutations and combinations that such possibilities provide, it becomes obvious that it would require an oppressively complicated schema, virtually a self-parodying critical apparatus, to do justice to the narrative situation in many passages of *Ulysses.*

And yet, amazingly, the engaged reader is for the most part quite capable of responding to and enjoying these nuances. I return, then, to where I began, in my introduction, with the acknowledgment that, fortunately, our reading of any rich text is richer than the categories and labels that we foist upon it. This was something I had heard by the hearing of my ear, but now know by the seeing of my eye to be true of Joyce's wonderful novel.

Notes

1. Literary Mimesis and the Realism of the Novel

1. From a letter to Richard Holt Hutton, 8 August 1863, in *The George Eliot Letters*, 4:97. Eliot is speaking of *Romola*, which preceded *Middlemarch* by several years. For Isaiah Berlin's famous evocation of this inherently unformalizable medium that arises from "the permanent relationships of things, and the universal texture of human life" (67), prompted mainly by Tolstoy's *War and Peace*, see the long final paragraph of section 6 of *The Hedgehog and the Fox* (65–71).

2. While all fictive texts evoke a world, some do so more deftly or more richly than others. When we praise the economy of the *Dubliners* stories, we acknowledge Joyce's selection of precisely those details that evoke a rich and detailed picture in the mind of the reader. Perhaps the most famous statement about this is Ernest Hemingway's: "If a writer of prose knows enough about what he is writing about he may omit things that he knows and the reader, if the writer is writing truly enough, will have a feeling of those things as strongly as though the writer had stated them. The dignity of movement of an iceberg is due to only one-eighth of it being above water" (*Death in the Afternoon*, 192).

William Trevor has said, "What interests me most of all about writing is the relationship between you and the unknown reader and the sort of link you have with that person, *the way in which that person actually picks up something which isn't in the story*" ("PW Interviews," 81; my emphasis).

3. We appreciate more fully our capacity to construct a whole fictive world from the text-on-the-page if we consider the unsuccessful attempts of artificial intelligence researchers to render explicit what is involved in such simple tasks as ordering a meal in a restaurant or preparing breakfast for someone—or reading a children's story. It appears that while very complex cognitive processes, such as solving mathematical problems or playing chess, are formalizable, the most ordinary social activities are not. And yet even a young child has assimilated and can reenact an astounding array of implicit contexts and information for a wide variety of life situations.

For a solid, convincing discussion of this issue, see Hubert L. Dreyfus, *What Computers STILL Can't Do* (1992), esp. x–lii and 57–62. Dreyfus speaks specifically of "the failure of attempts to program an understanding of children's stories. The programs lacked the common sense of a four-year old, and no one knew how to give them the background knowledge necessary for understanding even the simplest stories" (x).

My appreciation of the process of literary/cultural evocation has been heightened by watching my grandchildren acquire language and respond to literary texts. It is impressive how soon a child becomes able to project from a simple literary text an imaginative world so complete that it enables her to infer conditions or to raise questions about relationships not explicitly given in the work—questions about why a character did something, or even why he did not do something, which requires a fuller and more complex sense of the implicit conditions and norms of the fictive world.

Dealing with such questions makes us realize that we cannot understand any literary work without invoking psychological levels and cultural schemata that are not specified by the literal text but are nonetheless an essential part of the world of the novel, just as such levels and schemata are an integral part of any actual cultural domain.

4. Robert Champigny distinguishes historical narration from fictional, saying that, while "a historical narration is always incomplete" (i.e., there are facts and events that the given narrative does not include), "The statements of a novel are, on the contrary, complete. If a commentator *adds events,* he is acting as a would-be novelist, not as a commentator" ("Implicitness in Narrative Fiction," 988; my emphasis). But while Champigny is correct that readers cannot fabricate *totally new events* (e.g., an episode in which Bloom talks with Deasy), his describing the statements of a novel as "complete," and his focus on events, obscures and simplifies the subtle interrelationships between the fictive and the real world, for every novel consists not simply of "events" but of an entire cultural milieu.

A work such as Paul van Caspel's *Bloomers on the Liffey* continuously testifies to the extensive cultural world that we necessarily project in reading *Ulysses;* in resolving various cruxes in the novel, van Caspel draws upon an array of customs, assumptions, schemata that are nowhere explicitly given by the text. Bernard Benstock is quite right when he says that *Ulysses* "suggests events that never take place within the text, nor could possibly take place even if the text were expanded many times over" (*Narrative Con/Texts,* 127).

5. For some ingenious speculations about the circumstances and motives behind the moving of the furniture, see Hugh Kenner's "Molly's Masterstroke"; Kenner says that "Joyce was always pleased to have the foreground action he dwelt on backed up by unseen happenings we can extrapolate" (20). On the elision of the conversation in which Molly tells Bloom the time of Boylan's visit, see Frederick V. Wellington, "A Missing Conversation in *Ulysses*," and Margaret McBride, "At Four She Said" and "At Four She Said: II." Kenner explores the interdependence of the imaginative and experiential worlds in *Ulysses* more fully in "The Rhetoric of Silence"; there he says that Joyce expects us to understand that "interpenetrating the imagined world of the book is a real world our experience of which is pertinent" (383).

6. Michel Foucault, "What Is an Author?" in *Language, Counter-Memory, Practice,* 113–38. See also Roland Barthes, "The Death of the Author," in *Image—Music—Text,* 142–48.

7. Henry James says that "the air of reality (solidity of specification) seems to me to be the supreme virtue of a novel," and "the novel seems to me the most magnificent form of art" (*Theory of Fiction,* 35, 41). David Lodge, critic and

novelist, objects to a statement of Robert Scholes and Robert Kellogg in *The Nature of Narrative* about the novel "being pushed in the direction of realism while still remaining somehow a novel," by saying that "it is difficult to conceive of there being a conflict of interests between the novel and realism." Lodge further argues, "The novel supremely among literary forms has satisfied our hunger for the meaningful ordering of experience *without* denying our empirical observation of its randomness and particularity" (*Novelist at the Crossroads,* 4).

Similarly, David Goldknopf says, "Realism is the generic commitment of the novel, its contract with the reader," and that realism is "the historical commission of the novel, which came into existence as a record of the mind's circulation through the world-as-it-is." He adds that "the art of the novel is finally, by tradition and generic commitment, realistic" (*Life of the Novel,* 178, 179).

8. J. Hillis Miller says (in discussing George Eliot) that the concept of realism in fiction is "fundamentally paradoxical and contradictory" ("Narrator as General Consciousness," 80), and David Goldknopf, speaking of more recent fiction, says that "even the general sense of the word 'realism' has become increasingly obscure" (*Life of the Novel,* 179).

9. We see here a fledgling example of the stance that emerges more fully later in the century in those three great masters of what Paul Ricoeur calls the "school of suspicion"—Marx, Nietzsche, and Freud—i.e., the idea that austere minimalism is the pathway to truth and that it can be pursued only by those who are brave enough to forgo the self-indulgence of wishful (i.e., imaginative) thinking. Ricoeur explores the conflict between a hermeneutics of reductionism and demystification, as over against a hermeneutics of belief, in his *Freud and Philosophy,* esp. 32–36. For a discussion of Ricoeur's "hermeneutics of suspicion" see Don Ihde, *Hermeneutic Phenomenology: The Philosophy of Paul Ricoeur,* chap. 6.

10. J. Hillis Miller makes the same point about Eliot in "The Narrator as General Consciousness," 80–85. Quoting from the famous chap. 17 of *Adam Bede* ("In Which the Story Pauses a Little"), Miller shows that Eliot's understanding of realism at that time (i.e., 1859) involved "the faithful representing of commonplace things," and the aim "to give a faithful account of men and things as they have mirrored themselves in my mind. . . . The mirror is doubtless defective; the outlines will sometimes be disturbed, the reflection faint or confused; but I feel as much bound to tell you as precisely as I can what that reflection is, as if I were in the witness-box narrating my experience on oath" (81). Miller then says, "The puzzles of realism in *Adam Bede* are resolved in *Middlemarch* by the frank recognition that a novel is the world turned inside out and taken into a subjective realm by something like that 'inward mirror' of which Meredith speaks" (82). He quotes from chap. 16 of *Middlemarch,* where Eliot describes the narrator's mind as an "ideally illuminated space [in which] the imagination reveals subtle actions inaccessible by any sort of lens" (82).

11. For example, Ezra Pound's various critical dicta show his confusion (or at least his ambivalence) about these issues; on the one hand, he proclaims that "[Art] means constatation of fact. It presents. It does not comment," or "the arts, litera-

ture, poesy, are a science, just as chemistry is a science. . . . Bad art is inaccurate art. It is art that makes false reports." But at other times, when he was less under the influence of the scientistic paradigm and more attuned to the inherently interpretive nature of literature, he describes art as above all the "expression of emotional values" (all quoted in S. Schwartz, *The Matrix of Modernism*, 65–67). Schwartz tries to reconcile such comments, arguing that "Pound was actually attempting to bridge the distinction between subjective and objective domains" (67). But these and other similar statements suggest that Pound was torn between dichotomous views. Schwartz goes on to discuss Eliot's objections to "photographic" realism (174–75).

12. The term is Charles Taylor's, in *Sources of the Self*. Of the "'punctual' or 'neutral' self," he says that it "is defined in abstraction from any constitutive concerns and hence from any identity . . . . Its only constitutive property is self-awareness. This is the self that Hume set out to find and, predictably, failed to find" (49). Taylor elaborates in chap. 9, "Locke's Punctual Self," 159–76. For Hume's argument that personal identity is illusory and fictitious, see book I, part IV, section vi of his *Treatise of Human Nature* (1739).

2. Point of View, Narrative Voice, Authorial Omniscience

1. As early as 1955 Norman Friedman's *PMLA* essay "Point of View in Fiction: The Development of a Critical Concept" listed a large number of relevant books and articles; his essay is still useful for tracing the historical roots and the early development of the concept. Friedman shows that critical concern with point of view has been inextricably linked with the assumption that authorial effacement— i.e., showing rather than telling—is desirable. Of the many books on this subject, those of most use to me have been Wayne Booth, *The Rhetoric of Fiction* (1961, 1983); Dorrit Cohn, *Transparent Minds* (1978); Seymour Chatman, *Story and Discourse* (1978); and Roy Pascal, *The Dual Voice* (1977). Monika Fludernik's *The Fictions of Language and the Languages of Fiction* (1993), which is a very broadly based study of free indirect discourse, contains a comprehensive bibliography (465–523).

2. Consider, for example, (fictional) novelist Philip Quarles's statement in his Notebook recorded at the opening of chap. 22 of Huxley's *Point Counter Point*: "The novelist can assume the god-like creative privilege and simply elect to consider the events of the story in their various aspects—emotional, scientific, economic, religious, metaphysical, etc. He will modulate from one to the other—as, from the aesthetic to the physico-chemical aspect of things, from the religious to the physiological or financial. But perhaps this is a too tyrannical imposition of the author's will. Some people would think so. But need the author be so retiring? I think we're a bit too squeamish about these personal appearances nowadays."

Similarly, E. M. Forster in *Aspects of the Novel*, after talking about the special prerogatives of the novelist over the dramatist, says, "'How did the writer know that?' it is sometimes said. 'What's his standpoint? He is not being consistent, he's shifting his point of view from the limited to the omniscient, and now he's edging back again'. Questions like these have too much the atmosphere of the law courts about them. All that matters to the reader is whether the shifting of attitude and the secret life are convincing . . ." (84).

Perhaps the most vociferous authorial protest at such critical categories and constraints is D. H. Lawrence's in the "Wie es Ihnen Gefällt" chapter of *Aaron's Rod*. After exploring Aaron's preconscious feelings for several pages, Lawrence explains that Aaron was a musician and these are word-translations of what he felt, and then says, "Don't grumble at me then, gentle reader, and swear at me that this damned fellow wasn't half clever enough to think all these smart things, and realise all these fine-drawn-out subtleties. You are quite right, he wasn't, yet it all resolved itself in him as I say, and it is for you to prove that it didn't" (164).

3. In "Illusion, Point of View, and Modern Novel-Criticism," Fogle says that the concept of fictional illusion "is a principle, a living law, a genuine critical issue, and an end in itself. Point of view [by contrast] is a rule, a particular application of the principle or a means of law enforcement, the appropriateness of which must be carefully considered" (350). Leo Bersani proclaims, "point-of-view analysis is the literary-criticism version of hide-and-seek. It is the paranoid response to what might be called the ontological irreducibility of voice in literature to location and identities" ("Against *Ulysses*," 6).

4. On the term *implied author*, see the passages in *The Rhetoric of Fiction* indexed under "Implied author." Chatman extends Booth's discriminations in his *Story and Discourse*, especially chap. 4.

5. In *"Ulysses": The Mechanics of Meaning* (1982), chap. 5 and "Ten Years After Thoughts." I discuss this more fully below, in chap. 3. For reasons explained there, I find *presenter* a more appropriate term than *arranger*. I will characterize these secondary narrators in subsequent chapters.

6. That other critics do the same suggests that they too find considerable congruity among these entities—or may simply be an acknowledgement that all of them stem from Joyce. Hugh Kenner, in *Joyce's Voices*, often makes no distinction between Joyce and the narrator (29, 30–31). Arnold Goldman speaks in successive sentences of "the voice of the narrator" and of "Joyce describing Stephen thinking" (*Joyce Paradox*, 79). He also refers to the *narrator* of the "Cyclops" episode, but then says that *Joyce* interrupts the flow of the narrative to give us the interpolated passages (92). Ellmann uses the term *narrator* to refer to the first-person speaker of the "Cyclops" episode, to the voice of the first half of "Nausicaa," and to the presenter of "Eumaeus" (*JJII*, 357), and then says that a passage in "Calypso" might be supposed to be Joyce talking for Bloom (363).

7. In "Joyce versus Joyce: Moderns and Post-Moderns," 20. See also the section of Michael Levenson's *Genealogy of Modernism* entitled "The modernist narrator on the Victorian sailing ship" (1–10), where he discusses "the use of the narrator as part of the subjectivist perspective" (3) in Conrad's *The Nigger of the "Narcissus."* In this discussion Levenson criticizes George Eliot's mode of presentation in *Middlemarch*, saying, "The narrator is not another character, but a disembodied presence, moving freely over the dramatic scene, and granted prerogatives not

allowed to mere mortals. Without becoming implicated in the recorded scene, the narrator becomes an assimilating, amalgamating force who makes transparent the opacities between individuals, who lets moral evaluation mingle freely with description, who sees hidden thoughts quite as clearly as natural landscapes, who hears distinctly the faintest whispers of introspection" (8). Turning to Conrad, he says, "The rejection of omniscience was a complicated matter." (I discuss these claims of Levitt and Levenson in the first chapter of *The Antimodernism of Joyce's "Portrait."*)

J. Hillis Miller, in "The Narrator as General Consciousness," says, "The theological overtones of the word 'omniscient' suggest that such a narrator is like a God, standing outside the time and space of the action, looking down on the characters with the detachment of a sovereign spectator who sees all, knows all, judges all, from a distance" (63)—but he argues that the implication is inaccurate for many Victorian novels.

Similarly, Bruce Morissette says, "It was Flaubert who sought to destroy the omniscient narrator who knew everything about everyone in his book, who, in his God-like way, described both the exterior and interior of all his scenes and characters. . . . It was his effort to remove *himself* from the narrative that led Flaubert to the discovery that if the omniscient *author* is eliminated, the only remaining basis for the 'point of view' that justifies the text has to be the *consciousness* of someone: a character in the novel, or a plausible observer placed at the realistic level of the action within the novel" ("The New Novel in France," 4).

8. James Weber Linn and Houghton Wells Taylor say, "The frankly omniscient story-teller has well nigh disappeared from modern fiction" (*Foreword to Fiction*, 1935, 33). But the crucial word here is *frankly*; what is missing from modern fiction is not the omniscient perspective, but its traditional trappings. Attention to this point reveals that most modern novels employ some significant form of omniscience, often involving overt exposition/interpretation about characters or themes and frequently involving evaluations and qualitative descriptions that cannot be attributed to a character. This is true of much of the work of Joseph Conrad, E. M. Forster, Dorothy Richardson, Virginia Woolf (see the following note), D. H. Lawrence, Theodore Dreiser, Stephen Crane, F. Scott Fitzgerald, and William Faulkner. And according to John E. Tilford, Jr., it is true even of so austere a text as James's *The Ambassadors;* see his "James the Old Intruder."

Moreover, Robert Humphrey points out that stream-of-consciousness technique "is description by an omniscient author" (*Stream of Consciousness*, 33), and Dorrit Cohn concurs with him on this point (*TM*, 271). For a discussion of modernist omniscience, see Barbara K. Olson, *Authorial Divinity in the Twentieth Century* (1997), esp. chaps. 1 and 4.

9. J. Hillis Miller recognizes omniscience in *Mrs. Dalloway*, but argues, "In *Mrs. Dalloway* nothing exists for the narrator which does not first exist in the mind of one of the characters, whether it be a thought or a thing"; he acknowledges, however, that "The sermon against 'Proportion' and her formidable sister 'Conversion' is one of the rare cases where the narrator speaks for his own view,

or even Virginia Woolf's own view, rather than by way of the mind of one of the characters" ("Virginia Woolf's All Souls' Day," 104).

10. Similarly, in his "Three Problems of Fictional Form," Miller refers to "that public mind for which the omniscient narrator is a spokesman" (31).

11. Several comments quoted by Richard Stang in *The Theory of the Novel in England, 1850–1870* support Miller's claim about these writers' evocation of a public mind. Charles Kingsley, for example, defended his own narrative practice by saying that "the author's business is . . . to speak, if he can, the thoughts of many hearts, to put into words for his readers what they would have said for themselves if they could" (qtd. in Stang, 99).

Trollope in *Framley Parsonage* similarly called himself the "leader of the chorus," and Stang says, "His own comments on the action become in some sense impersonal because they are not merely his own individual opinions; they belong to all right-thinking readers, just as the comments of the Greek chorus were not merely personal opinions of the playwright" (99).

In the passage I quoted above, Miller attributes belief in a "transindividual mind" to *Victorian* novelists; interestingly, in the opening of the next chapter in *The Form of Victorian Fiction*, Miller says of the collective mind, "That mind, as James Joyce says of a different kind of narrator, 'flow[s] round and round the persons and the actions like a vital sea' [*Portrait*, 215]. It enters into those persons and lives their experiences from within" (93). Regrettably, Miller does not develop this idea, nor does he explain what he means by "a different kind of narrator." He does, however make a case for a collective mentality in *Mrs. Dalloway,* saying, "Like the omniscient narrators of *Vanity Fair, Middlemarch,* or *The Last Chronicle of Barset,* the omniscient narrator of *Mrs. Dalloway* is a general consciousness or social mind which rises into existence out of the collective mental experience of the individual human beings in the story" ("Virginia Woolf's All Souls' Day," 105).

Similarly, David Lodge acknowledges that omniscience may reflect an omniscient deity, but adds, "In the realistic novel the third-person omniscient mode is more often used to assert or imply the existence of society, or of history, than of heaven or hell" (*Modes of Modern Writing,* 51).

12. For examples of the strange idea that Joyce's fictions wrote themselves, or are written by Stephen Dedalus, see Shari Benstock, "Who Killed Cock Robin? The Sources of Free Indirect Style in *Ulysses*" (1980); Shari Benstock and Bernard Benstock, "The Benstock Principle" (1982); and John Paul Riquelme, *Teller and Tale in Joyce's Fictions* (1983), esp. 51–52 and 61–64.

In the 1980 essay Shari Benstock says, "The technical devices that collectively become the means for rendering plot and establishing tone and point of view *are generated from subject matter and context* rather than imposed from above (or behind) by an authorial presence hovering close to the narrative product," and of "Aeolus," "These headlines arise in the text of *Ulysses* as they do in most newspapers, *from the context of the day's news*" (261, 271; my emphases).

The 1982 essay articulates "The Benstock Principle": "*Fictional texts that ex-*

ploit free indirect speech (the narrational mode most common to *Ulysses*) *establish the contextual supremacy of subject matter, which influences the direction, tone, pace, point of view, and method of narration"* (18).

3. Authorial Voice and Point of View in *Ulysses*

1. Discussions of this issue—chronologically listed by author and publication date—include the following (see the bibliography for full citations): Arnold Goldman, 1966; David Hayman, 1970; rev. ed., 1982; Richard Ellmann, 1972; Erwin R. Steinberg, 1973; Wolfgang Iser, 1974; Ben D. Kimpel, 1975; Marilyn French, 1976; William B. Warner, 1977; Hugh Kenner, 1978; "Narrative in *Ulysses*," 1979; Shari Benstock, 1980; Roy K. Gottfried, 1980; Hugh Kenner, 1980; rev. ed. 1987; Karen Lawrence, 1981; Marilyn French, 1982; Brook Thomas, 1982; Shari Benstock and Bernard Benstock, 1982; John Paul Riquelme, 1983; Erwin R. Steinberg, 1985; Monika Fludernik, "Narrative . . . in *Ulysses*," 1986; Brian McHale, 1990; James McMichael, 1991, esp. chap. 1; and John Somer, 1994.

2. For a discussion of this division among critics of *Ulysses,* see Stanley Sultan's "The Adventures of *Ulysses* in Our World." Critics who have treated the style of *Ulysses*—or its concern with its own narrative processes—as its subject matter include several of those listed in the preceding note, but especially Michael Groden, 1977; Karen Lawrence, 1981; Brook Thomas, 1982; John Paul Riquelme, 1983; and several contributors to D. Attridge and D. Ferrer, *Post-Structuralist Joyce: Essays from the French* (1984). Wolfgang Iser has said point-blank: "In spectacular fashion, *Ulysses* puts an end to representation" (*"Ulysses* and the Reader,"* 1).

Groden's *"Ulysses" in Progress* argues that Joyce's interest shifted away from the "novelistic" elements of plot and character during the composition of *Ulysses,* but as his account progresses, Groden continually defers the time when Joyce supposedly lost interest in these elements, and in fact he detects a novelistic interest in vividness, dramatization, the characters' personal histories, and the web of realistic details even in the very last phase of composition (see, e.g., 195 and 196–97).

Monika Fludernik in "*Ulysses* and Joyce's Change of Artistic Aims" comes to the opposite conclusion from Groden—i.e., "that Joyce did not abruptly change his intentions at any point during the writing of *Ulysses,* but that he gradually elaborated a plan, which had existed from the start" (186). She reaches this same conclusion from a different angle in "Narrative and Its Development in *Ulysses*," 36.

Ellmann notes, "Some critics have asserted that Joyce changed his plans radically after writing the first half of the book," but he disagrees (*JJII,* 790), explaining his views in an essay-review entitled "The New *Ulysses*" (1986).

John Somer argues that "the arranger is the dominant character in *Ulysses* and that the decisions it makes and the actions it takes constitute the essential plot of the novel, a plot measured not by a narrator's developing portrait of reality, but by an arranger's growing mastery of style" ("The Self-Reflexive Arranger," 76 and 78–79).

Though the idea that *Ulysses* is about its own styles still represents the main current of critical opinion, there are voices of dissent among contemporary critics. David Trotter says, "The orthodox view, now, is that [in reading *Ulysses*] we should suspend our appetite for relevance, and simply take pleasure in the hyperbole, the excess, the 'play' of language. My argument is that the appetite for relevance is not easily suspended, as Joyce very well knew, and that our response to stylistic excess is likely to involve not only pleasure but fatigue, boredom, frustration and, yes, disgust" (*The English Novel in History*, 219).

Later Trotter says of a "textual" (i.e., reflexive) reading of *Ulysses*, "Its major shortcoming is that it drastically underestimates the strength of our desire for relevance, and Joyce's recognition of that desire. 'Textual' readings imagine a reader marvelling at, or ecstatically dispersed among, kaleidoscopic combinations and recombinations of language. I imagine a reader whose appetite for relevance is fed by the initial style, and frustrated by its successors. Joyce was as interested in the appetite as in the means by which it might be frustrated" (295).

3. The term *initial style* derives from Joyce's letter to Harriet Shaw Weaver of 6 August 1919. After explaining some of the intricacies of the style of "Sirens," he says, "I understand that you may begin to regard the various styles of the episodes with dismay and prefer the initial style much as the wanderer did who longed for the rock of Ithaca" (*Sel Lts*, 242).

4. In a section of *The Rhetoric of Fiction* entitled "The Author's Many Voices" (16–20), Wayne Booth emphasizes how pervasively the author exists in his fictional creation, concluding, "though the author can to some extent choose his disguises, he can never choose to disappear" (20).

Leon Edel quotes Henry James as saying that the artist is present in every page of every book from which he tries to eliminate himself (*Stuff of Sleep and Dreams*, 20). Elsewhere James says, "We take for granted by the general law of fiction a primary author [e.g., implied author], take him so much for granted that we forget him in proportion as he works upon us, and that he works upon us most in fact by making us forget him" (*Theory of Fiction*, 253; cf. also 174–80).

Christopher Butler says that even in reading postmodernist, reflexive novels— Barth or Robbe-Grillet, e.g.—we are reminded "not of the author's disappearance but of his varying status, and of the cunning ways in which his hand may be hidden" ("Joyce and the Displaced Author," 71).

Accordingly, many critics have acknowledged Joyce's pervasive presence in *Ulysses*. Marilyn French says, "Whatever role he momentarily plays, Joyce, in *Ulysses*, is probably the most intrusive author ever to write a piece of fiction" (*Book as World*, 267); Hugh Kenner says, "Joyce, let us make no mistake, is always present in *Ulysses*, and no talk of that dyad of technicians, the self-effacing narrator and the mischievous Arranger, should permit us wholly to forget that fact" (*Ulysses*, 1987, 68–69); and John Paul Riquelme argues similarly in "Enjoying Invisibility," 22–24.

5. See, for example, Phillip Herring's claim that Joyce "maintain[s] a consistent moral neutrality in his novel" (*Joyce's "Ulysses" Notesheets*, 15)—surprising since the statement occurs in his discussion of "Cyclops" and seems to contradict Herring's own observation that "most of the notes for 'Cyclops' ridicule Fenianism, Ireland, Catholicism, and, above all, the Establishment" (16). David Fuller, working from this same material and even citing Herring, says, "That Joyce intended the ["Cyclops"] episode to have moral meanings of the kind his letters identify in *Dubliners* is clear from his preparatory notesheets" (*JJ's "Ulysses,"* 25, 109).

In spite of the skepticism of avant-garde critics, there have always been readers who have recognized that *Ulysses* does involve values—among them Frank Budgen, Ellsworth Mason, Richard Ellmann (e.g., *JJII*, 371–72, 379), Stanley Sultan, S. L. Goldberg, Marilyn French, Louis D. Rubin, Jr., Dominic Manganiello, G. J. Watson, and others. And it is not surprising that a new generation of critics endorses an enantiodromic swing away from the earlier claims of Joyce's high-modernist moral neutrality or indifference, to the idea that, far from paring his fingernails, Joyce in *Ulysses* has a distinct (postmodernist?) cultural/political agenda—e.g., Mark Harman's "Joyce and Kafka" or Enda Duffy's *The Subaltern "Ulysses."*

Generally, those critics who see *Ulysses* as involving stylistic relativism, or as "self-reflexive," either elide value issues or see the novel as relativistic morally as well as stylistically. For critics who would deny any moral aspect to *Ulysses*, "Cyclops" is often a stumbling block, since it so clearly elicits a judgment against the citizen and his chauvinism.

6. In *The Antimodernism of Joyce's "Portrait"* (42–45) I discuss Joyce's concern for the *potential* of his characters (and his fellow citizens) as the fulcrum for all of his value judgments. When he judges against institutions (church or state), attitudes (chauvinism, sentimentality), modes of discourse (journalese, the "Nausicaa" style), it is because they inhibit or paralyze the individual's potential.

7. My terminology here obviously reflects David Hayman's "arranger," but I prefer "presenter" because "arranger" implies that the persona has authority over the events and interrelationships in the novel, whereas "presenter" confines his authority to the mode of stylistic presentation.

In the 1970 edition of *"Ulysses": The Mechanics of Meaning*, Hayman described the role of the arranger briefly, but in terms ascribing more authority to it than I would to the presenter. For example, he sees the arranger as responsible for interrelationships among the episodes as well as for the fact that both Bloom and Stephen are keyless and for various other "givens" of the novel that I would attribute to the author (1970, 72–73; 1982, 86).

Hayman also argues, "By the book's second half he [the narrator] will have become a creature of many faces but a single impulse, a larger version of his characters with a larger field of vision and many more perceptions to control, the figure I am calling the arranger" (1970, 78; 1982, 93). These are more extensive roles than I would assign the various presenters, who are confined within individual episodes and whose scope is limited to the style of the presentation.

These quoted passages are identical in the two editions, but in 1982 Hayman adds a section titled "Ten Years After Thoughts" (122–36), in which he acknowledges the "problem of the extent of the arranger's role in *Ulysses*" (123). He characterizes the arranger more fully, and assigns him a more extensive role, saying that "we should probably think of the arranging presence as subtly interpenetrating the fabric of the narrative at a variety of points and in a variety of ways" (124). For a critique of the vagueness of the term and a discussion of Hayman's considerable extension of the arranger's role in his 1982 edition, see Christine O'Neill, *Too Fine a Point*, 117–22.

4. The Initial Style of *Ulysses*

1. Most critics assume that Joyce aspired to effacement and objectivity—see, for example, the discussion later in this chapter of Stephen's famous claim in *Portrait* that the author is "refined out of existence." Brian McHale, in "Constructing (Post)Modernism," assumes there is a dualism between our mobile mind and a stable world "outside consciousness" and that Joyce accepts this dualism and dramatizes it through his techniques (see esp. 3–5).

2. Many thinkers have recognized the pervasiveness of the Cartesian dualisms in modern Western thought, and the costs they have exacted. Charles Taylor's *Sources of the Self* provides an extensive, cogent analysis of these issues, showing the modern Western provincialism of these dualistic ideas that seem to us so absolute, and detailing the depleting effects they have had on our understanding of self and world (see *Sources of the Self*, esp. 114).

Fredric Jameson speaks of the gap between public and private, social and psychological, society and individual, that maims our existence and paralyzes our thinking about time and change (*The Political Unconscious*, 20). I explore these ideas more fully in a manuscript in progress, *The Roots of Modernism: A Study in Cultural Temperament*.

3. Christopher Butler discusses Joyce's resistance to certain contemporary ideas, saying, "His philosophical allegiances are to the pre-moderns, for example to Aquinas" ("Joyce, Modernism, and Post-Modernism," 265). And in 1917 Joyce told Georges Borach, "The greatest thinker of all times, in my opinion, is Aristotle" (qtd. in W. Potts, *Portraits of the Artist*, 71).

Joyce's rejection of empiricist/Enlightenment thinking in favor of an Aristotelian/Thomistic (or even a mystical) tradition has been argued by many scholars, including Robert Boyle in *James Joyce's Pauline Vision* (1978), Beryl Schlossman in *Joyce's Catholic Comedy of Language* (1985), Cordell Yee in *The Word According to James Joyce* (1997), and Colleen Jaurretche in *The Sensual Philosophy: Joyce and the Aesthetics of Mysticism* (1997).

4. Erwin R. Steinberg, in his detailed and thoughtful *Stream of Consciousness and Beyond in "Ulysses,"* consistently describes the presentation as omniscient; see, for example, the section entitled "Omniscient Author's Sentences in Proteus and Lestrygonians," 92–96 (cf. also 251, 252, 253). Michael Groden, in *"Ulysses" in Progress,* speaks repeatedly of Joyce's omniscience, expressed in excursions into the characters' minds, in the Homeric parallels, the "Aeolus" subheads, etc. (32, 34, 37, 40, et passim). John Somer says pointedly of the opening sentence of the novel that it "is the work of an omniscient narrator" ("The Self-Reflexive Arranger," 71). And Beckson and Ganz, in their *Literary Terms: A Dictionary,* exemplify omniscient narration by citing *Ulysses* (3rd ed., 1989, 210).

But other critics—expressing the disdain of omniscience discussed above in chap. 2—describe the authorial voice as "objective" or deny the existence of any such voice or narrator. See, for example, Seymour Chatman, *Story and Discourse,* 155; David Fuller, *JJ's "Ulysses,"* 37; H. A. Kelly, "Consciousness," 5; and Melvin Friedman, *Stream of Consciousness,* 224.

5. Surprisingly, Erwin R. Steinberg (though acknowledging an omniscient author in the episode) sees this last passage in "Lestrygonians" (*U,* 8.937–1027) as a violation of technique, complaining that "even for a few lines after Bloom reappears the reader does not resume his position in Bloom's mind" and puzzling "that Joyce should violate the technique of an entire chapter because it was convenient" (*SoC&B,* 111–12). But we must presume what Joyce does here to be intentional and ask ourselves why he does it. Rather than an inadvertent "violation," such a passage is clear evidence that Joyce's narrator is not simply a figural spokesperson but is omniscient.

6. Bernard DeVoto comes close to this austere standard when he suggests that descriptive passages in a novel should always relate to an individual's perspective, and he disdains passages that "set the mood" or "create atmosphere," saying, "But what is a mood, what is atmosphere, *apart from someone who is feeling it?*" (*World of Fiction,* 240; my emphasis). DeVoto's nominalism is also reflected in his saying that in the opening of "Telemachus" we do not see the scene through Buck, and so the reader "is still neutral, waiting for the means of perception to be established" (230), which is done when Stephen emerges on the scene—essentially similar to the claims Michael Levenson makes that were noted above and in chap. 2. DeVoto's strictures clearly exemplify modernist skepticism about any collective mind or psychic medium such as I am claiming Joyce intentionally evokes in *Ulysses.*

7. See Brivic's "Joyce's Consubstantiality," 149. Among the many critics who have presumed this aim to be Joyce's are Robert Humphrey (*Stream of Consciousness,* 15); Erwin R. Steinberg (*SoC&B,* 258–59); and Melvin Friedman (*Stream of Consciousness,* 224).

8. Baruch Hochman says that *Ulysses* dramatizes "the slipperiness not only of individual consciousness, but of the communal consciousness as well" ("Beyond Portraiture," 199). Robert M. Adams, noting how the characters' thoughts and personalities interpenetrate, says, "When other people's words turn up in Bloom's

monologues, or his in theirs, it isn't a 'dropping out of character' but a deliberate dropping of character *into some other continuum*" ("Hades," 110; my emphasis).

Sheldon Brivic discusses the "Author" in *Ulysses* in ways that sound very much like a collective mind in his *The Veil of Signs*, esp. in chap. 2, "The Author as Other." Later Brivic says, "The lines Stephen and Bloom share throughout the novel and the predictions in which they are involved, like the mythological and structural references that pop up in people's minds . . . serve to make it clear that the individuals are part of a larger mental continuum" (107); and the idea of a "multimind" is the main theme of Brivic's *Joyce the Creator* (1985).

David Hayman makes a number of observations about *Ulysses* (often in contrast to *A Portrait*) that recognize some such communal element in the novel; see his *MM*, 1982, 87–88. But in spite of such acknowledgements of a psychic milieu, this dimension of the book has never been taken as seriously as it deserves.

9. Sheldon Brivic speculates on the many elements common to the minds of Stephen and Bloom in *Joyce between Freud and Jung*, 170–73, and his *Joyce the Creator* has a lengthy list of "Synchronicities in *Ulysses*" (145–53). David Fuller also discusses the many links between Stephen and Bloom; see his *JJ's "Ulysses,"* 31 and 109, nn. 4 and 5. Craig Smith points out more than a dozen links between the thoughts of Bloom and Gerty in "Nausicaa" ("Twilight in Dublin," 634).

Joyce was familiar with "Magic," in which Yeats expresses his view of the social or collective psyche under three doctrines: "(1) That the borders of our mind are ever shifting, and that many minds can flow into one another, as it were, and create or reveal a single mind, a single energy. (2) That the borders of our memory are as shifting, and that our memories are a part of one great memory, the memory of Nature herself. (3) That this great mind and great memory can be evoked by symbols" (*Essays and Introductions*, 28; Joyce's Trieste library contained the 1905 edition of *Ideas of Good and Evil*, which contains this essay; see Ellmann, *Consciousness of Joyce*, 134).

Frank Budgen in his "Further Recollections of James Joyce" says that "it is sometimes forgotten that in his early years in Dublin Joyce lived among the believers and adepts in magic gathered round the poet Yeats," and Budgen says that Joyce talked with him about ideas in "Magic" (*JJMU*, 361). Craig Carver agrees that Joyce knew Yeats's essay and explores Joyce's interest in a Universal Memory in "James Joyce and the Theory of Magic."

10. Stephen's description of the effaced author as "flowing round and round the persons and the action like a vital sea" has affinities with Virginia Woolf's famous injunction that the novelist capture the "semi-transparent envelope surrounding us from the beginning of consciousness to the end." Woolf's statement deserves quoting, both because the novelistic quality that she calls for suggests a circumambient collective psyche, and because she recognizes this very quality in Joyce's work: "Life is not a series of gig lamps symmetrically arranged; but a luminous halo, a semi-transparent envelope surrounding us from the beginning of consciousness to the end. Is it not the task of the novelist to convey this varying, this unknown and uncircumscribed spirit, whatever aberration or complexity it

may display, with as little mixture of the alien and external as possible? . . . It is, at any rate, in some such fashion as this that we seek to define the quality which distinguishes the work of several younger writers, among whom Mr. James Joyce is the most notable, from that of their predecessors" ("Modern Fiction," in *The Common Reader,* 155).

Three sentences later Woolf refers specifically to *Ulysses,* "now appearing in the *Little Review*"; by April 1919, the date of Woolf's essay, only the first eight episodes of *Ulysses* had appeared ("Aeolus" lacking the headlines), so whatever "uncircumscribed spirit" Woolf detected in the novel was evoked by the initial style of the novel.

11. Some of Joyce's revisions of the opening episodes involve replacing distinctive terms that the reader might attribute to a persona. For example, an earlier version of *U,* 1.123 read, "He folded his razor and with the feeling *polpastrelli* of the fingers of his right hand touched his jaws and chin." Joyce revised this to read, "He folded his razor neatly and with stroking palps of fingers felt the smooth skin." In the earlier version, *polpastrelli* leaps out at the reader and attracts attention to itself; the revised version by contrast deftly conveys Mulligan's action (see *Lts,* 1:109 for the letter of 6 December 1917 to Claude Sykes detailing this change).

12. See chap. 2 of Kenner's *Joyce's Voices.* The device is by no means unique to Joyce. Dorrit Cohn cites a 1922 essay by Leo Spitzer in which he described the phenomenon of "stylistic contagion," "when he discovered that a narrator's style is sometimes peppered with elements of figural dialect or vulgarity" (*TM,* 33). And it is not easy to draw a line between this and what Cohn calls "narrated monologue" (i.e., free indirect discourse—13, 107, 109), which she describes as "the technique for rendering a character's thought in his own idiom while maintaining the third-person reference and the basic tense of narration" (100).

13. Anthony Burgess characterizes what he unabashedly calls traits of *Joyce's* style in *Ulysses* in "The Joyce Sentence," in *Joysprick;* see esp. 69–76, where he discusses the diction and syntax of the opening lines of the novel, and of passages in "Proteus," "Calypso," and "Lotus Eaters." Burgess brilliantly demonstrates a distinctive Joycean quality in these passages, even when they present quite different persons and situations—and even in "Wandering Rocks," where a secondary narrator has largely taken over the organization or arrangement of the chapter, but cannot be credited with the quality of all of the prose.

Philip Toynbee expresses a common view that Joyce has no style of his own: "The mature Joyce differed from his predecessors in refusing to have any single personal style" ("Study of James Joyce's *Ulysses,*" 252)—and yet in the same paragraph he calls a passage from "Telemachus" "Joyce's *only* definite personal style"! But if we turn aside from the shibboleths of Joyce's effacement and objectivity and follow Burgess's brilliant lead, we will discover in the early episodes of *Ulysses* a style that deserves to be called Joyce's own.

14. Kenner says that "while the first voice [of "Telemachus"] attends to the chapter's housekeeping, a second narrative voice is uttering passages like the fol-

lowing: "Woodshadows floated silently by through the morning peace from the stairhead seaward where he gazed . . ." (*Joyce's Voices*, 71). But in spite of the third-person presentation, and of Kenner's explicit caveat a few sentences later— "These thoughts of woodshadows floating are not Stephen's, not quite"— Stephen, not a secondary narrator, is the source of the images and cadence of the passage; "woodshadows" comes directly from Stephen's extended reflection on "the shadow of the wood" in the Yeats poem Mulligan has just sung (literal woodshadows are not possible at the Martello tower).

Others who have detected the eruption of the secondary narrator in these early episodes include Dermot Kelly and John Somer. I reject this claim, both because I believe that such passages involve coloring of the primary narrative voice by local conditions or lie fully within the range of the primary narrator's deftness of language, unusual syntax, etc., and because these passages are characterized by a sympathetic tone rather than the irony that marks the secondary voice in its earliest clear manifestations—i.e., in "Aeolus," "Scylla and Charybdis," and "Wandering Rocks."

15. Others who describe the style in similarly fragmented terms include Brian McHale, "Constructing (Post)Modernism," 4; H. A. Kelly, "Consciousness," 9– 10; Michael Groden, *"Ulysses" in Progress*, 15; Derek Bickerton, "Modes of Interior Monologue," 237, and "James Joyce and the Development of Interior Monologue," 45; David Fuller, *JJ's "Ulysses,"* 37–38; Jerry Dibble, "Stephen's Aesthetic and Joyce's Art," 37; Melvin Friedman, *Stream of Consciousness*, 223–25; David Hayman, *MM*, 1982, 84; David Trotter, *The English Novel in History*, 98; and John Somer, "Self-Reflexive Narrator," 71.

16. I must put "interior monologue" into quotation marks, because the first-person aspect of Joyce's initial style is so blended with other modes that simply to label it "interior monologue" is seriously misleading. Only in "Penelope" does Joyce use unalloyed interior monologue—and there (as we shall see in chap. 5) he reveals the limitations of that technique.

17. A few critics have described the method of *Ulysses* as essentially similar to or continuous with that of *Portrait*—e.g., Robert Ryf, *A New Approach to Joyce*, 94–97; and Melvin Friedman, *Stream of Consciousness*, 217. But the differences are significant and raise valid questions about why Joyce develops a new technique in *Ulysses*. Michael Groden notes that the introduction of interior monologue is "the major technical difference between *A Portrait* and *Ulysses*," but says only that it "adds an entirely new dimension to the characterization of Stephen" (*"Ulysses" in Progress*, 25). Zack Bowen says that the stream-of-consciousness technique as Joyce uses it in *Ulysses* "allows Joyce a freedom to approximate the human mind, which a third-person narration would not do" (*"Ulysses,"* 434).

18. Others who acknowledge that the first-person mode in *Ulysses* involves preverbal experience include Bernard DeVoto (*World of Fiction*, 233), Seymour Chatman (*Story and Discourse*, 154–55), and Arnold Goldman (*Joyce Paradox*, 79).

19. Erwin R. Steinberg demonstrates that the associative patterns within the psychic flow of Stephen, Bloom, and Molly are not simply verbal. They are gov-

erned by relationships such as similarity, contiguity, and recentness; by grammatical categories; and by memories (see esp. chap. 7, "Patterns of Association," in *SoC&B*). Patrick Colm Hogan, in his *Joyce, Milton, and the Theory of Influence*, also discusses the associative links at work within the characters' minds. Asserting, "There are many sorts of associations that Joyce implies in the course of the novel" (116), Hogan lists semantics, sound similarities, perception, modes of empirical knowledge, and associations determined by the characters' "abiding concerns" (117).

20. Further evidence that the "interior monologue" is not purely verbal is its simulation of music. When in "Lotus Eaters" Bloom recalls "*Là ci darem la mano / La la lala la la,*" the rhythm of the second line shows that he is singing the duet to himself (*U*, 5.227). Other instances of Bloom's silently singing a melody are "Glowworm's la-amp is gleaming, love" (*U*, 8.590), and "*Comes lo-ove's old . . .*" (*U*, 5.161).

21. See Ellmann, *JJII*, 126 and 520 (drawing on Frank Budgen, *JJMU*, 94, and *Lts*, 2:409). Joyce came across Dujardin's novel in 1903; later, he inscribed a copy of *Ulysses* to Dujardin: "A Édouard Dujardin, annonciateur de la parole intérieur, le larron impénitent, JJ."

22. A number of critics have noted the qualitative differences between Dujardin's and Joyce's styles. Ellmann says that Dujardin's "novel is a soliloquy without any interposition by the author. The technique makes for some clumsiness when the hero has to describe outer circumstances, and Joyce had to modify it" (*JJII*, 126, n.). Ellmann later asserts, "The method of the *monologue intérieur* was of consequence only because Joyce saw what could be done with it" (520, n.). H. A. Kelly notes the great awkwardness and unrealism of Dujardin's method and says, "Joyce did not follow Dujardin's lead in the matter" ("Consciousness," 6); Leon Edel agrees (*Modern Psychological Novel*, 31).

On the penchant of this mode for solipsism, David Lodge notes, "It has been said that the stream-of-consciousness novel is the literary expression of solipsism . . ." (*Art of Fiction*, 42); Taylor Stoehr concurs when he describes one strand of modern art as "a mandarin art turning in on itself in stream of consciousness, wordplay, lyricism, and other symptoms of self-reflexive formalism" (*Word and Deed*, 170). But while such criticisms are appropriate to Dujardin's style, they are utterly misplaced in regard to Joyce's.

23. Arnold Goldman says, "Any particular instance not part of actual dialogue may be Stephen thinking, Joyce describing Stephen thinking, Joyce describing how Stephen might have thought, or some indeterminate state between these" (*Joyce Paradox*, 79). Derek Attridge discusses the "familiar novelistic device [in which] the narrator's style has given way to one that mimics the speech and thought patterns of the character" and says that this technique "goes by many names—free indirect discourse, narrated monologue, empathetic narrative, *style indirect libre, erlebte Rede*—and is perhaps best regarded as a cluster of techniques ranging from precisely recoverable thoughts to a slight colouring of the narrator's style by that

of the character" ("Reading Joyce," 5, 29). Fortunately, as Attridge astutely points out, "our activities as readers are usually more complex than the terms in which we represent those activities to ourselves" (5).

24. Zack Bowen discusses this paragraph similarly in his *"Ulysses,"* 433–34. Apart from minor differences in terminology and emphasis, we agree on the distinctiveness of Joyce's blend of authorial and figural perspectives in this passage. Bowen says, "Such a blend of the narrative line with interior monologue is in itself unique among Joyce's books" (434). I see this as a defining trait of the initial style.

25. For many years I tried assiduously to separate "authorial" and "figural" elements in the initial style—as the annotations and markings in my first copy of *Ulysses* attest. I was puzzled and offended by Joyce's employing such a chameleonic narrative voice and mixing the authorial and the figural so indiscriminately. Only later did I acknowledge that so pervasive a feature of the initial style must fulfill some important purpose, and begin to explore what that purpose might be. As a result I realized how effectively the narrative technique subverts various modernist dichotomies and simulates a collective psyche that surrounds and sustains the individual characters.

26. Many other critics have testified to the inextricable blending of figural and authorial perspective in *Ulysses.* Anthony Burgess observes that "Joyce's refusal to separate, by some device of punctuation or relineation, the récit from the monologue led early readers of *Ulysses* to complain," and he notes that "it is not really possible to separate the observed from the observer" (*Joysprick,* 50–51); Bernard DeVoto says of a passage presenting Stephen in "Telemachus" that it is "both inside and outside, both thought and exposition" (*World of Fiction,* 231), and then he quotes the opening paragraphs of "Calypso" to illustrate the virtual impossibility of separating authorial from figural elements (234–35); David Hayman notes that Stephen's voice "at times blends inextricably with the narrator's" in "Proteus," and "their voices almost imperceptibly mingle" in "Telemachus" (*MM,* 1982, 94 and 107); and Bernard Benstock says that in "Telemachus" "The hard line that should separate narration proper from internalization has been effectively softened" (*Narrative Con/Texts,* 23).

Others who note this blending of perspectives include Arnold Goldman (*Joyce Paradox,* 79); Sheldon Brivic (*Veil of Signs,* 50–51); Franz Stanzel (*Narrative Situations,* 156); and Robert Humphrey (*Stream of Consciousness,* 28).

27. As we shall see in the discussion of "Circe" in chap. 6, Jung's view of the relationship between subconscious and conscious is much more permeable and symbiotic than Freud's. The terms *focal* and *subsidiary* come from the epistemology of Michael Polanyi, who argues that human perception, human knowledge, always involves elements that are in conscious focus, as well as those that are necessarily peripheral or subsidiary and less than conscious. A shift of attention reconfigures what is focal and what is subsidiary, but the basic focal/subsidiary structure remains. Thus every perception, every experience, every act of understanding inherently involves both conscious and unconscious elements, in symbi-

otic relationship. See Polanyi's *Personal Knowledge*, esp. 55–65, and *The Tacit Dimension*, esp. chap, 1, "Tacit Knowing."

28. Derek Bickerton concurs when he says that one important reason for the change of technique in *Ulysses* was that in all his earlier works Joyce had told the story from a single character's viewpoint, so that it mattered little that he filtered that character's inner speech through the narrator's mind in free indirect speech; but in *Ulysses* Joyce wishes to present a wide variety of characters, whose idiolects can be better individuated by the method of free direct speech (Bickerton's term for interior monologue; "James Joyce and the Development of Interior Monologue," 45–46).

David Hayman relevantly compares *Portrait* and *Ulysses*, saying that in *Ulysses* Joyce wished to convey "the unity of mankind and the uniqueness of individuals," "the multi-personal reality within the orderly frame of daily life in a large city" (*MM*, 1982, 87). Hayman explains, "He had already evolved ways of disclosing the nature of the individual [in *Portrait*]. Here he would go further, exhibiting as well qualities that underlie and undercut individuality, the common substratum of historical and psychic experience" (87); "In the *Portrait*, Joyce had to convey the quality of a developing mind and an evolving identity . . . . The problem was immensely more complex in *Ulysses* . . . where he had to modulate from one sort of consciousness to another, from unity in diversity to diversity in unity" (87–88).

29. While the tables of correspondences that Joyce constructed during the composition of *Ulysses* extensively elaborate the Odyssean (and other) allusions, including the episode titles, that material is of course not a part of the text—though it is clear that Joyce was quite willing to have it strongly present within his reader's mind. Kenner hyperbolically claims that the seven-letter title *Ulysses* is "the sole *remark* the author (otherwise invisible, paring his fingernails) permits himself amid a quarter-million words" (*Joyce's Voices*, 59).

30. Jennifer Levine, speaking not only of this episode, says, "Stephen may be cast as Telemachus, but he thinks he is playing Hamlet. One might argue that he never does find out he is emoting on the wrong stage" ("*Ulysses*," 132). This is a more sympathetic judgment than Kenner's of more than forty years ago. In *Dublin's Joyce* (1955), he said that while Bloom does not know that he is Odysseus and an analogue of Christ, "Stephen on the other hand is aware that he is Hamlet, but the awareness is put to the wrong uses. It provides him with no insight. It merely feeds his morbidity. It is a role in which he is imprisoned" (209).

31. One technical dilemma here deserves fuller exploration than I can afford. It seems unavoidable that we equate the character's *conscious* awareness with *explicit* reference in the text, but this is doubly inadequate. That is, we know on the one hand that the characters have thoughts and conversations during the day that we are not apprised of (discussed above, in chap. 1). And on the other hand, we have seen that not everything that is presented as interior monologue is conscious to the character, but may involve unarticulated thoughts, images, visceral sensations, etc. But since we are dealing here with a literary convention, we can only rely

on relevant context (usually contiguous, but sometimes many pages removed) to try to determine whether a given passage is "conscious" or "subconscious" for a character. Scrutiny of *Ulysses* with this specific issue in mind would doubtless show how subtly Joyce is exploring the liminal terrain between conscious and unconscious.

32. An extensive critical literature has developed around Stephen's theory of Shakespeare, dealing mainly with whether his remarks comprise a coherent theory, with how seriously he is proposing it, and with how the theory is relevant to our understanding of *Ulysses*. I believe that his theory does have considerable coherence and that he proposes it out of serious motives. Moreover, we must not forget that this theory exists in the novel not primarily as a vehicle for Joyce's ideas, but as a dramatized expression of Stephen's own struggle for self-understanding.

33. On "The Dead" see "The Backgrounds of 'The Dead,'" in *JJII*, esp. 246. On Martha Fleischmann see Senn's "Nausicaa," 287–90. Ellmann says of Stephen's Shakespeare theory that "Joyce made Stephen Dedalus emphasize in *Ulysses* that the artist and his life are not distinct," and that the theory "hints at what is, in fact, true: that nothing has been admitted into the book [*Ulysses*] that is not in some way personal and attached" (*JJII*, 364). Erwin R. Steinberg says that "Joyce liked his little joke and was perfectly capable of writing into a passage private meanings that no one save himself and one or two other people could understand" (*SoC&B*, 40).

34. The saturation of Stephen's psyche with Shakespearean material makes it impossible to draw a clear line between what is conscious and what is not. E. R. Steinberg says that Stephen "knows Shakespeare's plays so well that he uses quotations from them quite naturally in his thinking," and that "Stephen's thoughts tend not to be references to Shakespeare . . . but rather to use Shakespeare to express what is in Stephen's mind" (*SoC&B*, 72). Steinberg speculates that "although he certainly would recognize them *if they were brought to his attention*, Stephen may not even be aware that some of the phrases he uses are borrowings" (72–73; my emphasis), which testifies both to Stephen's extensive use of the Shakespeare mythos as a means of self-understanding and to how such material remains subliminal or, in Michael Polanyi's terms, subsidiary.

35. On Stephen's misogyny, see Sheldon Brivic, *Joyce between Freud and Jung*, esp. chap. 8; Brivic says that the role Stephen assigns to Anne Hathaway expresses misogyny (136). David Fuller, discussing the Shakespeare theory, makes a similar point about another of Stephen's foibles: "Stephen's rejection of physical fathers is consequent on his own emotional needs. *Stephen does not recognize this himself,* but Joyce implies it by having Stephen recognize a parallel evasion in Eglinton" (*JJ's "Ulysses,"* 51; my emphasis). Stephen's denial of his own father, and his consequent obsession with the issue of paternity, is, then, another highly charged, subliminal aspect of his Shakespeare theory.

36. In fact, on 16 June 1904 Rudy would be ten, since he was born on 29 December 1893 (*U*, 17.2280). But, strangely, three places in the text say he would

be eleven: Bloom thinks, "He would be eleven now if he had lived" (*U*, 4.420); "Circe" depicts Rudy as "*a fairy boy of eleven*" (*U*, 15.4957); and Molly thinks, "thats 11 years ago now yes hed be 11" (*U*, 18.1307). Is this persistent error influenced or generated by the Shakespeare parallel—i.e., by the fact that Hamnet was eleven when he died? Kenner says, "Eleven is a recurrent Joyce-number. Bloom's son in *Ulysses* lived 11 days and would be in his eleventh year if he were alive on Bloomsday" ("*Ulysses,*" 1987, 18). (Is it possible that the date in "Ithaca" is wrong—one of the many errors in that episode?) Puzzlingly, John Henry Raleigh says, "it is true that by June 16, 1904, Rudy would have been eleven, since he was born on December 29, 1893" (*Chronicle of Leopold and Molly*, 133).

37. See Richard M. Kain, "James Joyce's Shakespeare Chronology," 350, 353. Joyce twice notes the birth of Elizabeth in 1608, and labels her "(grand daughter)" (353). This chronology was compiled probably in 1916 when Joyce was writing "Scylla and Charybdis" (see Kain, "Shakespeare Chronology," 345); William H. Quillian concurs that it was "apparently compiled specifically for the writing of 'Scylla and Charybdis'" ("Shakespeare in Trieste," 16).

38. A number of critics have recognized the intricate, polyvalent interrelationships between Shakespeare and the novel's characters, especially Bloom. William M. Schutte points out many of these links in his *Joyce and Shakespeare*, esp. 126–35. Erwin R. Steinberg also notes the bewildering array of possible identifications between the novel's characters, and persons or characters evoked by the schemata, but he remains skeptical of their meaningfulness; he reminds us that Mulligan has earlier parodied these paradoxes in his gibe that Stephen "proves by algebra that Hamlet's grandson is Shakespeare's grandfather and that he himself is the ghost of his own father" (*U*, 1.555; Steinberg, *SoC&B*, 234–36). Steinberg also notes the link between Shakespeare and Odysseus, suggested by Stephen explicitly (*U*, 9.403), and in the reference to the boar's wound (*U*, 9.459), thus hinting of intricate ramifications among the novel's allusive schemata.

Richard Brown explores the palimpsest of narrative situations and identities in an extensive two-page chart, titled "Shakespeare and company: the palimpsest of identity" (*James Joyce*, 78–79). Noting Stephen's linking of a number of mythic narratives, Brown says, "And beyond the character of Stephen, Joyce himself adds analogies to Stephen's life, the life of Bloom, the life of Odysseus, the lives of Aristotle and Socrates and, of course, the life of Joyce himself" (77–78). Brown later says, "Since for Joyce to write *Ulysses* was to rely on the famous Homeric compositional scaffold, to read the book can also be to embark on a vast cultural Odyssey searching for this and for others of the kinds of analogies *that are keyed together in the Shakespeare theory*" (80; my emphasis). David Fuller says, "Unknown to Stephen, Shakespeare in his theory is also parallel to Bloom" (*JJ's "Ulysses,"* 50).

5. Voices and Values in the Later Episodes of *Ulysses*

1. A move in this direction is evident as early as Ellmann's 1959 *James Joyce*, where he says, "Joyce hit upon the . . . radical device of the undependable narrator

with a style adjusted to him. He used this in several episodes of *Ulysses,* for example in *Cyclops,* where the narrator is so obviously hostile to Bloom as to stir up sympathy for him, in *Nausicaa,* where the narrator's gushiness is interrupted and counteracted by Bloom's matter-of-fact reporting, and in *Eumaeus,* where the narrator writes in a style that is constabular" (1959 ed., 367; repeated in the 1982 ed., 357).

Then Arnold Goldman in *The Joyce Paradox* (1966) notes that only after norms are established for Stephen and Bloom in the first six chapters does Joyce begin "systematic exploitation of technical experimentation" (81). Goldman says, "We begin, in Chapter Seven, to grasp that the words (and techniques) of *Ulysses* stand between us and the Dublin action" (83), and he says that the novel's "symbolic dimension (including its 'styles') wars with its human dimension" (95).

In 1970 David Hayman coined the term "arranger" to indicate some intervening presence (*MM,* 1982, esp. 88–93 and 122–25). Ben D. Kimpel concurs: "As for the various narrators, they are generally reliable as to matters of fact but either clearly prejudiced (as in Oxen of the Sun) or noncommittal (as in Ithaca)" ("The Voices of *Ulysses,*" 1975, 311). As we shall see in discussion of specific episodes, a number of critics have pursued this idea.

2. French discusses Joyce's purported change of attitude about the possibility of a normative style from *Dubliners* to *Ulysses* in "Joyce and Language," 247–48 and 251–52. She also says that *Ulysses* "is written in many styles, and from many points of view, none stamped with the author's guarantee of certitude. The ground is shifted under the reader's feet so frequently and extremely that one does not know where one is" ("Joyce and Language," 251). Hugh Kenner describes the book's strategy as "to clown through various systems of local presentation, all cohesive, hence Styles, and all wrong" (*Joyce's Voices,* 84).

Shari Benstock says, "The facade of objective norm, against which the behavior of characters and the method of narration is retroactively judged in *Ulysses,* is pretense from the outset. The narrative equivocates, never establishing models against which its later incarnations can be measured or restructured. The authority assumed behind the narrative voice is no more present on the first page of Telemachus than it is on the last page of Penelope" ("Who Killed Cock Robin?" 264).

3. Other critics question whether there is any "reality" beneath the stylistic surface of some of the later episodes—e.g., Kenner on "Oxen of the Sun" and especially "Circe" (Kenner's *Ulysses,* 1987, 121–27)—though Kenner has himself written engagingly about one event utterly beyond the text of the novel (see chap. 1, above). Brian McHale seems to concur in this skepticism ("Constructing [Post]Modernism," 6 ff.) and yet says of the disagreement between Kenner and Janusko about a scene in "Oxen" that "Kenner is probably right" (7), thus acknowledging some basis of appeal.

But these critics are confused about the nature of the fictive plenum that literary works involve (discussed in chap. 1, above), and as a result they fail to appreciate that it is impossible to interpret any literary work without invoking implicit aspects of the characters' psychology and of the fictive world of the text. Try to imagine an analysis of Hamlet, for example, that does not involve claims about what is going on in his mind beneath what is presented in the text. Such textual nominalism is not only barren but self-contradictory.

4. In each of the following statements the critic (explicitly or implicitly) discriminates between form and content, between style and subject matter, and even recognizes that some styles are better vehicles of a given subject matter than others. Several of them acknowledge that the later styles are an impediment to our engagement with the fictive world of *Ulysses* (my emphases highlight the often implicit assumptions).

Disparity between the matter and the manner of the later episodes of *Ulysses* is the strongest criticism that Edmund Wilson levels against *Ulysses* ("James Joyce," esp. 172–74). Philip Toynbee says of "Eumaeus," "Had [Joyce] described the moments spent at the cabman's shelter with the economy and compression of the opening in the Martello tower I am convinced that *he could have achieved all his effects* in fifteen pages instead of fifty" ("Study of *Ulysses*," 281).

David Hayman says of "Oxen of the Sun" that "the verbal texture . . . *impedes* rather than facilitates our attempts *to follow the action*" (*MM*, 1982, 100). Marilyn French says more generally, "The many styles leave us feeling that we have somehow not seen *the real scene* at all" (*Book as World*, 182). Hugh Kenner says, again of "Oxen of the Sun," "What anyone *really says* in these paragraphs 'style' keeps us from discerning" (*"Ulysses,"* 1987, 109).

Arnold Goldman asserts, "Though a chapter is written entirely in clichés, we do not believe that the characters spoke entirely in clichés" (*Joyce Paradox*, 83). Michael Groden in *"Ulysses" in Progress* says explicitly that the style does not represent an impediment (44), but then goes on to talk repeatedly as if it does (e.g., 46, 49, 50, 53, 62).

Susan Bazargan says of a passage in "Oxen" that "Joyce's primary intention is not to reveal his character's thoughts but to explore the various ways language can *shape and reshape* our *perception of any situation*," and then adds, "As prolific symbols words can be used for purposes of enlightenment . . . but they can also be *abused* in a variety of ways. In 'Oxen,' I think the *corruption* occurs mainly when discourse draws attention primarily to its own verbal antics, bloats itself and gathers wool as it goes along" ("Oxen of the Sun," 276).

Karen Lawrence frequently speaks of the style impeding our sense of "*events that do occur*" and even speaks of "the *incongruity between style and object*" (*Odyssey*, 124), apparently unaware of how poorly such statements mesh with her claim of the relativity of all style. A similar inconsistency exists in Andrew Gibson's review of "Circe" criticism, which begins by condemning all realist approaches, and ends by explaining a number of the more elusive "real actions" within the episode (Introduction to *Reading Joyce's "Circe,"* 3–14 and 20–23).

Moreover, a great many critics and novelists acknowledge that though form and content cannot be *separated*, they can and must be *distinguished*. Arnold Goldman says that *Ulysses* forces us to see a distinction between the way it talks about things and the things that are talked about (thus recognizing a form/substance distinction), and that the words and techniques of *Ulysses* stand between us and the Dublin action (*Joyce Paradox*, 82, 83, 92). He even claims, "The theory of the 'organic whole' of style and subject will not work for *Ulysses*, whose symbolic dimension (including its 'styles') wars on its human dimension" (95).

Michael Mason speaks in passing of "the inappropriateness, by ordinary standards, of the style to the subject-matter in so many places" in *Ulysses* (*JJ: "Ulysses,"* 25). Gerald L. Bruns says of the "Eumaeus" narrator that "the posturing of the storyteller works to conceal as much as to present the narrative" ("Eumaeus," 369). I quote so many such statements because this issue remains a source of confusion and contradiction in *Ulysses* criticism.

5. Many critics have seen the opening episodes as in some sense normative. Arnold Goldman, for example, says that the "first three chapters give us a norm for Stephen," and Bloom provides "an equal and opposite apprehension" (*Joyce Paradox*, 81). He also claims that "the style of the novel required a gradual *lead into* these extravagances [of the later episodes]" (89; Goldman's emphasis). Richard Brown asserts that "Joyce clearly needs three full episodes for each character's story and reservoir of mental associations to be established and indeed to establish a kind of semantic norm of narration and inner monologue on which later departures can be based" (*James Joyce,* 72).

David Hayman argues that we use our knowledge of Stephen and Bloom to reorient ourselves in passages where their thought is jumbled, distorted, or absent (*MM*, 1982, 97), and that Joyce's "dislocations are possible and effective . . . because we have accumulated an awareness of Bloom's mind and the Dublin scene" (98); Paul van Caspel claims, "The first nine episodes of *Ulysses* have conditioned the reader sufficiently to enable him to recognize and appreciate the device of interior monologue" (*Bloomers,* 151).

Erwin R. Steinberg argues that the earliest episodes prepare the reader for the long stream-of-consciousness passages (*SoC&B*, 33). David Fuller says that Joyce "reserv[ed] the more radical experiments of *Ulysses* for later episodes," and he says that the early episodes lay the foundations of the characters (*JJ's "Ulysses,"* 31, 38). Richard Ellmann contends that Joyce "laid the groundwork for the later chapters in the earlier, even in the *Little Review* version" ("The New *Ulysses*," 549). David G. Wright acknowledges Joyce's consideration of the reader in preparing us for the "more bizarre portions of *Ulysses*," and says, "It is difficult to imagine ourselves confronting a novel which began with the 'Circe' or the 'Ithaca' episode, for example" (*Ironies of "Ulysses,"* 110).

David Trotter feels that our "appetite for relevance is fed by the initial style, and frustrated by its successors" (*English Novel in History,* 220). Even Michael Groden seems to concur: "Joyce changed his focus of interest from his characters to his styles, knowing that the first nine episodes provided support to sustain the characters as much as necessary through the successive elaborations" (*"Ulysses" in Progress,* 50–51).

Karen Lawrence's description of the "initial style" of *Ulysses* sounds as if she regards it as normative, referring to it as "the nonparodic style that establishes the decorum of the novel" (*Odyssey*, 43). But she subsequently says that we "realize that it too was a choice among many possibilities, a mode of presentation" (43), and she detects in "Telemachus" mimicry and parody, manifested in a "narrator [who] dons a stylistic mask of innocence to parody the very enterprise of telling a story" (47).

6. The coherence and continuity of the characters, in spite of the intervention of the secondary narrative voices, have been affirmed by many critics. Gerald L. Bruns (speaking of the narrator in "Eumaeus") notes that "we have seen these characters, Bloom and Stephen, born of other narrators in previous episodes, and accordingly they tend to have for us an existence that is independent of any story-teller" ("Eumaeus," 369). Denis Donoghue, speaking also of "Eumaeus," says, "Bloom has indeed an anterior existence and *the narrator comes into temporary existence only with these words in this chapter*" ("Is There a Case Against *Ulysses?*" 33; my emphasis).

Similarly, David Fuller notes, "As Telemachus does for Stephen, Calypso lays the foundations of Bloom's character" (*JJ's "Ulysses,"* 38); Clive Hart, speaking of the successive styles in "Oxen of the Sun," says, "We see *Stephen* and *Bloom* as they might have been at other periods of history, and as *they might have appeared* to other authors" (*JJ's "Ulysses,"* 69; my emphases). Fritz Senn acknowledges this continuity of character "on the basis of some supposed internal entelechy," and then says, "We think we can discern Bloomness even in the most outrageous distortive presentations of some later chapters" ("In Quest of a *nisus formativus Joyceanus,*" 39).

7. Critics of "Aeolus" and of "Ithaca" have noticed such an intensification of or defection from their agenda in those voices, and Katie Wales recognizes a similar personalized quality in the narrator of "Circe." She notes that the voice of the stage directions "is far from a neutral or objective monologic voice" ("'Bloom Passes Through Several Walls,'" 263), that "As the episode progresses these directions become longer, become mini-narratives" (257), and that "As the episode progresses to its climax and close, the action described becomes more and more cosmic, apocalyptic" (259).

8. While Suzette Henke has called the tone of "Nausicaa" and of Gerty's portrait "enigmatic" ("Gerty MacDowell," 132), surely we sympathize with Gerty and deplore the effects upon her of this banal style. Peggy Ochoa's defense of Gerty's "psychologically rewarding" narcissism ("Joyce's Nausicaa," 784) is charitably intended, but acquiesces in a condescendingly low standard for Gerty. Joyce's aim is to expose and subvert the paralyzing linguistic forces that constrain Dubliners to so limited an existence as Gerty's.

9. As an example of the good writer's resentment of inferior language, the following comment from Henry James seems especially relevant to the "pictorial" style of "Nausicaa": James E. Miller, Jr., says, "James's concern for style manifested itself in his earliest reviews. He was fond of attacking pretentious and un-natural styles in the popular books of the day. In an 1865 review of Harriet Eliza-

beth Prescott's *Azarian: An Episode,* he said: 'If the dictionary were a palette of colors, and a goose-quill a brush, Miss Prescott would be a very clever painter. But as words possess a certain inherent dignity, value, and independence, language being rather the stamped and authorized coinage which expresses the value of thought than the brute metal out of which forms are moulded, her pictures are invariably incoherent and meaningless'" (*Theory of Fiction,* 19).

10. For a review of critical discussions of "Eumaeus," see Christine O'Neill, *Too Fine a Point,* 12–41.

11. This need to "naturalize" the narrative voice—i.e., to find a character whose perspective the voice presents, on the assumption that Joyce would not employ a disembodied or conventional voice—is a recurrent (though specious) issue in discussions of the later episodes. (I borrow the term from David Hayman, who says that the headlines in "Aeolus" represent the first time that we "face a presence that the reader cannot naturalize" ["Cyclops," 266, n. 14]. Presumably Hayman feels no need to "naturalize" the voice that opens the novel.)

This search for a source-character for each voice involves a resurfacing of the problem explored in chap. 4, where we saw that Joyce's careful effacement of the primary voice caused some critics to deny the existence of any narrator in the opening episodes. In these later episodes, the obvious presence of a qualitatively different voice forces critics to turn to other tactics—e.g., attributing the language to some character. But the evidence shows that Joyce (or *Ulysses*) simply does not share the modernist assumption that such a conventional suprafigural narrative perspective is forbidden, and it seems far simpler to acknowledge the existence of a narrative persona in these episodes.

12. Attridge says that "Eumaeus" takes its bearings from "some of the dialects of turn-of-century public utterance in English, spoken and written (journalism, essays, speeches, pedagogic oratory)" (*Peculiar Language,* 182–83). He abjures the "strategy of reading which demands some kind of linkage between a particular style—especially if it is an unusual style—and an imaginary human being, whether narrator or character" (174), and yet his intelligent discussion necessarily treats the style of this episode as unified and coherent ("the Eumaean style," 179), and he uses intentionalistic language in discussing it—"we encounter the *self-conscious* use of 'elegant variation,'" (176)— and even speaks of the "narrator" (three times in the footnote on p. 179).

13. When presented through indirect discourse, the thoughts and even the dialogue of all of the characters are recast into the Eumaean style (e.g., Stephen's thoughts, *U,* 16.269 and 16.1142; Skin the Goat's dialogue, *U,* 16.983). When given directly, the dialogue of the characters is not recast into the narrator's idiom (Stephen and Corley, *U,* 16.155; the Italians, *U,* 16.314; the sailor, *U,* 16.370; the keeper and responder, *U,* 16.1352). But Bloom's dialogue sometimes *seems* to be recast (*U,* 16.245, 16.279, 16.777). Derek Attridge acknowledges that "it is frequently impossible to decide whether a given locution is Bloom's or the reporting narrator's" (*Peculiar Language,* 179).

14. Some critics have detected a "breakdown" of the initial style within the

body of "Aeolus": Dermot Kelly sees this in locutions such as "Burke's sphinx face reriddled" of *U*, 7.589 (*Narrative Strategies,* 19). But even in the first six episodes, the primary voice has never been objective or totally colorless; it has always been characterized by certain distinctive traits of syntax and diction, of taking cues from the characters or the situation, and we have seen the impossibility of knowing whether what appears as "authorial" is not in fact a reflection of a character or even of a quality of the scene itself.

Hayman pinpoints certain distinctive traits of the primary narrative voice from the earliest episodes through "Lotus Eaters" and "Hades" and "Aeolus" into "Scylla and Charybdis" and even "Sirens" before it is usurped by the arranger (*MM,* 1982, 88–93). In terms of the underlying tone and techniques of psychic presentation, the style of the body of the "Aeolus" episode is of a piece with what precedes and follows.

15. Michael Groden shows that the headlines were not added until the placard stage—August 1921—and even later; see *"Ulysses" in Progress,* 105 ff. In a letter of 7 October 1921 to Harriet Shaw Weaver, Joyce says, "*Eolus* is recast" (*Lts,* 1:172).

16. R. B. Kershner makes the point that Arthur Harmsworth, founder of the *Daily Mail* and the *Daily Mirror,* "gave new emphasis, informality, and brevity to newspaper headlines, a feat Joyce reflects and parodies in 'Aeolus'" (*Joyce, Bakhtin, and Popular Literature,* 5); Kershner goes on to say, "A major theme of Joyce's work is the confrontation of the literary with the journalistic" (7).

Joyce was of course not alone among contemporary writers in viewing journalism critically. Attacks on the journalistic style and mentality form a persistent theme of W. B. Yeats's writings. In his essay "Ellen O'Leary" Yeats calls journalism the "great abyss of inane facility" (*Letters to the New Island,* 129), and in "The Old Stone Cross" we read, "A journalist makes up his lies / And takes you by the throat." John P. Frayne says of Yeats, "His articles, his memoirs, and his private correspondence all express the view that journalism is the most oppressive form of Adam's curse. . . . He found in Irishmen a fatal susceptibility to newspaper writing since it appealed to what he considered the Irishman's love of immediate effects without prolonged toil" (*Uncollected Prose,* 1:19).

Frayne later describes the *Daily Mail,* founded by Alfred Harmsworth in 1896, as "the notorious halfpenny paper, the success of which . . . had astounded and disturbed established literary and journalistic circles" (2:246–47). See also E. M. Forster's authorial critique of the "gutter press" and his distinction between "Journalism" and "Literature" in *Howards End* (1910), 65.

17. Both Stuart Gilbert and Frank Budgen tell us that this was Joyce's favorite episode (Gilbert, *JJ's "Ulysses,"* 370; Budgen, *JJMU,* 264), but this does not mean that he sanctioned its style or agenda. And other comments by Joyce are less affirmative; to Claude Sykes he wrote, "Struggling with the aridities of Ithaca—a mathematico-astronomico-physico-mechanico-geometrico-chemico sublimation of Bloom and Stephen (devil take 'em both) to prepare for the final amplitudin-

ously curvilinear episode Penelope" (spring 1921; *Lts*, 1:164); to Harriet Shaw Weaver he wrote, "I am very very slow and have just energy enough to write the dry rocks pages of Ithaca" (7 October 1921; *Lts*, 1:173); in letters to both Valery Larbaud and Robert McAlmon he called it "very strange" (*Lts*, 1:169, 175).

Virtually all commentary on the episode begins with Joyce's statement in a letter to Frank Budgen: "I am writing *Ithaca* in the form of a mathematical catechism. All events are resolved into their cosmic physical, psychical etc. equivalents . . . so that not only will the reader know everything and know it in the baldest coldest way, but Bloom and Stephen thereby become heavenly bodies, wanderers like the stars at which they gaze" (*Sel Lts*, 278; end of February 1921).

18. Benstock's review of the criticism is on 92–105 and 108–20. Another extensive review of the critical literature is provided by Andrew Gibson in the introduction to *Joyce's "Ithaca*," edited by Gibson (3–27).

19. For examples of Stephen's perceptions or thoughts, see *U*, 17.109, 17.135, 17.776, 17.783, 17.1203; for instances of facts or information not known by either, see *U*, 17.164 (Roundwood reservoir) and *U*, 17.1362 (the details of Bloom's books).

20. The only places in "Ithaca" where we have unmediated access to the language of Bloom or Stephen are the Gaelic line that Stephen recites (*U*, 17.727), the Hebrew that Bloom responds with (*U*, 17.729), the anthem that Bloom chants (*U*, 17.763), the ballad that Stephen sings (*U*, 17.802), his intoning of the psalm (*U*, 17.1030), and (perhaps) the mental echoes heard by each from the ringing of the bell of St. George's church (*U*, 17.1230). Everywhere else the "actual language" of their dialogue or reflection is recast into the Ithacan idiom. Moreover, asking what Stephen or Bloom "really said" is no different than discussing what "actually happens" in this chapter, as Karen Lawrence does, below.

21. Failure to acknowledge this recasting by the narrative voice causes Avrom Fleishman to misread Stephen's mental processes. Taking the style of the passage that describes Stephen's watching Bloom via four different images of "a man" (*U*, 17.109–12) as veridical, Fleishman makes the surprising claim that "The contents of Stephen's mind, then, include no sense of continuity, much less of the identity of the actor, Bloom"; and he goes on to say that the account "manages to give an accurate impression of the state of Stephen's mind" in regard to Bloom, and that "With equal passivity, he collects discrete images from his memory in the pages that follow" ("Science in 'Ithaca,'" 142).

But even in Stephen's lethargic condition, what this Ithacan language gives us is nothing approaching the subtlety or continuity of the mental processes going on in his mind, but a Humean/scientistic reduction of experience to a series of discrete states. Note the Humean bias of the question: "What *discrete succession of images* did Stephen meanwhile perceive," which Fleishman concurs in, by saying, "With equal *passivity*, he collects *discrete images*" (my emphasis in both). This is, after all, the same Stephen whose subtle, complex mental operations we have seen in earlier episodes.

22. Several critics have even claimed that our sense of the characters' humanity is *enhanced* by the impersonality of the prose: see Litz ("Ithaca," 393); S. L. Goldberg (*Classical Temper*, 190—in a statement cited below); and Clive Hart (*JJ's "Ulysses,"* 74).

23. See his "Joyce's Unreliable Catechist." James H. Maddox, Jr., speaks of the "self-evident and purposeful inadequacies of the 'Ithaca' style" and says that there is "enough error in 'Ithaca' to at least suggest the use of error as a motif" (*Assault upon Character*, 188, 189). J. F. Byrne also points out a number of errors of computation, fact, diction, etc.; see *Silent Years*, 159–62.

24. Other errors in the episode include Bloom's having purchased the soap thirteen hours previously (*U*, 17.232), when it has been at least fifteen hours; University College's being located on Stephen's Green north, when it is south (*U*, 17.146); an erroneous calculation of the BTU's required to heat water (*U*, 17.270); that the solstice (June 21) is only three days following (*U*, 17.655); a miscalculation of kinship (*U*, 17.1876); that Bloom's bee sting on May 23 was two weeks and three days previous (*U*, 17.1448); Bloom's dream house having a carbon monoxide gas supply throughout, when it would surely be methane (*U*, 17.1549); the population of Ireland for 1901 is different than that given in Thoms (*U*, 17.1708; see Gifford and Seidman); Brigid's tree is said to be an elm, when it is an oak (*U*, 17.1977); the bodies of Bloom and Molly are being carried eastward, not westward (*U*, 17.2308); and several other errors that might or might not be attributable to the perspective of a character (e.g., the incomplete budget, the list of Molly's lovers).

25. Interestingly, in the case of the first phrase, the narrator soon recovers his wonted objectivity: "it was not a heaventree, not a heavengrot, not a heavenbeast, not a heavenman" *(U*, 17.1139). Commentators have noted this anomalous passage—e.g., Maddox, *Assault upon Character*, 201—but none has satisfactorily explained it.

Karen Lawrence says, "The one statement we can make about this line is that no matter what it is supposed to mean, we know from the sounds, the verbal compression, the images, and the allusion to *The Divine Comedy* that this is poetry" (*Odyssey*, 185). It is not easy, however, to reconcile Lawrence's observations about such passages with her insistence that "instead of the human voice of a narrative persona, ['Ithaca'] offers a catalogue of cold, hard facts" (181) and that "Joyce does everything possible in 'Ithaca' to destroy our sense of a narrating, human voice" (183–84).

26. For example, in his 6 August 1919 letter to Harriet Shaw Weaver (*Sel Lts*, 242), he describes the episode in terms of "recitative" and "the eight regular parts of a *fuga per canonem*"; in a conversation with Georges Borach, he said, "I wrote this chapter with the technical resources of music. It is a fugue with all musical notations: *piano, forte, rallentando,* and so on" (qtd. in W. Potts, *Portraits of the Artist*, 72). Harry Blamires says the style represents "an elaborate attempt to imitate musical form in words" and lists a number of specific techniques that are

imitated (*New Bloomsday Book,* 1988, 100). For full-scale analyses of the musical techniques of the episode, see Zack Bowen, "The Bronzegold Sirensong" and Heath Lees, "The Introduction to 'Sirens'."

27. Derek Attridge declines to posit a narrator for this episode, saying that he uses the term "narrator" only as a convenience, a "shorthand way of indicating the third-person passages that interweave with the representations of thought, speech, and song—not that the distinction between these categories is always clear" (*Peculiar Language,* 166). But even this practice acknowledges a difference between this "narrator," and whatever is the source of all the material *other than the third-person passages* (call it author, implied author, primary narrator), and it ignores the unity and distinctiveness of the style of this episode. Most critics are less austere in this regard, invoking the narrator, or the author, or Joyce.

28. In a note on this, editor Cedric Watts quotes the relevant passage from Pater and says that this notion "had become an aesthetic commonplace by the 1890s" (131). Colin MacCabe says, "It was a common conceit at the end of the nineteenth century that music could be understood as the supreme expressive medium, as a perfect voice," and he adds that while Joyce may have shared this belief in his youth, later "he was to say that Rimbaud, although he had the artistic temperament, was 'hardly a *writer* at all' (letter to Stanislaus Joyce about 24 September 1905)" (*JJ and the Revolution of the Word,* 88–89; see *Lts,* 2:110).

George Steiner criticizes the ideal of musical form as a retreat from language and from the kinds of meaning best conveyed by words, and he sets this issue in a larger philosophical and cultural context in "The Retreat from the Word" (*Language and Silence,* 12–35).

29. Others who abjure what they presume to be Joyce's intention are L. A. G. Strong in *The Sacred River,* esp. 37, and S. L. Goldberg, who says of "Sirens," "The attempt at a *fuga per canonem* form, for example, is not only unsuccessful in practice; more fundamentally, it is meaningless in conception" (*Classical Temper,* 281).

30. Yeats shared Joyce's skepticism about this idea. In "The Musician and the Orator" (in *Discoveries,* 1907) Yeats notes that "Walter Pater says music is the type of all the arts," but disagrees, saying, "Music is the most impersonal of things, and words the most personal, and that is why musicians do not like words. They masticate them for a long time, being afraid they would not be able to digest them, and when the words are so broken and softened and mixed with spittle that they are not words any longer, they swallow them" (*Essays and Introductions,* 267–68).

Also, according to a note in the *Literary Digest* of 11 March 1911, Yeats in a lecture spoke of music as the "deadly foe" of poetry, asking, "How can true poetry be written to music . . . for the sake of which the word 'love' must be drawled out with 15 o's?" (vol. 42, no. 10, 461; he develops this idea also in "Speaking to the Psaltery," in *Essays and Introductions*). Such effects within "Sirens" are exemplified below.

31. David Hayman, however, has suggested that the first-person narration emanates not from Kiernan's pub at about 5:00, but rather is told retrospectively at 9:00 p.m. or later ("Cyclops," 265), at some other (unspecified) pub to an unnamed and uncharacterized listener, who accompanies the narrator even in his urination—artfully timed to coincide narratorily with his earlier urination! (At one point Hayman attributes even the entrances and exits of the episode's characters and the artful interweaving of topics discussed to this narrator ["Cyclops," 261].)

But Hayman's claims about the narrative situation create more problems than they solve, and it seems best to accept the direct address of the narrator and the veridical dialogue simply as conventional prerogatives of a first-person narrator. That our nameless "I" could talk for more than an hour without any reference to the (later) situation in which Hayman presumes him to be speaking, and without any response whatsoever from his listener, strains credulity.

Hayman proposes this view in his "Cyclops" essay, and more briefly in *MM* (1982); it is challenged by Herbert Schneidau and reiterated by Hayman in the Fall 1978/Winter 1979 issue of the *James Joyce Quarterly*. Charles Peake calls Hayman's position "ingenious" but says that "the need for ingenuity disappears if one regards the gossiping voice as a technique for presenting the narrator's stream of consciousness, as proper to him as Gerty Macdowell's convention is to her" (*JJ: Citizen and Artist*, 234). For all its innovation, *Ulysses* remains in many ways a conventional novel.

32. Appropriately, Hugh Kenner uses quotations from "Cyclops" to exemplify his scathing comment that "The Irish as Joyce presents them . . . are such Pyrrhonists they are apt to be set snickering by the mere suspicion that an idea has entered the room" (*Joyce's Voices*, 53).

33. Vivian Mercier, after acknowledging the high proportion of satire in traditional Irish literature, says, "Even the most superficial observer can hardly fail to notice the vein of harsh ridicule running through twentieth-century Irish writing" (*Irish Comic Tradition*, 105). Subsequently he quotes Frank O'Connor's disappointment that so little modern Irish satire rises to the level of "a stiletto to run into the vitals of some pompous ass," but rather that "Irish anger is unfocused; malice for its own sweet sake, as in the days of the bards" (182). Mercier briefly mentions malicious autobiographies and autobiographical romans à clef, which he sees as "a spurious form of satire in that their ultimate aim is to inflate their authors rather than to deflate the foolish and the evil" (184).

How much Irish the citizen knows is questionable. David Hayman says that the pub denizens "know that the Gaelic which he reserves for the dog or uses in curses to ornament his speech is an affectation. Can he really speak a language few of them can understand?" ("Cyclops," 247).

34. "Preface: Fragments of an Autobiography," in *The Matter with Ireland* (1962), 8–9. The novel was written in 1879 and first published in 1930; the preface was written in 1921. In a similar vein, Seumas Shields, in O'Casey's *The*

Shadow of a Gunman, says, "That's right, that's right—make a joke about it! That's the Irish people all over—they treat a joke as a serious thing and a serious thing as a joke" (84).

35. Marilyn French acknowledges that the point of view in this episode is "very strange" and is "less distinguishable than any other in the novel" (*Book as World,* 109). She says that it "seems to follow the form of the basic style with a few exceptions," but is "an extremely derisive style" (109); finally, though, she sees it as very close to Stephen, pointing out (imprecisely) that "everyone is mocked except Stephen" (109; but cf. "Stephen sneered" [*U,* 9.16], "Stephen said superpolitely" [*U,* 9.56], and "Stephen said rudely" [*U,* 9.228])—and saying that the "narrator has donned Stephen's clothes" (110).

Robert Kellogg acknowledges a narrator—"The narrator of 'Scylla and Charybdis' is similar to the one who tells the first three chapters of *Ulysses* and all of *A Portrait of the Artist*" ("Scylla and Charybdis," 149)—but believes that the narrator reflects Stephen's point of view "faithfully" (159), and feels that the tone of mockery reflects both Stephen and the narrator (148–49). Paul van Caspel says, "The narrator keeps as close as possible to Stephen's point of view, and in the narrative passages he often takes his cue from the dialogue. His descriptive phrases are such as might have been used by Stephen, had he been asked to describe the action" (*Bloomers,* 137).

David Hayman acknowledges the mixed nature of the episode, finding "a certain comforting consistency in the persona behind the action of *the first eleven chapters*" of the novel (*MM,* 1982, 88; my emphasis), but seeing this relatively objective voice complemented in "Scylla and Charybdis" by a "sharper, irreverent commentator reflecting on the action from Stephen's point of view. This puckish commentator contributes, not only the caricatural asides, but also the increasingly numerous typographical eccentricities" (96).

36. Several critics have noted this "dramatic" proclivity. Patrick McGee several times refers to Stephen's performance (*Paperspace,* 47, 47, 50), and John Gordon says that this chapter is "largely an Elizabethan production" ("Obeying the Boss," 237). Charles Peake notes that "the way in which things are said reflects, in a very selfconscious manner, what is said, as though the speakers were actors" (*JJ: Citizen and Artist,* 208); "The theatrical character of the dialogue is supported by a few devices of lay-out" (206); and "most remarkably the authorial narrative itself is infected with theatricality" (207). Paul van Caspel says of the narrator that "in the narrative passages he often *takes his cue* from the dialogue" (*Bloomers,* 137; my emphasis). David Hayman attributes the episode's typographical eccentricities to the "puckish commentator" and says, "Such devices suggest that the subject matter of the discussion is in itself dramatic" (*MM,* 1982, 96, 97).

37. A. Walton Litz says, "'Penelope' does not contribute to the sequence of styles which is one of our chief interests in *Ulysses*. Instead, the novel subsides into *an appearance of naturalness,* and our final impression is that of a voice, curious, lively, undiscriminating" ("Ithaca," 404; my emphasis). But the pure interior

monologue of "Penelope" is an integral part of Joyce's exploration of the assets and liabilities of various modes of presenting literary material.

38. Brian McHale surprisingly says that "Penelope" "regress[es] to the narrative form of the first half" of *Ulysses* ("Constructing [Post]Modernism," 2), making no distinction between its unmediated interior monologue and the complex mode of presentation of the initial style!

39. I am drawing here upon Dorrit Cohn, who discusses Joyce's various choices and tactics to make this an optimal situation for "autonomous interior monologue." She calls the "Penelope" episode "the most famous and the most perfectly executed specimen of its species" (*TM*, 217).

40. We saw earlier that the psychic range of first-person interior monologue is not confined to what the character verbally articulates. But my impression here is that "Penelope" does restrict itself to an almost-verbalized level of Molly's psyche. Doubtless these verbalizations exist in a somatic context—e.g., Molly feels the need to urinate, her period begins, and she drifts into sleep—but in contrast to the first-person material within the initial style, there is little attempt to incorporate subliminal material here.

But some critics disagree. For example, Arnold Goldman says that the style of "Penelope" is "an approximation to a level of consciousness (or *un*consciousness) which is during the day working below the level of the 'stream' reproduced for Stephen and Bloom in 'the initial style'. Its verbalization by Molly is something of a pretext . . ." (*Joyce Paradox*, 110). Naomi Segal says that Molly is only half-awake and that her monologue exists "throughout at a level very close to that of unconsciousness" ("*Style indirect libre*," 102).

41. Cohn says that Molly's thoughts move a bit faster than our reading or reciting of them, in keeping with "the common view that thoughts move faster than speech" (*TM*, 220). This raises again the issue of whether this "unmediated" technique is replication or simulation, and of what. While even this presentation involves a conventional technique (as does the "interior monologue" of Stephen and Bloom), the whole of this chapter can readily be seen as Molly's silently verbalized, conscious reflections, telling us only what Molly herself could tell us.

42. W. J. Lillyman sees interior monologue as "the culmination of the trend to remove the narrator's voice from the novel or, more precisely, to remove those features of narration which make the reader aware of the narrator's mediating voice. I make this distinction since all parts of all novels are obviously 'narrated'" ("Interior Monologue," 47). Perhaps this explains Joyce's ending *Ulysses* with this technique—as close to narrative ground zero as possible—yet still highly contrived and controlled. Joyce may be undercutting here the presumption that sheer, unmediated interior monologue involves total *authorial* effacement.

43. Earlier, I challenged the claim that stream-of-consciousness technique is inherently solipsistic, but the charge has some justification in regard to unmediated interior monologue, since that technique presumes to convert everything into reflections and sensations of the character's "inner world." Dorrit Cohn reflects

this in her simultaneous praise and criticism of this mode: "The perfect adherence to unity of place creates the condition for a monologue in which *the mind is its own place:* self-centered and therefore self-generative to a degree that can hardly be surpassed" (*TM,* 222; my emphasis). Cohn's allusion to Satan's boast in *Paradise Lost,* 1:254 suggests the solipsistic implications of the mode.

6. "Wandering Rocks," "Oxen of the Sun," and "Circe"

1. In his comprehensive essay on this chapter, Clive Hart refers frequently to a narrator, but his characterization of that narrator is inconsistent. He speaks, for example, of Joyce's assuming here "the persona of a harsh and awkward narrator whose difficult personality is the most salient thing about the chapter" ("Wandering Rocks," 186), which supports my claim for an unsanctioned presenter, but exaggerates our awareness of a narrative persona as we read the episode.

At other times Hart speaks as if this narrative persona were the mind of Dublin itself: "The consciousness which presents 'Wandering Rocks' is in a sense that of Dublin itself, and the spirit is endowed with a distinctive personality" (189); "The mind of this city is both mechanical and maliciously ironic" (193); "the city's mentality is mercurial and unpredictable" (193) (other references to the narrator occur on 190, 193, 193, 193, 196, 202).

But while virtually all of his references to the narrator and to the mind of the city are negative and make the episode seem mechanical or even malevolent, Hart nonetheless says that this episode is "*Joyce's* most direct, most complete *celebration* of Dublin" (181; my emphases), implying a divergence between Joyce's view and the narrator's. Nowhere does Hart discuss this narrative voice vis-à-vis the other voices of the novel, or how this voice relates to Joyce's larger intentions within this episode or the novel. We shall see that most critics assume that there is a narrator in this episode and characterize him negatively.

2. Budgen also records Joyce's famous comment about being able to reconstruct the city from his novel (*JJMU,* 69). Others who see the city as the subject include Kathleen McCormick, *"Ulysses," "Wandering Rocks," and the Reader,* 17; Richard Ellmann, *JJII,* 452; and David Hayman, *MM,* 1982, 86.

3. "Aeolus" and "Cyclops" involve interruptions of the action, but not separate sections. Stuart Gilbert says that the structure of this episode is "unique in *Ulysses*" (*JJ's "Ulysses,"* 227).

4. There is often some connection between vignette and interpolation, but such links are likely to be trivial or perfunctory, reflecting the mechanical and ironic agenda of the narrator. Clive Hart tries assiduously to discover substantial links, but concludes that some are specious or indiscernible ("Wandering Rocks," 203–14). His appendix B (215–16 and the foldout chart) shows that most but not all of the interpolations are simultaneous with the vignette they interrupt.

5. Blamires, for example, describes the episode as "a small-scale labyrinth" (*New Bloomsday Book,* 87). Budgen also uses the term, and says that while writing the episode, Joyce bought and played with Lucia a game called Labyrinth

(*JJMU*, 125). Kathleen McCormick says, "Not only does the Dublin represented in the chapter seem to be labyrinthine, but so too does the chapter itself" (*"Ulysses," "Wandering Rocks," and the Reader*, 21). Leo Knuth makes much of the labyrinthine quality of the episode in his long, arcane chapter in *The Wink of the Word*.

6. We might array the characters in terms of how fragmentary or superficial a view the narrator provides of them: (1) persons who are physically incomplete (the one-legged sailor) or whom we glimpse only parts of (Molly's arm, Artifoni's leg); (2) persons referred to by physical trait (one-legged sailor, blind stripling); (3) characters never named (the two cocklepickers, the elderly woman at the law courts); (4) characters referred to (ironically) by name and epithet (Marie Kendall, Maginni); (5) persons identified by a "professional" label (Constable 57C, the lackey, the sandwich men); (6) persons known by name and profession only (Mrs. M'Guiness, pawnbroker); (7) persons confusingly identified or unidentified (Crotty, Sam Lambert, Jack Mooney's brother-in-law [i.e., Bob Doran], Bloom the dentist); (8) nonce-persons (Susy Nagel, Shannon, Neary, etc.); (9) characters we hear only brief dialogue from (the bookseller); (10) characters for whom we have a single brief glimpse of their thoughts (Boylan, and *perhaps* the blond girl in Thornton's—*U*, 10.330); (11) characters whose thoughts are presented minimally (Miss Dunne); (12) characters whose thoughts are presented more fully (Conmee, Kernan, Master Dignam, Stephen, Bloom). These last two characters of course elude the narrator's ironic devices—but what if we knew them only through these vignettes?

7. I attribute this condescending tone to the narrator; C. H. Peake, however, attributes it to Joyce, and consequently judges against Father Conmee and Mr. Kernan (*JJ: Citizen and Artist*, 211–12). Clive Hart more ambiguously says that "Joyce insists very strongly on [Conmee's] unpleasantness by writing in a style of the most irritating smugness" (*JJ's "Ulysses,"* 61).

8. "Eliot, Pound, Joyce: Unreal City?" 145. Long says of the image of the city in Pound's *Cantos*: "This vision never achieved, nor ever merited, the fame and authority of Eliot's; but it strengthened the received idea of Modernism's city, the received idea of the metropolis as a kind of hell" (146).

9. Critics who have developed this theme include John Wenke, "Charity"; Vincent Sherry, "Distant Music" ; and John Gordon, *James Joyce's Metamorphoses*, 63. Gordon's list of charitable acts includes Boylan's sending a gift to Molly!

10. Several critics have noted this reduction of Stephen and Bloom to the status of "minor characters." Richard M. Kain observes that Stephen and Bloom "are lost in the constant traffic of persons on the streets of the city" (*Fabulous Voyager*, 26). David Hayman says that in this episode, "the arranger begins to reduce these protagonists to the condition of the other characters" (*MM*, 1982, 97). Similarly, Richard Brown says of Stephen and Bloom that in this episode, "their importance is leveled to that of several other 'background' characters" (*James Joyce*, 67). Kathleen McCormick develops this point for a full paragraph (*"Ulysses," "Wandering Rocks," and the Reader*, 17–18).

11. In a letter to Harriet Shaw Weaver on 25 February 1920, Joyce said, "I am working now on the *Oxen of the Sun* the most difficult episode in an odyssey, I think, both to interpret and to execute" (*Sel Lts,* 249). He had not yet, of course, completed the later episodes.

12. Bernard Benstock, in his wish to deny any suprafigural voice in the novel, is an exception, making the assumption that "all factual materials derive from Bloom's consciousness (and that the style of 'Oxen' therefore is an extension of the possibilities and limitations of interior monologue)" (*Narrative Con/Texts,* 128). I do not fully understand this last phrase; once again, it seems simpler to acknowledge a narrative persona who is given responsibility for the *presentation* of this episode, which he does in terms of the theory of imitative form.

13. *Sel Lts,* 251–52. This corrected version of the letter differs from that given in the earlier edition of Joyce's *Letters* (1957) and from that quoted by several critics.

14. Stuart Gilbert apparently did not have access to this letter when he wrote *JJ's "Ulysses"* (1930), but he did draw on Joyce's schema to discuss the embryological parallels in the episode. Frank Budgen, in *JJMU* (1934), quotes part of the letter and uses it in his discussion.

By far the most determined attempt to read the episode in terms of Joyce's directive is A. M. Klein's 1949 essay "The Oxen of the Sun," in which he posits an extensive number of parallels with the development of the embryo and with geologic evolution, without questioning the presumed attempt to ground the literary structure of this episode in these physical processes. Robert Janusko spends several pages showing the wrong-headedness of Klein's article and cites other critics who are skeptical of it (*Sources and Structures of JJ's "Oxen,"* 3–4 and 41–43).

A more recent attempt to vindicate the style and to find thematic appropriateness in the various authors invoked is John Gordon's "Obeying the Boss in 'Oxen of the Sun'" (1991). Gordon argues that even in this episode "changes at the level of events determine stylistic variants . . . calling into question the whole idea that *Ulysses* abandons its earlier project of rendering the actual" (234). Robert Scholes calls it basically a simple narrative segment of the day and gives a summary of it, obviously assuming that tangible events and exchanges among characters exist beneath the narrator's verbal facade (*"Ulysses:* A Structuralist Perspective," 124, 125).

15. Harry Levin, *James Joyce* (1941), 105–6; the passage is the same in the 1960 revision. Franz Stanzel says of "Oxen," "Although one cannot fail to recognize the virtuosity of the pasticcio itself, one may still ask whether the author's expressive intention has achieved adequate formal realization. Evidently Joyce, who until now has avoided this trap again and again with great skill, falls prey after all to the 'fallacy of imitative form'" (*Narrative Situations,* 134). S. L. Goldberg expresses similar skepticism, calling this episode a "generally admitted failure" (*Classical Temper,* 284).

More recently Leo Bersani has said of "Oxen of the Sun," "The episode is perhaps the most extraordinary example in the history of literature of meaning unrelated to the experience of reading and to the work of writing. . . . And so we have a series of imitative fallacies. . . . Finally, the idea of some significant connection between Mrs. Purefoy's gestation *or* the history of English prose styles to Stephen's development or emergence as an artist is so absurd that it is difficult even to find the terms in which to object to it" ("Against *Ulysses*," 25–26).

Jennifer Levine says that the chapter may be an embarrassing lapse ("*Ulysses*," 153) and acknowledges that at the end of the episode the writing reverts to opacity (154). She says, "The question remains of course whether the identification of particular styles with particular stages of foetal development does not push the concept of imitative form over the brink, into absurdity" (152).

16. Atherton, "The Oxen of the Sun," 320. Atherton modestly adds, "This may, of course, be simply the result of my own lack of perception" (320), but others share his doubts. Anthony Burgess says candidly, "The parallel between the growth of a foetus and the growth of a language does not really work, nor is it maintained consistently" (*Joysprick*, 124), and elsewhere he says of this episode that "it is a pity that Stephen and Bloom have to get lost in the process of glorifying an art that is supposed to be their servant" (*Re Joyce*, 156). Similarly, C. H. Peake repeatedly expresses misgivings about Joyce's purported program (*JJ: Citizen and Artist*, esp. 250–51, 262–63).

17. In the same vein Atherton says that "conscientious objection to contraception appears several times in Joyce's works, but on each occasion the tone of the passage in which the condemnation occurs leaves one in doubt as to its seriousness" ("The Oxen of the Sun," 324). Suzette A. Henke agrees that Joyce's condemnation of contraception must be understood emotionally and spiritually rather than literally (*Joyce's Moraculous Sindbook*, 174–77).

18. Wolfgang Iser says that the central theme is love and even contends, "Each individual style projects a clearly recognizable idea of love, procreation, or birth" (*The Implied Reader*, 190), but he does not demonstrate this. Marilyn French claims that "the episode is a meditation on sex," but then she adds, "the chapter is also about literature" (*Book as World*, 169). French attempts to bring these divergent subjects into proximity by referring to "the two main subjects of the chapter, procreation and language" (173), but this still leaves unaddressed the relationship between content and style. Susan Bazargan claims that "the central themes engaging Joyce" in this episode are "maternity, language, and history" (271).

19. Frances L. Restuccia develops an interesting corollary argument in "Transubstantiating *Ulysses*." Restuccia argues that "in an attempt to establish the correct version—that is to say, the Church version—of the model on which he bases his art, Joyce presents in *Ulysses* erroneous conceptions of this mystery [the Eucharist] by way of contrast. What these false views appear to share (we shall observe) is an overemphasis on matter; they all, it might be said, involve what Jacques Maritain has called the 'sin of materialism'" (329).

20. Etymologically the papal "bull" is quite distinct from the animal, but the context of *U*, 14.625–39 shows that Adrian's bull is a sacred cow.

21. In Anatole France's *L'Affaire Crainquebille* (1901), which Joyce read (see *Lts*, 2:212; *Sel Lts*, 148), Crainquebille is arrested on the false charge of having said, "Mort aux vaches" (Joyce, *James Joyce in Padua*, ed. L. Berrone, 121–22).

22. On our role as extender of the creation, consider Carl Jung's statement that "man is indispensable for the completion of creation . . . in fact, he himself is the second creator of the world . . ." (*Memories, Dreams, Reflections*, 256). And William Blake is even more categorical on this point: "God only Acts and Is, in existing beings, or Men" (*The Marriage of Heaven and Hell*).

23. Atherton too notes the ineptness of several of these passages. Hugh Kenner agrees and devotes several pages to showing how "unMacaulayesque" the passage based on Macaulay is, concluding, "Little is left of Macaulay," and "it is difficult, given Saintsbury's critical pointers, and Joyce's mimetic skill, to account such infidelities inadvertent" (*Joyce's Voices*, 106–9). And in his *"Ulysses"* (1987), Kenner says of these passages, "The considerable mimetic powers of James Joyce are not at work here" (108).

24. We know from one of his Padua essays of Joyce's unwillingness to read Western culture in evolutionary terms: "The theory of evolution, in the light of which our society basks, teaches us that when we were little we were not yet grown up. Hence, if we consider the European Renaissance as a dividing line, we must come to the conclusion that humanity up to that epoch possessed only the soul and body of a youth, and only after that epoch did it develop physically and morally to the point of meriting the name of adult. It is quite a drastic conclusion, and not very convincing. In fact (if I were not afraid to seem a *laudator temporis acti*) I should like to attack it with drawn sword" ("The Universal Literary Influence of the Renaissance," in *James Joyce in Padua*, 19). The idea of English prose style being "fetal" until Ruskin seems equally outlandish.

25. Among the problems raised by such literalism is the question of what we are to make of that portion of the episode occurring after the presumed birth has been effected—to which A. M. Klein answers ("The Oxen of the Sun," 31), it is the afterbirth!

26. In *The Rhetoric of Religion*, 18. Were I to develop these ideas further, one ally I would invoke is Owen Barfield. In his *History, Guilt, and Habit* he discusses the dire effects of the modern Western confusion of physical and spiritual categories. See esp. chap. 2, appropriately entitled "Modern Idolatry: The Sin of Literalness."

27. Andrew Gibson's review of "Circe" criticism shows how difficult it is to sustain the claim that the episode is ontologically discontinuous with the rest of the novel. He begins by censuring early critics who naively indulged in "reason; realism; and 'totalization'" (Introduction to *Reading Joyce's "Circe,"* 14)—i.e., who regarded certain aspects of the episode as realistic and reliable. But soon after, Gibson offers his own eminently realistic explanations for various events: "(The 'grouse' that 'wings clumsily through the underwood,' for instance, is clearly the cushion that Florry throws to Kitty,)" (20, citing *U*, 15.3410–14).

John Gordon, however, makes a strong, unapologetic case for a resolutely realistic reading of the episode, and convincingly traces a great deal of the "hallucinatory" material to "actual events" ("Approaching Reality in 'Circe'"). Critics who presume to give an account of the events include (in addition to Gordon), Paul van Caspel (*Bloomers,* 210); Harry Blamires (who often distinguishes between the real and hallucinatory events in his *New Bloomsday Book*); Clive Hart (who says that "The external action of this extremely long chapter is very simple," *JJ's "Ulysses,"* 70); and Fargnoli and Gillespie in *James Joyce A to Z,* 37–40.

28. The "ontological" problems felt by some critics may be inherent in the conventions of expressionistic drama. It is doubtful whether we can subsume to any single plane of experience (or level of reality), all that happens even in a relatively simple expressionistic work such as O'Neill's *The Hairy Ape*— e.g., Yank's labor at the furnaces of the ship, and yet his being unperceived by the strollers on Fifth Avenue. But the fact that all of the play's events cannot be accommodated on a single level is no reason to say that every element in it is equally real (Kenner), or utterly to deny (literary) reality to any events within it (Benstock). This is simply how expressionistic drama works.

29. In her essay on stage directions in "Circe," Katie Wales cites several kinds of evidence for "the subjectivity and authority" of an omniscient voice that is 'directing' more than the action and its actors" ("'Bloom Passes Through Several Walls,'" 275). Clive Hart describes some of the hallucinatory material of the episode as "the author's expressionistic commentary" (*JJ's "Ulysses,"* 70).

30. Nadel cites several critics who have described the episode as expressionist, including Marilyn French, R. M. Adams, Mark Shechner, and Hugh Kenner (Nadel, 142). Others who have done so include R. M. Kain, *Fabulous Voyager,* 31; Clive Hart, *JJ's "Ulysses,"* 70; Karen Lawrence, *Odyssey,* 148–49; and Dermot Kelly, who says "the expressionism of 'Circe' is absolutely necessary to dramatize Bloom's secret fears and yearnings" (*Narrative Strategies,* 2). Fritz Senn says of "Circe," "The episode turns everything inside out, makes it plainly visible and audible, pushes it to the surface; it *expresses*. Expressionist drama has been adduced as one of its prototypes" ("'Circe' as Harking Back," 74).

31. Ira Nadel discusses the prominence of distortion in expressionistic drama and painting and specifically calls attention to "images of circus dwarfs, isolated men, and potential violence" ("Joyce and Expressionism," 145) in the expressionistic paintings of Jack B. Yeats, which Joyce admired (Joyce purchased two Jack Yeats paintings in 1929).

32. Critics have puzzled over the most appropriate term for the "hallucinations," calling them variously hallucinations or fantasies or dramatizations. One problem with any single term for these episodes is that, as Kenner says, they "obey an elusive variety of principles" (*"Ulysses,"* 1987, 123). Some involve only a few lines, others many pages; some are rooted in an individual's psyche, others are public or communal; some seem self-contained, others are more responsive to ongoing events. Moreover, any technical psychological term (such as *hallucination*) is misleading, because the "hallucinations" in "Circe" are not phenomena such as a psychoanalyst would encounter; they are a literary device, by which the

dramatist presents his (Freudian) conception of the unconscious. Since the Gorman-Gilbert schema describes the technic of the episode as "Hallucination," that is the term I shall use.

33. In his first claim, Cribb is echoing a criticism made by Jung, who said, "Freud's teaching is definitely one-sided in that it generalizes from facts that are relevant only to neurotic states of mind; its validity is really confined to those states. . . . In any case, Freud's is not a psychology of the healthy mind" ("Freud and Jung—Contrasts," in *Modern Man in Search of a Soul,* 117).

Frank Budgen concurs with Cribb's broader point: "There are hints of all practices in *Ulysses*—cubism, futurism, simultanism, dadaism and the rest—and this is the clearest proof that he was attached to none of the schools that followed them" (*JJMU,* 198).

34. In response to a *Times Literary Supplement* questionnaire about overrated and underrated works of the first seventy-five years of the twentieth century, Erich Heller responded: "The most overrated works of the epoch are, I believe, those of Sigmund Freud. . . . The most fatal of the 'overrating' assumed the form of a superstition: the trust in the medically 'scientific' character of the discipline, the deceptive belief in metaphors derived from the physical world, notions such as 'deep' and 'sub' and 'over'" (*TLS,* 21 January 1977, 67–68).

Bibliography

Adams, Robert M. "Hades." In Hart and Hayman, *James Joyce's "Ulysses,"* 91–114.

———. *Surface and Symbol: The Consistency of James Joyce's "Ulysses."* New York: Oxford University Press, 1962.

Atherton, J. S. "The Oxen of the Sun." In Hart and Hayman, *James Joyce's "Ulysses,"* 313–39.

Attridge, Derek. *Peculiar Language: Literature as Difference from the Renaissance to James Joyce.* London: Methuen, 1988.

———. "Reading Joyce." In Attridge, *Cambridge Companion,* 1–30.

———, ed. *The Cambridge Companion to James Joyce.* Cambridge: Cambridge University Press, 1990.

Attridge, Derek, and Daniel Ferrer, eds. *Post-Structuralist Joyce: Essays from the French.* Cambridge: Cambridge University Press, 1984.

Barfield, Owen. *History, Guilt, and Habit.* Middletown, Conn.: Wesleyan University Press, 1979.

Barnes, Djuna. "James Joyce." In *Djuna Barnes: Interviews,* ed. Alyce Barry, 288–96. Washington, D.C.: Sun and Moon Press, 1985. Originally in *Vanity Fair* (April 1922).

Barthes, Roland. *Image—Music—Text.* Trans. Stephen Heath. New York: Hill and Wang, 1977.

Bazargan, Susan. "Oxen of the Sun: Maternity, Language, and History." *James Joyce Quarterly* 22 (Spring 1985): 271–80.

Beach, Joseph Warren. *The Twentieth Century Novel: Studies in Technique.* New York: Appleton, 1932.

Beckson, Karl, and Arthur Ganz. *Literary Terms: A Dictionary.* 3d ed., rev. and enl. New York: Farrar, Straus and Giroux, 1989.

Beja, Morris, Phillip Herring, Maurice Harmon, and David Norris, eds. *James Joyce: The Centennial Symposium.* Urbana: University of Illinois Press, 1986.

Benstock, Bernard. "Anna Livia and the City Builder." *Notes and Queries* 206 (September 1961): 352–53.

———. *Narrative Con/Texts in "Ulysses."* Urbana: University of Illinois Press, 1991.

———, ed. *The Seventh of Joyce.* Bloomington: Indiana University Press, 1982.

Benstock, Bernard, and Shari Benstock. "The Benstock Principle." In Benstock, *The Seventh of Joyce,* 10–21.

———. *Who's He When He's at Home: A James Joyce Directory.* Urbana: University of Illinois Press, 1980.

Benstock, Shari. "Who Killed Cock Robin? The Sources of Free Indirect Style in *Ulysses.*" *Style* 14 (Summer 1980): 259–73.

Berlin, Isaiah. *The Hedgehog and the Fox: An Essay on Tolstoy's View of History.* Introduction by Michael Walzer. New York: Simon and Schuster, 1986. First published in 1953.

Bersani, Leo. "Against *Ulysses.*" *Raritan* 8 (1988): 1–32.

Bickerton, Derek. "James Joyce and the Development of Interior Monologue." *Essays in Criticism* 18 (1968): 32–46.

Blamires, Harry. *The New Bloomsday Book: A Guide through "Ulysses."* Rev. ed. London: Routledge, 1988.

Booker, Keith. "The Horror of Mortality: Conrad's Dialogue with Mastery in *Heart of Darkness.*" *Arkansas Quarterly* 2:1 (1993): 1–29.

Booth, Wayne. *The Rhetoric of Fiction.* Rev. ed. Chicago: University of Chicago Press, 1983. First published in 1961.

Borach, Georges. "Conversations with James Joyce." In Potts, *Portraits of the Artist in Exile,* 69–72.

Bowen, Zack. "The Bronzegold Sirensong: A Musical Analysis of the Sirens Episode of *Ulysses.*" In his *Bloom's Old Sweet Song: Essays on Joyce and Music,* 25–76 and 140–44. Gainesville: University Press of Florida, 1995. Essay first published in 1967.

———. "*Ulysses.*" In *A Companion to Joyce Studies,* ed. Zack Bowen and James F. Carens, 421–558. Westport, Conn.: Greenwood Press, 1984.

Boyd, Ernest. *Ireland's Literary Renaissance.* New rev. ed. New York: Barnes and Noble, 1968. First published in 1922.

Boyle, Robert. *James Joyce's Pauline Vision.* Carbondale: Southern Illinois University Press, 1978.

Brandabur, Edward. *A Scrupulous Meanness: A Study of Joyce's Early Work.* Urbana: University of Illinois Press, 1971.

Briggs, Austin. "'Roll Away the Reel World, the Reel World': 'Circe' and Cinema." In *Coping with Joyce: Essays from the Copenhagen Symposium,* ed. Morris Beja and Bernard Benstock, 145–56. Columbus: Ohio State University Press, 1989.

Brivic, Sheldon. *Joyce between Freud and Jung.* Port Washington, N.Y.: Kennikat Press, 1980.

———. "Joyce's Consubstantiality." In Beja, Herring, Harmon, and Norris, *James Joyce: The Centennial Symposium,* 149–57.

———. *Joyce the Creator.* Madison: University of Wisconsin Press, 1985.

———. *The Veil of Signs: Joyce, Lacan, and Perception.* Urbana: University of Illinois Press, 1991.

Brooke-Rose, Christine. *Stories, Theories, and Things.* Cambridge: Cambridge University Press, 1991.

Brown, Richard. *James Joyce.* New York: St. Martin's Press, 1992.

Bruns, Gerald L. "Eumaeus." In Hart and Hayman, *James Joyce's "Ulysses,"* 363–83.

Budgen, Frank. *James Joyce and the Making of "Ulysses" and Other Writings.*

Introduction by Clive Hart. London: Oxford University Press, 1972. First published in 1934.

———. *Myselves When Young.* London: Oxford University Press, 1970.

Burgess, Anthony. *Joysprick: An Introduction to the Language of James Joyce.* London: Andre Deutsch, 1973.

———. *Re Joyce.* New York: W. W. Norton, 1965.

Burke, Kenneth. *The Rhetoric of Religion: Studies in Logology.* Boston: Beacon Press, 1961.

Butler, Christopher. "Concept of Modernism." In *Essays for Richard Ellmann: Omnium Gatherum,* ed. Susan Dick, Declan Kiberd, Dougald McMillan, and Joseph Ronsley, 49–59, 443–44. Montreal: McGill-Queens University Press, 1989.

———. "Joyce and the Displaced Author." In *James Joyce and Modern Literature,* ed. W. J. McCormack and Alistair Stead, 56–73. London: Routledge and Kegan Paul, 1982.

———. "Joyce, Modernism, and Post-Modernism." In Attridge, *Cambridge Companion,* 259–82.

Byrne, J. F. *Silent Years: An Autobiography with Memoirs of James Joyce and Our Ireland.* New York: Farrar, Straus and Young, 1953.

Carver, Craig. "James Joyce and the Theory of Magic." *James Joyce Quarterly* 15 (Spring 1978): 201–14.

Champigny, Robert. "Implicitness in Narrative Fiction." *PMLA* 85 (October 1970): 988–91.

Chatman, Seymour. *Story and Discourse: Narrative Structure in Fiction and Film.* Ithaca: Cornell University Press, 1978.

Cohn, Dorrit. *Transparent Minds: Narrative Modes of Presenting Consciousness in Fiction.* Princeton: Princeton University Press, 1978.

Collier, Peter, and Judy Davies, eds. *Modernism and the European Unconscious.* New York: St. Martin's, 1990.

Connolly, Thomas E. *The Personal Library of James Joyce: A Descriptive Bibliography.* Buffalo: University of Buffalo Bookstore, 1957.

Conrad, Joseph. *The Nigger of the "Narcissus."* 1897. Edited by Cedric Watts. London: Penguin Books, 1988.

Cope, Jackson I. *Joyce's Cities: Archaeologies of the Soul.* Baltimore: Johns Hopkins University Press, 1981.

———. "Sirens." In Hart and Hayman, *James Joyce's "Ulysses,"* 217–42.

Cribb, Tim. "James Joyce: The Unconscious and the Cognitive Epiphany." In Collier and Davies, *Modernism and the European Unconscious,* 64–78.

Cummins, Maria Susanna. *The Lamplighter.* 1854. Edited by Nina Baym. New Brunswick, N.J.: Rutgers University Press, 1988.

Curtius, E. R. "James Joyce and his *Ulysses.*" In his *Essays on European Literature,* trans. Michael Kowal, 327–54. Princeton: Princeton University Press, 1973. First published in 1929.

Dahl, Lisa. "The Linguistic Presentation of the Interior Monologue in James Joyce's *Ulysses.*" *James Joyce Quarterly* 7 (Winter 1970): 114–19.

Deming, Robert H., ed. *James Joyce: The Critical Heritage.* 2 vols. New York: Barnes and Noble, 1970.

DeVoto, Bernard. *The World of Fiction.* Boston: Houghton Mifflin, 1950.

Dibble, Jerry Allen. "Stephen's Aesthetic and Joyce's Art: Theory and Practice of Genre in *A Portrait of the Artist as a Young Man.*" *Journal of Narrative Technique* 6 (Winter 1976): 29–40.

Donoghue, Denis. "Is There a Case Against *Ulysses?*" In *Joyce in Context,* ed. Vincent Cheng and Timothy Martin, 19–39. Cambridge: Cambridge University Press, 1992.

Dreyfus, Hubert L. *What Computers STILL Can't Do: A Criticism of Artificial Reason.* Cambridge: M.I.T. Press, 1992.

Duffy, Enda. *The Subaltern "Ulysses."* Minneapolis: University of Minnesota Press, 1994.

Dujardin, Édouard. *"The Bays are Sere" and "Interior Monologue."* Trans. Anthony Suter. London: Libris, 1991. *Les Lauriers sont coupés* was first published in 1887; *Le Monologue intérieur, son apparition, ses origines, sa place dans l'oeuvre de James Joyce* was first published in 1931.

Edel, Leon. *The Modern Psychological Novel.* Rev. and enl. New York: Grosset and Dunlap, 1964.

———. *Stuff of Sleep and Dreams: Experiments in Literary Psychology.* New York: Harper and Row, 1982.

Eliot, George. *Adam Bede.* 1859. Ed. Valentine Cunningham. Oxford: Oxford University Press, 1996. World's Classics.

———. *The George Eliot Letters, Volume IV: 1862–1868.* Ed. Gordon S. Haight. New Haven: Yale University Press, 1955.

———. *Middlemarch.* 1871–72. Ed. W. J. Harvey. London: Penguin Books, 1965.

Ellmann, Richard. *The Consciousness of Joyce.* New York: Oxford University Press, 1977.

———. *James Joyce.* Rev. ed. New York: Oxford University Press, 1982. First edition, 1959.

———. "The New *Ulysses.*" *Georgia Review* 40 (Summer 1986): 548–56.

———. *"Ulysses" on the Liffey.* New York: Oxford University Press, 1972.

Fargnoli, A. Nicholas, and Michael Patrick Gillespie. *James Joyce A to Z: The Essential Reference to the Life and Work.* New York: Facts on File, 1995.

Fitzpatrick, William P. "The Myth of Creation: Joyce, Jung, and *Ulysses.*" *James Joyce Quarterly* 11 (Winter 1974): 123–44.

Fleishman, Avrom. "Science in 'Ithaca'." In his *Fiction and the Ways of Knowing: Essays on British Novels,* 136–48. Austin: University of Texas Press, 1978. Essay first published in 1967.

Fludernik, Monika. *The Fictions of Language and the Languages of Fiction: The Linguistic Representation of Speech and Consciousness.* London: Routledge, 1993.

———. "Narrative and Its Development in *Ulysses.*" *Journal of Narrative Technique* 16 (Winter 1986): 15–40.

———. "*Ulysses* and Joyce's Change of Artistic Aims: External and Internal Evidence." *James Joyce Quarterly* 23 (Winter 1986): 173–88.

Fogle, Richard Harter. "Illusion, Point of View, and Modern Novel-Criticism." In Halperin, *The Theory of the Novel*, 338–52.

Forster, E. M. *Aspects of the Novel*. 1927. New York: Harcourt, Brace and Company, 1954.

———. *Howards End*. 1910. New York: Vintage Books, 1989.

Foucault, Michel. *Language, Counter-Memory, Practice: Selected Essays and Interviews*. Ed. Donald F Bouchard. Trans. Donald F. Bouchard and Sherry Simon. Ithaca: Cornell University Press, 1977.

French, Marilyn. *The Book as World: James Joyce's "Ulysses."* Cambridge: Harvard University Press, 1976.

———. "Joyce and Language." *James Joyce Quarterly* 19 (Spring 1982): 239–55.

Friedman, Melvin. *Stream of Consciousness: A Study in Literary Method*. New Haven: Yale University Press, 1955.

Friedman, Norman. "Point of View in the Novel: The Development of a Critical Concept." In *Approaches to the Novel*, ed. Robert Scholes, 113–42. San Francisco: Chandler Publishing Company, 1961. First published in *PMLA* in 1955.

Fuller, David. *James Joyce's "Ulysses."* New York: St. Martin's Press, 1992.

Galilei, Galileo, et al. *The Controversy on the Comets of 1618*. Trans. Stillman Drake and C. D. O'Malley. Philadelphia: University of Pennsylvania Press, 1960.

Gaskell, Philip, and Clive Hart. *"Ulysses": A Review of Three Texts: Proposals for Alterations to the Texts of 1922, 1961, and 1984*. Princess Grace Irish Library 4. Totowa, N.J.: Barnes and Noble Books, 1989.

Gibson, Andrew, ed. *Joyce's "Ithaca."* European Joyce Studies 6. Amsterdam: Rodopi, 1996.

———, ed. *Reading Joyce's "Circe."* European Joyce Studies 3. Amsterdam: Rodopi, 1994.

Giedion-Welcker, Carola. "Meetings with Joyce." In Potts, *Portraits of the Artist in Exile*, 256–80.

Gifford, Don, with Robert J. Seidman. *"Ulysses" Annotated: Notes for James Joyce's "Ulysses."* 2d ed. Berkeley: University of California Press, 1988.

Gilbert, Stuart. *James Joyce's "Ulysses."* New York: Vintage Books, 1956. First published in 1930; rev. ed., 1952.

Gillespie, Michael Patrick. *Inverted Volumes Improperly Arranged: James Joyce and His Trieste Library*. Ann Arbor: UMI Research Press, 1983.

———. *James Joyce's Trieste Library: A Catalogue of Material at the Harry Ransom Humanities Research Center, The University of Texas at Austin*. Austin: Harry Ransom Humanities Research Center, 1986.

Goldberg, S. L. *The Classical Temper: A Study of James Joyce's "Ulysses."* London: Chatto and Windus, 1961.

Goldknopf, David. *The Life of the Novel.* Chicago: University of Chicago Press, 1972.

Goldman, Arnold. *The Joyce Paradox: Form and Freedom in His Fiction.* Evanston: Northwestern University Press, 1966.

Gordon, Caroline, and Allen Tate. *The House of Fiction: An Anthology of the Short Story with Commentary.* 2d ed. New York: Charles Scribner's Sons, 1960.

Gordon, John. "Approaching Reality in 'Circe.'" *Joyce Studies Annual 1994,* ed. Thomas F. Staley, 3–21. Austin: University of Texas Press, 1994.

———. *James Joyce's Metamorphoses.* Dublin: Gill and Macmillan, 1981.

———. "Obeying the Boss in 'Oxen of the Sun'." *ELH* 58 (Spring 1991): 233–59.

Gottfried, Roy K. *The Art of Joyce's Syntax in "Ulysses."* Athens: University of Georgia Press, 1980.

Grace, Sherrill. "Midsummer Madness and the Day of the Dead: Joyce, Lowry, and Expressionism." In *Joyce/Lowry: Critical Perspectives,* ed. Patrick A. McCarthy and Paul Tiessen, 9–20. Lexington: University Press of Kentucky, 1997.

Groden, Michael. *"Ulysses" in Progress.* Princeton: Princeton University Press, 1977.

———, gen. ed. *The James Joyce Archive.* 63 vols. New York: Garland Publishing, 1977, 1978.

Halperin, John, ed. *The Theory of the Novel: New Essays.* New York: Oxford University Press, 1974.

Harman, Mark. "Joyce and Kafka." *Sewanee Review* 101 (Winter 1993): 66–84.

Harmon, William, and C. Hugh Holman, eds. *A Handbook to Literature.* 7th ed. Upper Saddle River, N.J.: Prentice Hall, 1996.

Hart, Clive. *James Joyce's "Ulysses."* Sydney: Sydney University Press, 1968.

———. "Wandering Rocks." In Hart and Hayman, *James Joyce's "Ulysses,"* 181–216.

Hart, Clive, and David Hayman, eds. *James Joyce's "Ulysses": Critical Essays.* Berkeley: University of California Press, 1974.

Hayman, David. "Cyclops." In Hart and Hayman, *James Joyce's "Ulysses,"* 243–75.

———. "Two Eyes at Two Levels: A Response to Herbert Schneidau on Joyce's 'Cyclops'." *James Joyce Quarterly* 16 (Fall 1978/Winter 1979): 105–9.

———. *"Ulysses": The Mechanics of Meaning.* Rev. ed. Madison: University of Wisconsin Press, 1982. First published in 1970.

Heller, Erich. "Reputations Revisited." *Times Literary Supplement: 75th Anniversary Number,* 21 January 1977, 67–68.

Hemingway, Ernest. *Death in the Afternoon.* 1932. New York: Charles Scribner's Sons, 1955.

Henke, Suzette. "Gerty MacDowell: Joyce's Sentimental Heroine." In *Women in Joyce,* ed. Suzette Henke and Elaine Unkeless, 132–48. Urbana: University of Illinois Press, 1982.

———. *Joyce's Moraculous Sindbook: A Study of "Ulysses."* Columbus: Ohio State University Press, 1978.

Herr, Cheryl. "Art and Life, Nature and Culture, *Ulysses.*" In Newman and Thornton, *Joyce's "Ulysses": The Larger Perspective,* 19–38.

———. *Joyce's Anatomy of Culture.* Urbana: University of Illinois Press, 1986.

Herring, Phillip F. *Joyce's Uncertainty Principle.* Princeton: Princeton University Press, 1987.

———, ed. *Joyce's Notes and Drafts for "Ulysses": Selections from the Buffalo Collection.* Charlottesville: University of Virginia Press, 1977.

———, ed. *Joyce's "Ulysses" Notesheets in the British Museum.* Charlottesville: University of Virginia Press, 1972.

Hochman, Baruch. "Beyond Portraiture: *Ulysses* and the Streaming World." In his *The Test of Character: From the Victorian Novel to the Modern,* 195–212. Rutherford, N.J.: Fairleigh Dickinson University Press, 1983.

Hoffman, Frederick J. "Infroyce." In his *Freudianism and the Literary Mind,* 2d ed., 116–50. Baton Rouge: Louisiana State University Press, 1957.

Hoffman, Michael J., and Patrick D. Murphy, eds. *Essentials of the Theory of Fiction.* Durham: Duke University Press, 1988.

Hoffmeister, Adolph. "Portrait of Joyce." In Potts, *Portraits of the Artist in Exile,* 127–36.

Houston, John Porter. *Joyce and Prose: An Exploration of the Language of "Ulysses."* Lewisburg, Pa.: Bucknell University Press, 1989.

Howard, Tom. *Hardy Country.* London: Regency House Publishing, 1995.

Hume, David. *An Enquiry Concerning Human Understanding.* 1748. La Salle, Ill.: Open Court Publishing Company, 1958.

———. *A Treatise of Human Nature.* 1739. Ed. L. A. Selby-Bigge. Oxford: Clarendon Press, 1888.

Humphrey, Robert. *Stream of Consciousness in the Modern Novel.* Berkeley: University of California Press, 1954.

Huxley, Aldous. *Point Counter Point.* 1928. Intro. by Nicholas Mosley. Normal, Ill.: Dalkey Archive Press, 1996.

Ihde, Don. *Hermeneutic Phenomenology: The Philosophy of Paul Ricoeur.* Foreword by Paul Ricoeur. Evanston: Northwestern University Press, 1971.

Iser, Wolfgang. *The Implied Reader: Patterns of Communication in Prose Fiction from Bunyan to Beckett.* Baltimore: Johns Hopkins University Press, 1974.

———. "*Ulysses* and the Reader." *James Joyce Broadsheet* 9 (October 1982): 1–2.

Jacobi, Jolanda. *Complex/Archetype/Symbol in the Psychology of C. G. Jung.* Trans. Ralph Mannheim. Bollingen Series 17. Princeton: Princeton University Press, 1959.

James, Henry. *Theory of Fiction: Henry James.* Ed. James E. Miller, Jr. Lincoln: University of Nebraska Press, 1972.

James, William. *Varieties of Religious Experience: A Study in Human Nature.* 1902. New York: Modern Library, n.d.

Jameson, Fredric. *The Political Unconscious: Narrative as a Socially Symbolic Act.* Ithaca: Cornell University Press, 1981.

Janusko, Robert. *The Sources and Structures of James Joyce's "Oxen."* Ann Arbor, Mich.: UMI Research Press, 1983.

Jaurretche, Colleen. *The Sensual Philosophy: Joyce and the Aesthetics of Mysticism.* Madison: University of Wisconsin Press, 1997.

Joyce, James. *The Critical Writings of James Joyce.* Ed. Ellsworth Mason and Richard Ellmann. New York: Viking Press, 1959.

———. "Daniel Defoe." Ed. and trans. by Joseph Prescott. *Buffalo Studies* 1 (December 1964): 1–27.

———. *Dubliners.* Ed. Robert Scholes and A. Walton Litz. Rev. ed. New York: Penguin Books, 1996. Viking Critical Edition.

———. *James Joyce in Padua.* Ed. and trans. Louis Berrone. New York: Random House, 1977.

———. *Letters of James Joyce.* 3 vols. Vol. I ed. Stuart Gilbert (1957); vols. II and III ed. Richard Ellmann. New York: Viking Press, 1966.

———. "A Portrait of the Artist." In Scholes and Kain, *The Workshop of Daedalus* (1965), 60–68; also printed in Anderson's Viking Critical Edition of *A Portrait.*

———. *A Portrait of the Artist as a Young Man.* Ed. Chester G. Anderson. New York: Viking Press, 1968. Viking Critical Edition.

———. *Selected Letters of James Joyce.* Ed. Richard Ellmann. New York: Viking Press, 1975.

———. *Stephen Hero.* Ed. Theodore Spencer, John J. Slocum, and Herbert Cahoon. New York: New Directions, 1963.

———. *Ulysses.* Corr. text. Ed. Hans Walter Gabler et al. New York: Random House, 1986.

Joyce, Stanislaus. *The Complete Dublin Diary of Stanislaus Joyce.* Ed. George H. Healey. Ithaca: Cornell University Press, 1971.

———. *My Brother's Keeper: James Joyce's Early Years.* Ed. Richard Ellmann. New York: Viking Press, 1958.

Jung, Carl G. *Memories, Dreams, Reflections.* New York: Vintage Books, 1963.

———. *Modern Man in Search of a Soul.* Trans. W. S. Dell and Cary F. Baynes. New York: Harcourt, Brace and World, 1933.

———. "On the Nature of the Psyche." In his *The Structure and Dynamics of the Psyche,* 2d ed., trans. R. F. C. Hull, 159–234. Princeton: Princeton University Press, 1972. Vol. 8 of the *Collected Works.*

Kahler, Erich. *The Inward Turn of Narrative.* Trans. Richard and Clara Winston. Foreword by Joseph Frank. Bollingen Series 83. Princeton: Princeton University Press, 1973.

Kain, Richard M. *Fabulous Voyager: A Study of James Joyce's "Ulysses."* New York: Viking Press, 1959. First published in 1947.

———. "James Joyce's Shakespeare Chronology." *Massachusetts Review* 5 (Winter 1964): 342–55.

Kellogg, Robert. "Scylla and Charybdis." In Hart and Hayman, *James Joyce's "Ulysses,"* 147–79.

———. "Translating Dublin." Typescript of an unpublished paper delivered at the First International Academic Conference on James Joyce in China, July 1996.

Kelly, Dermot. *Narrative Strategies in Ulysses.* Ann Arbor, Mich.: UMI Research Press, 1988.

Kelly, H. A. "Consciousness in the Monologues of *Ulysses.*" *Modern Language Quarterly* 24 (1963): 3–12.

Kenner, Hugh. "Circe." In Hart and Hayman, *James Joyce's "Ulysses,"* 341–62.

———. *Dublin's Joyce.* London: Chatto and Windus, 1955.

———. *Joyce's Voices.* Berkeley: University of California Press, 1978.

———. "Molly's Masterstroke." *James Joyce Quarterly* 10 (Fall 1972): 19–28.

———. "The Rhetoric of Silence." *James Joyce Quarterly* 14 (Summer 1977): 382–94.

———. *"Ulysses."* Rev. ed. Baltimore: Johns Hopkins University Press, 1987. First published in 1980.

Kershner, R. B. *Joyce, Bakhtin, and Popular Literature: Chronicles of Disorder.* Chapel Hill: University of North Carolina Press, 1989.

Kimpel, Ben D. "The Voices of *Ulysses.*" *Style* 9 (Summer 1975): 283–319.

Klein, A. M. "The Oxen of the Sun." *Here and Now* 1 (January 1949): 28–48.

Knuth, A. M. L. *The Wink of the Word: A Study of James Joyce's Phatic Communication.* Amsterdam: Rodopi, 1976.

Lawrence, D. H. *Aaron's Rod.* 1922. Ed. Mara Kalnins. Cambridge: Cambridge University Press, 1988.

———. Introduction to *Mastro-don Gesualdo*, by Giovanni Verga. In *Phoenix II: Uncollected, Unpublished, and Other Prose Works by D. H. Lawrence.* Ed. Warren Roberts and Harry T. Moore. New York: Viking Press, 1970.

Lawrence, Karen. *The Odyssey of Style in "Ulysses."* Princeton: Princeton University Press, 1981.

Leaska, Mitchell A. "The Concept of Point of View." In Hoffman and Murphy, *Essentials of the Theory of Fiction,* 251–66.

Lees, Heath. "The Introduction to 'Sirens' and the *Fuga per Canonem.*" *James Joyce Quarterly* 22 (Fall 1984): 39–54.

Levenson, Michael H. *A Genealogy of Modernism: A Study of English Literary Doctrine, 1908–1922.* Cambridge: Cambridge University Press, 1984.

Levin, Harry. *James Joyce.* Rev. and aug. edition. Norfolk, Conn.: New Directions, 1960. First published in 1941.

Levine, George. "Realism Reconsidered." In Hoffman and Murphy, *Essentials of the Theory of Fiction,* 336–48.

Levine, Jennifer. *"Ulysses."* In Attridge, *Cambridge Companion,* 131–59.

Levitt, Morton P. "Joyce versus Joyce: Moderns and Post-Moderns." In his *Modernist Survivors: The Contemporary Novel in England, the United States, France, and Latin America,* 3–21, 257–58. Columbus: Ohio State University Press, 1987.

Lillyman, W. J. "The Interior Monologue in James Joyce and Otto Ludwig." *Comparative Literature* 23 (1971): 45–54.

Linn, James Weber, and Houghton Wells Taylor. *A Foreword to Fiction.* New York: D. Appleton-Century Company, 1935.

Litz, A. Walton. *The Art of James Joyce: Method and Design in "Ulysses" and "Finnegans Wake."* London: Oxford University Press, 1961.

———. "The Genre of *Ulysses.*" In Halperin, *The Theory of the Novel,* 109–20.

———. "Ithaca." In Hart and Hayman, *James Joyce's "Ulysses,"* 385–405.

Lodge, David. *The Art of Fiction Illustrated from Classic and Modern Texts.* London: Secker and Warburg, 1992.

———. *The Modes of Modern Writing: Metaphor, Metonymy, and the Typology of Modern Literature.* Ithaca: Cornell University Press, 1977.

———. *The Novelist at the Crossroads and Other Essays on Fiction and Criticism.* Ithaca: Cornell University Press, 1971.

Long, Michael. "Eliot, Pound, Joyce: Unreal City?" In *Unreal City: Urban Experience in Modern European Literature and Art,* ed. Edward Timms and David Kelley, 144–57. Manchester: Manchester University Press, 1985.

Lubbock, Percy. *The Craft of Fiction.* New York: Viking Press, 1957. First published in 1921.

Lukács, Georg. *The Theory of the Novel: A Historico-Philosophical Essay on the Forms of Great Epic Literature.* Trans. Anna Bostick. Cambridge, Mass.: M.I.T. Press, 1971.

MacCabe, Colin. *James Joyce and the Revolution of the Word.* New York: Harper and Row, 1979.

Maddox, James H., Jr. *Joyce's "Ulysses" and the Assault upon Character.* Brunswick, N.J.: Rutgers University Press, 1978.

Manganiello, Dominic. *Joyce's Politics.* Boston: Routledge, 1980.

Mann, Thomas. "Freud and the Future." In his *Freud, Goethe, Wagner,* 3–45. New York: Alfred A. Knopf, 1937.

Mason, Michael. *James Joyce: "Ulysses."* London: Edward Arnold, 1972.

McBride, Margaret. "At Four She Said." *James Joyce Quarterly* 17 (Fall 1979): 21–39.

———. "At Four She Said: II" *James Joyce Quarterly* 18 (Summer 1981): 417–31.

McCarthy, Patrick. "Joyce's Unreliable Catechist: Mathematics and the Narration of 'Ithaca'." *ELH* 51 (1984): 605–18.

McCormick, Kathleen. *"Ulysses," "Wandering Rocks," and the Reader: Multiple Pleasures in Reading.* Lewiston, N.Y.: Edwin Mellen Press, 1991.

McCormick, Kathleen, and Erwin R. Steinberg, eds. *Approaches to Teaching Joyce's "Ulysses."* New York: Modern Language Association of America, 1993.

McGee, Patrick. *Paperspace: Style as Ideology in Joyce's "Ulysses."* Lincoln: University of Nebraska Press, 1988.

McGowan, John. "From Pater to Wilde to Joyce: Modernist Epiphany and the Soulful Self." *Texas Studies in Literature and Language* 32 (Fall 1990): 417–45.

McHale, Brian. "Constructing (Post)Modernism: The Case of *Ulysses.*" *Style* 24 (Spring 1990): 1–21.

McKeon, Michael. *The Origins of the English Novel, 1600–1740.* Baltimore: Johns Hopkins University Press, 1987.

McMichael, James. *"Ulysses" and Justice.* Princeton: Princeton University Press, 1991.

Mercier, Vivian. *The Irish Comic Tradition.* Oxford: Clarendon Press, 1962.

Miller, J. Hillis. "The Narrator as General Consciousness." In his *The Form of Victorian Fiction: Thackeray, Dickens, Trollope, George Eliot, Meredith, and Hardy,* 52–90. South Bend, Ind.: Notre Dame University Press, 1969.

———. "Three Problems of Fictional Form: First-Person Narration in *David Copperfield* and *Huckleberry Finn.*" In Pearce, *Experience in the Novel,* 21–48.

———. "Virginia Woolf's All Souls' Day: The Omniscient Narrator in *Mrs. Dalloway.*" In *The Shaken Realist: Essays in Modern Literature in Honor of Frederick J. Hoffman,* ed. Melvin J. Friedman and John B. Vickery, 100–127. Baton Rouge: Louisiana State University Press, 1970.

Moffett, James, and Kenneth R. McElheny. *Points of View: An Anthology of Short Stories.* New York: New American Library, 1966.

Morrisette, Bruce. "The New Novel in France." *Chicago Review* 15 (Winter 1961/ Spring 1962): 1–19.

Nadel, Ira B. "Joyce and Expressionism." *Journal of Modern Literature* 16 (Summer 1989): 139–58.

"Narrative in *Ulysses.*" In *Joyce and Paris, 1902 . . . 1920–40 . . . 1975,* ed. Jacques Aubert and M. Jolas, 33–58. Publications de l'Université de Lille, 1979.

Newman, Robert D., and Weldon Thornton, eds. *Joyce's "Ulysses": The Larger Perspective.* Newark: University of Delaware Press, 1987.

O'Casey, Sean. *The Shadow of a Gunman.* In *Three Plays.* London: Macmillan, 1968.

Ochoa, Peggy. "Joyce's 'Nausicaa': The Paradox of Advertising Narcissism." *James Joyce Quarterly* 30/31 (Summer/Fall 1993): 783–93.

O Hehir, Brendan. *A Gaelic Lexicon for "Finnegans Wake" and Glossary for Joyce's Other Works.* Berkeley: University of California Press, 1967.

Olson, Barbara K. *Authorial Divinity in the Twentieth Century: Omniscient Narration in Woolf, Hemingway, and Others.* Lewisburg, Pa.: Bucknell University Press, 1997.

O'Neill-Bernhard, Christine. "Narrative Modes for Presenting Consciousness." A paper presented at the James Joyce Symposium in Monte Carlo in 1990.

———. *Too Fine a Point: A Stylistic Analysis of the Eumaeus Episode in James Joyce's "Ulysses."* Trier: Wissenschaftlicher Verlag Trier, 1996.

The Oxford English Dictionary. 2d ed. 20 vols. Oxford: Clarendon Press, 1989.

Pascal, Roy. *The Dual Voice: Free Indirect Speech and Its Functioning in the Nineteenth-Century European Novel.* Manchester: Manchester University Press, 1977.

Pater, Walter. *The Renaissance: Studies in Art and Poetry.* The 1893 text. Ed. Donald Hill. Berkeley: University of California Press, 1980.

Peake, C. H. *James Joyce: The Citizen and the Artist.* Stanford: Stanford University Press, 1977.

Pearce, Richard. "What Joyce after Pynchon?" In Beja, Herring, Harmon, and Norris, *James Joyce: The Centennial Symposium,* 43–46.

Pearce, Roy Harvey, ed. *Experience in the Novel: Selected Papers from the English Institute.* New York: Columbia University Press, 1968.

Perl, Jeffrey. *The Tradition of Return: The Implicit History of Modern Literature.* Princeton: Princeton University Press, 1984.

Platt, L. H. "*Ulysses* 15 and the Irish Literary Theatre." In Gibson, *Reading Joyce's "Circe,"* 33–62.

Polanyi, Michael. *Personal Knowledge: Towards a Post-Critical Philosophy.* New York: Harper and Row, 1964.

———. *The Tacit Dimension.* Garden City, N.Y.: Doubleday, 1966.

Potts, Willard, ed. *Portraits of the Artist in Exile: Recollections of James Joyce by Europeans.* New York: Harcourt Brace Jovanovich, 1986.

Power, Arthur. *Conversations with James Joyce.* Ed. Clive Hart. New York: Harper, 1974.

Quillian, William H. "Shakespeare in Trieste: Joyce's 1912 *Hamlet* Lectures." *James Joyce Quarterly* 12 (Fall 1974/Winter 1975): 7–63.

Raleigh, John Henry. *The Chronicle of Leopold and Molly Bloom: "Ulysses" as Narrative.* Berkeley: University of California Press, 1977.

———. "On the Way Home to Ithaca: The Functions of the 'Eumaeus' Section in *Ulysses.*" In *Irish Renaissance Annual* 2, ed. Zack Bowen, 13–114. Newark: University of Delaware Press, 1981.

Restuccia, Frances L. "Transubstantiating *Ulysses.*" *James Joyce Quarterly* 21 (Summer 1984): 329–40.

Rice, Thomas Jackson. *James Joyce: A Guide to Research.* New York: Garland, 1982.

———. "The (Tom) Swiftean Comedy of 'Scylla and Charybdis'." In *Joyce and Popular Culture,* ed. R. B. Kershner, 116–24 and 203–4. Gainesville: University Press of Florida, 1996.

Ricoeur, Paul. *Freud and Philosophy: An Essay on Interpretation.* Trans. Denis Savage. New Haven: Yale University Press, 1970.

———. "The Function of Fiction in Shaping Reality." *Man and World: An International Philosophical Review* 12 (1979): 123–41.

Riquelme, John Paul. "Enjoying Invisibility: The Myth of Joyce's Impersonal Narrator." In B. Benstock, *The Seventh of Joyce,* 22–24.

———. "*Stephen Hero, Dubliners,* and *A Portrait of the Artist as a Young Man:* Styles of Realism and Fantasy." In Attridge, *Cambridge Companion,* 103–30.

———. *Teller and Tale in Joyce's Fiction: Oscillating Perspectives.* Baltimore: Johns Hopkins University Press, 1983.

Ronen, Ruth. *Possible Worlds in Literary Theory.* Cambridge: Cambridge University Press, 1994.

Rubin, Louis D., Jr. "A Portrait of a Highly Visible Artist." In his *The Teller in the Tale,* 141–77. Seattle: University of Washington Press, 1967.

Ryf, Robert. *A New Approach to Joyce: The "Portrait of the Artist" as a Guidebook.* Berkeley: University of California Press, 1962.

Schlossman, Beryl. *Joyce's Catholic Comedy of Language.* Madison: University of Wisconsin Press, 1985.

Schneidau, Herbert. "One Eye and Two Levels: On Joyce's 'Cyclops'." *James Joyce Quarterly* 16 (Fall 1978/Winter 1979): 95–103.

Scholes, Robert. *The Fabulators.* New York: Oxford University Press, 1967.

———. "*Ulysses:* A Structuralist Perspective." In his *In Search of James Joyce,* 117–28. Urbana: University of Illinois Press, 1992.

———, ed. *Approaches to the Novel: Materials for a Poetics.* San Francisco: Chandler Publishing Company, 1961.

Scholes, Robert, and Richard M. Kain. *The Workshop of Daedalus: James Joyce and the Raw Materials for "A Portrait of the Artist as a Young Man."* Evanston: Northwestern University Press, 1965.

Scholes, Robert, and Robert Kellogg. *The Nature of Narrative.* New York: Oxford University Press, 1966.

Schutte, William M. *Index of Recurrent Elements in James Joyce's "Ulysses."* Carbondale: Southern Illinois University Press, 1982.

———. *Joyce and Shakespeare: A Study of the Meaning of "Ulysses."* New Haven: Yale University Press, 1957.

Schutte, William M., and Erwin R. Steinberg. "The Fictional Technique of *Ulysses.*" In *Approaches to "Ulysses": Ten Essays,* ed. Thomas Staley and Bernard Benstock, 157–78. Pittsburgh: University of Pittsburgh Press, 1970.

Schwartz, Sanford. *The Matrix of Modernism: Pound, Eliot, and Early Twentieth-Century Thought.* Princeton: Princeton University Press, 1985.

Segal, Naomi. "*Style Indirect Libre* to Stream of Consciousness: Flaubert, Joyce, Schnitzler, Woolf." In Collier and Davies, *Modernism and the European Unconscious,* 94–114.

Senn, Fritz. "'Circe' as Harking Back in Provective Arrangement." In Gibson, *Reading Joyce's "Circe,"* 63–92.

———. "In Quest of a *nisus formativus Joyceanus.*" *Joyce Studies Annual 1990,* ed. by Thomas F. Staley, 26–42. Austin: University of Texas Press, 1990.

———. "Nausicaa." In Hart and Hayman, *James Joyce's "Ulysses,"* 277–311.

———. "Righting *Ulysses.*" In *James Joyce: New Perspectives,* ed. Colin MacCabe, 3–28. Bloomington: Indiana University Press, 1982.

Shaw, Bernard. *The Matter with Ireland.* Ed. David H. Greene and Dan H. Laurence. London: Rupert Hart-Davis, 1962.

Shechner, Mark. *Joyce in Nighttown.* Berkeley: University of California Press, 1974.

Sherry, Vincent. "Distant Music: 'Wandering Rocks' and the Art of Gratuity." *James Joyce Quarterly* 31 (Winter 1994): 31–40.

Smith, Craig. "Twilight in Dublin: A Look at Joyce's 'Nausicaa,'" *James Joyce Quarterly* 28 (Spring 1991): 631–35.

Solomon, Margaret C. "Character as Linguistic Mode: A New Look at Streams of Consciousness in *Ulysses*." In *"Ulysses": Cinquante Ans Après,* ed. Louis Bonnerot, 111–30. Études Anglaises 53. Paris: Didier, 1974.

Somer, John. "The Self-Reflexive Arranger in the Initial Style of Joyce's *Ulysses*." *James Joyce Quarterly* 31 (Winter 1994): 65–79.

Staley, Thomas F. *An Annotated Critical Bibliography of James Joyce.* New York: St. Martin's Press, 1989.

———. "James Joyce." In *Anglo-Irish Literature: A Review of Research,* ed. Richard J. Finneran, 366–435. New York: Modern Language Association, 1976.

———. "James Joyce." In *Recent Research on Anglo-Irish Writers: A Supplement to Anglo-Irish Literature: A Review of Research,* ed. Richard J. Finneran, 181–202. New York: Modern Language Association, 1983.

Stang, Richard. *The Theory of the Novel in England, 1850–1870.* New York: Columbia University Press, 1959.

Stanzel, Franz. *Narrative Situations in the Novel: "Tom Jones," "Moby-Dick," "The Ambassadors," "Ulysses."* Trans. James P. Pusack. Bloomington: Indiana University Press, 1971. First pub., in German, in 1955.

Steinberg, Erwin R. "Author! Author!" *James Joyce Quarterly* 22 (Summer 1985): 419–24.

———. "Point of View, the Narrator(s), and Stream of Consciousness." In *Approaches to Teaching Joyce's "Ulysses,"* ed. Kathleen McCormick and Erwin R. Steinberg, 113–21.

———. *The Stream of Consciousness and Beyond in "Ulysses."* Pittsburgh: University of Pittsburgh Press, 1973.

———, ed. *Stream-of-Consciousness Technique in the Modern Novel.* Port Washington, N.Y.: Kennikat Press, 1979.

Steiner, George. *George Steiner: A Reader.* New York: Oxford University Press, 1984.

———. "The Retreat from the Word." In his *Language and Silence,* 12–35. New York: Athenaeum, 1976.

Stoehr, Taylor. *Words and Deeds: Essays on the Realistic Imagination.* New York: AMS Press, 1986.

Strong, L. A. G. *The Sacred River: An Approach to James Joyce.* London: Methuen, 1949.

Sultan, Stanley. "The Adventures of *Ulysses* in Our World." In Newman and Thornton, *Joyce's "Ulysses,"* 271–310.

———. *The Argument of "Ulysses."* Columbus: Ohio State University Press, 1964.

Taylor, Charles. *Sources of the Self: The Making of the Modern Identity.* Cambridge: Harvard University Press, 1989.

Thomas, Brook. "Formal Re-creation: Re-reading and Re-joycing the Re-rightings of *Ulysses*." In *Critical Essays on James Joyce's "Ulysses*," ed. Bernard Benstock, 277–92. Boston: G. K. Hall, 1989.

———. *James Joyce's "Ulysses": A Book of Many Happy Returns*. Baton Rouge: Louisiana State University Press, 1982.

Thomas, Ronald R. *Dreams of Authority: Freud and the Fictions of the Unconscious*. Ithaca: Cornell University Press, 1990.

Thornton, Weldon. *The Antimodernism of Joyce's "A Portrait of the Artist as a Young Man*." Syracuse: Syracuse University Press, 1994.

———. "Discovering *Ulysses*: The 'Immersive' Experience." In McCormick and Steinberg, *Approaches to Teaching Joyce's "Ulysses*," 122–28.

———. "The Roots of Modernism: A Study in Cultural Temperament." Unpublished typescript. Pp. 378.

———. "Voices and Values in *Ulysses*." In Newman and Thornton, *Joyce's "Ulysses*," 244–70.

Tilford, John E., Jr. "James the Old Intruder." *Modern Fiction Studies* 4 (Summer 1958): 157–64.

Toynbee, Philip. "A Study of James Joyce's *Ulysses*." In *James Joyce: Two Decades of Criticism*, ed. Seon Givens, 243–84. New York: Vanguard Press, 1948, 1963.

Trevor, William. "PW Interviews: William Trevor," interviewed by Amanda Smith. *Publisher's Weekly* 224 (28 October 1983): 80–81.

Trotter, David. *The English Novel in History, 1895–1920*. London: Routledge, 1993.

Tymoczko, Maria. *The Irish "Ulysses*." Berkeley: University of California Press, 1994.

Van Caspel, Paul. *Bloomers on the Liffey: Eisegetical Readings of Joyce's "Ulysses*." Baltimore: Johns Hopkins University Press, 1986.

Wales, Katie. "'Bloom Passes through Several Walls': The Stage Directions in 'Circe'." In Gibson, *Reading Joyce's "Circe*," 241–76.

Warner, John. *Joyce's Grandfathers: Myth and History in Defoe, Smollett, Sterne, and Joyce*. Athens: University of Georgia Press, 1993.

Warner, William B. "The Play of Fictions and Succession of Styles in *Ulysses*." *James Joyce Quarterly* 15 (Fall 1977): 18–35.

Watson, G. J. "The Politics of *Ulysses*." In Newman and Thornton, *Joyce's "Ulysses*," 39–58.

Watt, Ian. *Conrad in the Nineteenth Century*. Berkeley: University of California Press, 1979.

———. *The Rise of the Novel: Studies in Defoe, Richardson and Fielding*. Berkeley: University of California Press, 1957.

Wellington, Frederick V. "A Missing Conversation in *Ulysses*." *James Joyce Quarterly* 14 (Summer 1977): 476–79.

Wenke, John. "Charity: The Measure of Morality in 'Wandering Rocks'." *Eire-Ireland* 15 (Spring 1980): 100–113.

Whitehead, Alfred North. *Modes of Thought*. New York: Free Press, 1968.

Wilde, Oscar. *Oscar Wilde*. Ed. Isobel Murray. Oxford: Oxford University Press, 1989.

Wilson, Edmund. "James Joyce." In his *Axel's Castle: A Study in the Imaginative Literature of 1870–1930*, 155–89. London: Fontana Paperbacks, 1984. First published in 1931.

Woolf, Virginia. Introduction to *Mrs. Dalloway*. New York: Modern Library, 1927.

———. "Modern Fiction." In her *The Common Reader First Series*, 150–58. New York: Harcourt Brace, 1925.

———. *Mrs. Dalloway*. Ed. G. Patton Wright. London: Hogarth Press, 1990.

Wright, David G. *Ironies of "Ulysses."* Savage, Md.: Barnes and Noble Books, 1991.

Wright, Glenn Patton. "Narrative Point of View in *Ulysses:* A Study of the Novel's Implied Values." Ph.D. dissertation, University of North Carolina—Chapel Hill, 1977.

Yeats, W. B. *Essays and Introductions*. New York: Collier Books, 1968.

———. "A General Introduction for my Work." In his *Essays and Introductions* (1968), 509–26.

———. *The Letters of W. B. Yeats*. Ed. Allan Wade. London: Rupert Hart-Davis, 1954.

———. *Letters to the New Island*. Ed. Horace Reynolds. London: Oxford University Press, 1934.

———. [quoted in "The Evil of Too Much Print"] *Literary Digest* 42.10 (March 11, 1911): [461].

———. *The Poems*. Ed. Richard J. Finneran. Rev. ed. New York: Macmillan, 1989. Vol. I of *The Collected Works of W. B. Yeats*.

———. *Uncollected Prose 1: First Reviews and Articles, 1886–1896*. Ed. John P. Frayne. New York: Columbia University Press, 1970; *2: Reviews, Articles and Other Miscellaneous Prose, 1897–1939*. Ed. John P. Frayne and Colton Johnson. New York: Columbia University Press, 1976.

Yee, Cordell. *The Word According to James Joyce: Reconstructing Representation*. Lewisburg, Pa.: Bucknell University Press, 1997.

Zola, Emile. "The Experimental Novel." Excerpted as "The Novel as Social Science." In *The Modern Tradition: Backgrounds of Modern Literature*, ed. Richard Ellmann and Charles Fidelson, 270–89. Oxford: Oxford University Press, 1965.

Index

(Works are listed under their authors. *Ulysses* and its episodes have separate listings.)

Weldon Thornton is the William R. and Jeanne H. Jordan Professor of English at the University of North Carolina, Chapel Hill. He is author of several books, including *The Antimodernism of Joyce's "Portrait of the Artist as a Young Man"* (1994).